DAVID BOWIE

Series Editor: Anthony Elliott

Published:

Dennis Altman: Gore Vidal's America
Ellis Cashmore: Beckham 2nd edition
Ellis Cashmore: Tyson
Charles Lemert: Muhammad Ali
Chris Rojek: Frank Sinatra
Nick Stevenson: David Bowie

DAVID BOWIE

FAME, SOUND AND VISION

NICK STEVENSON

polity

First published in 2006 by Polity Press

Polity Press
65 Bridge Street
Cambridge CB2 1UR, UK.

Polity Press
350 Main Street
Malden, MA 02148, USA

ISBN10: 0-7456-2939-3
ISBN10: 0-7456-2940-7(pb)
ISBN13: 978-0-7456-2939-3
ISBN13: 978-07456-2940-7(pb)

A catalogue record for this book is available from the British Library.

Typeset in 11 on 13 pt Palatino
by SNP Best-set Typesetter Ltd, Hong Kong
Printed and bound in Great Britain by TJ International Ltd, Padstow

For further information on Polity, visit our website: www.polity.co.uk

CONTENTS

Acknowledgements   vi

one   INTRODUCTION: DAVID BOWIE IN THE AGE OF
          CELEBRITY   1

two   BOWIE IN THE SIXTIES: THE MAKING OF A STAR   7

three   POSTMODERN BOWIE   38

four   COMMODIFYING BOWIE   82

five   BOHEMIAN BOWIE   111

six   BOWIE FANS   147

seven   CONCLUSION: DAVID BOWIE TODAY   192

David Bowie Discography   196

Bibliography   198

Index   205

ACKNOWLEDGEMENTS

My experience in writing this book is delicately interwoven with revisiting my own past. This has been mostly generative although sometimes disconcerting. It created many new threads of thinking and feeling which have been supported by the generosity of others. Not least has been the support of Anthony Elliott (editor of this series) whose knowledge on the subject of all things Bowie often surpassed my own. I am particularly grateful to Anthony for the trip we took to see Bowie play live in Manchester during 2003. This was not only enjoyable, but helped keep me going on what proved to be a long process. He was always ready to lend a constructive ear and offer advice when it was required as I struggled to get my thoughts together. At different points the project received the necessary push in the right direction by David Rose and Diane Beechcroft. These proved to be necessary sparks that sustained me during periods when I was beginning to doubt the wisdom of the book. I would also like to thank Steve Gammon for his company at another Bowie concert in Manchester in 2002. I was particularly impressed by the way he withstood the rain and the rising level of mud. Both David Moore and Michael Kenny have offered me valuable insights on Bowie from different perspectives to my own. Their conversations enabled me to link Bowie to wider questions of culture and history than might otherwise have proved possible. I would also like to acknowledge the importance of some old friends. I am particularly grateful to Brian Comber and Chris Baber who not only shared my love of music but showed me how to think about it. I would also like to remember Bill Stokes for opening my ears all those years ago.

Along the way I had some very productive conversations in matters related to Bowie. In this respect I would like to thank Jim McGuigan, John Downey, Joanne Hollows, Mark Beaven, Joke Hermes, David Hesmondhaugh, Jason Toynbee, Chris Rumford, Mark Loughran, Tim O'Neil, Jagdish Patel, Angela McRobbie, Claire Anneseley, Nick Couldry, Robert Unwin, David Parker and Christian Karner amongst others. I would also like to thank Alan Walker for his level of enthusiasm for this project, and hope that he likes the final version. Thanks to my colleagues at Nottingham University for listening to a series of papers on this book as my ideas developed. Many of these interventions proved to be very helpful. Appreciation is also due to a number of students who helped fix up interviews with friends and family.

I would also like to thank the Bowie fans for sharing their enthusiasms with a comparative stranger. I continue to be struck by many people's willingness to give up their time to talk to a researcher about such personal involvements. In particular I would like to thank David Buckley for his writing and helpful e-mail correspondence. Finally the biggest thanks of all must go to my family Lucy, Eve and Ida James. They all had to endure rather more David Bowie than they might have wished. Indeed they are all thankful that Ziggy is finally dead. Yet without their help and support he might never have risen.

This book is dedicated to the memory of Liz Berney (1968–2005).

David Bowie: 'If I haven't made three good mistakes a week, then I'm not worth anything. You only learn from mistakes.'

Brian Eno: 'In England, the greatest crime is to rise above your station.'

David Bowie: 'Force yourself to buy your own groceries.'

Richard Hell: 'The artform of the future is celebrityhood.'

David Bowie: 'If anything maybe I've helped establish that rock 'n' roll is a pose.'

David Bowie: 'I've always been very chauvinistic even in my boy-obsessed days. But I was always a gentleman. I always treated my boys like real ladies.'

David Bowie: 'Who says the space people have got no eyes? You have – you've got one in every living room in the world. That's theoretical of course . . .'

one

INTRODUCTION: DAVID BOWIE IN THE AGE OF CELEBRITY

Modern societies are obsessed with celebrity. There is, it seems, no escape. Today we cannot turn on the television, open a magazine, flick on a computer or read a newspaper without being confronted with the smiling faces of celebrities. But what makes a celebrity? Are they simply the 'well-known' whose careers depend upon a public who take an interest in their successes and failures? Useful when they are endorsing a product or promoting a political campaign, but increasingly irritating as their careers go into decline, becoming ever desperate to be noticed by the media? Others have suggested that our interest in celebrity is less than innocent. Here celebrity is actually a celebration of the lives of the rich and famous. Celebrities seemingly have it all, money, success, fame and time, to enjoy leisurely consumption. While they may put their success down to 'hard work', we the audience know better. If only we had had their breaks we too could have become pop singers or top footballers. They encapsulate, if we could only admit it, how we ourselves would like to live. Celebrities have become a new aristocracy – figures of love and hatred, admiration and envy attracting admirers and detractors in equal measure. In this respect, celebrities could be said to embody a new form of cultural power attracting controversy and mediated conversation wherever they go, endorsing the popular idea that it is better to be talked about than ignored.

However, their positions are not as stable as many would like us to believe. Many public figures disappear just as quickly as they arrive. Today's overnight success quickly becomes yesterday's news. The currency of celebrity seemingly runs short very quickly. The art of keeping yourself embedded in the public imagination over time is something that very few have mastered. Indeed the more 'ordinary' celebrities appear to be, the more they are open to the ambivalence of the public. Why indeed should I spend my hard-earned money on someone who is merely talented? By contrast, stars are literally people to look up to. They seem to be extra-ordinary. There is no one quite like them. While celebrities are here today and gone tomorrow, stars are popular figures that last. Indeed while stars also have an economic function, their lives and performances become fascinating for different but related reasons. They are figures that seem to embody their time. Stars highlight the complications and contradictions of the cultures that made them. Major stars come along less often than celebrities and when they do it is hard not to be captured by their spell.

My contention in writing this book is that David Bowie is a star and not a celebrity. Yet for much of his early music career Bowie was just another would-be star in the making. But 'make it' he did. For this reason part of the fascination with Bowie is that he lasted in a music industry full of 'one-hit wonders'. Since the early seventies, Bowie has been a major star of popular music selling millions of albums all over the world. When he first appeared, Bowie captured public ambivalence about the end of the sixties and the death of the counter-culture. The public, it seemed, were ready for something new. Bowie's invented characters – Ziggy Stardust, Aladdin Sane and The Thin White Duke – brought a level of performativity and theatricality to popular music that had rarely been seen before. Bowie understood better than most that music is consumed through visual images. Star profiles, interviews with the press and the politics of image were not the added-on extra but absolutely key to getting yourself seen and noticed. Bowie also seemed to embody a new society that was being built where questions of sexuality and gender were open to question, and where the public were increasingly being encouraged to explore questions of identity. David Bowie above all was about change. Bowie articulated the pleasures of mutation. Why be who you were yesterday if you could become something different tomorrow? Indeed, as we shall see, the permanent possibility of transformation has become part of the common culture of overdeveloped societies. As Bowie fully understood in the seventies, no one in our society can afford to stand still. The remorseless logic of modernity that constantly threatens to destroy our current way of life means that we are all in danger of becoming obsolete. While the chances in the game of constant change and reinvention are unequally distributed, Bowie seems to remind his audiences that there is more than one way to play. We can, he suggests, turn the play of masks and endless self-invention into an artform. Yet however hard we might try and discard previous identities and selves, it seems that Bowie's story also serves to remind us that such playful strategies can never entirely mask more personal forms of pain. The fascination with Bowie is that we all share this drama of the self. If today we are compelled to reinvent ourselves to refresh fragile personal bonds, update our skills and maintain our market position, then it is not surprising that Bowie has appealed to so many people. David Bowie is the star of the individualized world.

This book, then, offers a different view of stars and celebrities to those that currently circulate in the media. My starting premise has been that in studying stars and celebrities we are also studying ourselves (Dyer 1979). The culture of celebrity has not come from 'nowhere' but has a history that deserves to be understood. By tracing Bowie's career I am hoping to demonstrate that he tells us a great deal about the times through which he (and many of us) lived. We are all products of our time, and stars are no different in this respect, the only difference being that Bowie, for a period at least, seemed to be ahead of his time. Yet on closer inspection we will see that he simply captured some of the cultural contradictions better than many of his contemporaries. Indeed, if Bowie is about change, he is also about contradiction. Bowie the popular entertainer, the avant-garde artist, the sexual provocateur, the cultural conservative, the bohemian radical, the businessman and the burnt-out pop star are all part of his story. In telling this tale, I have become aware of how much our society has changed. The new power, whether we are talking about successful business or political ventures, lies with those that capture the human imagination.

We no longer want to keep up with the Joneses, but want to become and invent ourselves. Just how we decide to do this is a matter of culture and politics. To be able to shape a sense of human possibility at the beginning of the twenty-first century is the most precious commodity of all. It is no overstatement to say that Bowie for millions of people is part of this story. The allure of performers like Bowie is central to the story of popular music. Part of that history is the dominance of a culture industry that seeks to manage and package music in the name of profits and product. There is also an equally important narrative that suggests that popular music is produced by and for outsiders. This is where many people's fascination with popular music comes from. Figures as diverse as David Bowie, Patti Smith, Bob Dylan, John Lydon, Morrissey and the current obsession with former libertine Pete Doherty can all be understood in these terms. These may not be the performers who ultimately sell the most records, and yet in terms of the column inches and everyday talk they inspire amongst their followers they offer something beyond an appreciation of sound and the brutal calculations of the economy. The attempt to explain the 'everyday magic' of such figures is part of what this book is about.

David Bowie's story will of course be already known to many of the people who read this book. However, the distinctiveness of this book is that I try both to connect Bowie to the culture of his times and to judge his various artistic ventures. Many of you reading these words will undoubtedly find much to agree and disagree with. However, the overall tone of the book is sympathetic, albeit at times sharply critical. In particular I want to comment on the meaning of his career and his music. Too many other books on Bowie (for my taste at least) become overly concerned with technical questions as to how the music is produced or merely seek to spill the dirt on Bowie's private life. Indeed, those looking for a detailed investigation into the complex layers of sound produced by Bowie might be better advised to look elsewhere. I have no formal musical training, but come to my subject as a sociologist interested in culture, history and meaning. There are of course other good books available on Bowie, the most comprehensive being David Buckley's

(1999) highly enjoyable biography. My book is less a biography and more an attempt to account for the significance that David Bowie has for our culture. This means that we need to go beyond questions of his individual genius to try and understand how and why he has had such an impact.

In chapter 2, I begin the story by seeking to locate David Bowie's emergence in the culture of the fifties and sixties. Looking back, this is a time of gender transformation when popular music was becoming linked to a number of radical ideas seeking to transform society. Here I look at David Bowie's early career and discover a struggling artist looking for that first big break. Much of the music that Bowie produced during the sixties has been deleted from his 'official' back catalogue, but is freely available on other collections. While Bowie's London of the sixties was literally the right place to be, it was not until the early seventies that Bowie would make his mark. In chapter 3, I seek to connect Bowie to a number of postmodern themes that suggest themselves in his artistic output. In particular, Bowie's own hero, Andy Warhol, is key, giving an example of an artist who believes little in his own authenticity, while experimenting with radical ideas and selling art. Further, I hope to outline how the theme of identity is central to any appreciation of David Bowie. In chapter 4, I look at Bowie's most overtly commercial period, the eighties. During this decade Bowie made his millions and became a global brand. However, there is another story here of artistic decline. It is perhaps impossible to sustain a long career in popular music without encountering a period when you simply lose your way. Chapter 5 looks at how Bowie not only resurrected his career but also rediscovered his creative spark. Again it is Bowie's ability to link the worlds of art and pop that are crucial. This chapter links the time he spent in Berlin, a new sense of artistic direction in the nineties, his flirtation with fascism and his later liberalism. Chapter 6 focuses on Bowie's fans and is essential to the overall argument of the book. If the cultures of stars and celebrities are about the visibility of certain individuals, then it is important to try and understand some of the people who are doing the looking. This chapter builds upon a number of interviews I have conducted with self-identified lifelong Bowie fans. Interest in David Bowie is after all more than just a matter of star images and strategies developed by the music industry, but crucially concerns the affective sensibilities of his many followers.

Unlike many of the books I have written, here I have directly felt the pull of my own biography. I have been a fan and a follower of Bowie since I discovered him at the age of seventeen. I have seemingly grown up with Bowie. During the course of writing this book, I have changed my mind about him several times. I think being a fan allows you the ability to edit out the parts of the story you don't like, a luxury less available to someone trying to write a more comprehensive study. Inevitably, however, I do concentrate on certain aspects of Bowie's career rather than others. Despite Bowie's career as a painter, narrator and actor, it is his popular music for which he is best known, and not surprisingly this forms the centrepiece of the book. While writing this book many people (friends and colleagues) have offered me their take on Bowie. It has been interesting to discover just how many have assumed that to be a fan means that you are uncritical. Of course it is a hard job to write a book on a subject with which you are completely out of sympathy; however, many people seem to manage it. The assumption seems to be that to express an interest in a star automatically converts you into an uncritical follower. Perhaps if I had not felt some affinity with Bowie at various points of my life I would have written about something else. However, at no point did I feel uncritical. In this respect, the most interesting experience for me has been the interviews I conducted with Bowie fans. Some readers will undoubtedly be surprised to discover just how critical as well as appreciative devoted fans can be. While popular media stereotypes often represent such people as dangerously obsessed, I discovered more complex patterns of devotion and dissonance. That I encountered similarly complex patterns within myself tells us that 'the writer' is never as separate from the 'object' of study as many would have us believe.

two

BOWIE IN THE SIXTIES:
THE MAKING OF A STAR

The 1960s remain a period of intense ideological contestation. Viewed from the political right, the emergence of the permissive society and anti-social individualism has led to increasing levels of drug abuse, crime and anti-social behaviour, family breakdown and social atomization. The lifestyle revolts of the sixties, in this view, fostered a host of liberal freedoms from which modern society is still learning to recover. The causes of social breakdown are variously blamed upon the rise of youth cultures, consumerism and the radical ambitions of the counter-culture. The enhancement of freedom as opposed to the conformity required by a well-ordered and regulated society is bemoaned by moralizers and populist right-wing commentators. Left-wing inspired accounts of the sixties, on the other hand, view the decade more progressively if no less ambivalently. The sixties witnessed the rise of new experiments in identity politics based upon questions of respect and recognition. The birth of the idea that the personal is political and that contemporary culture could offer arresting images and ideas all come from this decade. Yet most left-inspired readings of the sixties usually end with the triumph of commodification rather than liberation. The defeat of the counter-culture and the triumph of the ephemeral cultures of fashion and mass consumption led directly to the selfish neo-liberalism of modern times. The notion that popular music and culture seemed to offer possibilities of personal and collective transformation was soon displaced once these sentiments became incorporated into the system through commodification. This process ultimately ends with the stars of the sixties

7

enjoying glamorous lifestyles and global forms of visibility while trading upon the more 'authentic' sentiments of rebellion available within their earlier work.

These images of the sixties remain powerful within contemporary culture. Whereas the seventies are often seen as a period of lost innocence before the onset of the cynical, market-driven eighties, the sixties still evoke a clear sense of contestation. Yet the projections of both right and left arguably obscure as much as they reveal. Rather than reading the development of the counter-culture and rock music as either revolutionary or reactionary, I want to argue that popular culture needs to be understood more precisely within its political and cultural context. This means that the popular music of the period resists a unitary reading as either essentially radical or reactionary. Too many critics view the cultural productions of the sixties through simple binary oppositions. The mass appeal of popular music during this period can only be poorly understood as either a cheap form of distraction not really worthy of 'serious' forms of consideration or as the lost spirit of rebellion our own era would do well to recapture. By viewing popular music and culture as either a culture of containment or progress, we displace many other questions and concerns. In this chapter, I tell a story about how the sixties made David Bowie but also press the view that questions of culture are best understood through less sweeping, but no less critical, viewpoints.

While seeking to understand British and American society during the sixties, I shall suggest that there are a number of different ways of understanding this most contested of decades. Further, that while David Bowie is usually (and mostly correctly) thought of as the face of the seventies, it was undoubtedly the sixties that made him. As we shall see, the counter-culture, swinging London and the artistic underground all contributed to the making of David Bowie. If the sixties can be seen as the time when consumerism, mass communications, lifestyle experimentation and a new politics of gender and sexuality all came of age, then they all fed into the development of the international star image of David Bowie. Rather than understanding the sixties as the time of liberation or moral decline, the decade is better understood as a symbol of the desire for change. As we shall see, the idea that individuals or social movements could change themselves by refashioning their identities through commercial culture and radical ideas is a product of the sixties. The decade opened the possibility that ordinary consumer goods or services like the record player, the television set and the broadcast of popular music could threaten the established rules of authority and morality. The aesthetic changes in popular music pioneered through the star images of Elvis Presley, the Rolling Stones, the Beatles, Janice Joplin and Jimi Hendrix amongst others ultimately defeat the idea that the market automatically produces dumbed-down products for duped consumers. It was the coming together of radical politics, star images and the consumption of popular music that was to win out over the simplistic ideologies of both the right and the left.

The Reinvention of popular culture

The fifties was a period of middle-class stylistic revolts connected to the emergence of the beats in America and angry young men in Britain. Admittedly the numbers directly affected by these artistic and cultural movements were probably small but their impact upon later generations was immense. Just as the youth-orientated popular music of the fifties and sixties unsettled the established cultural order, these artistic movements had a similar effect. The beats – whose most famous members included the poet Allen Ginsberg and writers Jack Kerouac and William Burroughs – seemed to characterize those who tried to live outside the system. This was a mainly white, middle-class culture which protested against the blandness and conformity of American life. Bohemianism and rebelliousness were signified through the exploration of drugs, black culture, jazz and the image of the 'outsider'. Similarly, the angry young men of fifties' Britain, whose generation included John Osborne, Kingsley Amis and philosopher Colin Wilson, held a similar contempt for the domestic arrangements of middle-class suburbia. While the angry young men remained more distant from the impact of rock and popular music, they shared a similar anger with 'straight' family life. Many feminists, like Lynne Segal (1995), have argued that these literary formations can be understood as a specifically masculine rebellion against stifling domesticity. The men represented within this literature articulate a contempt for femininity and a sense of entrapment within unheroic suburban forms of masculinity. Reading the tirades of John Osborne's Jimmy Porter in *Look Back in Anger* or the masculine bravado of Jack Kerouac's Dean Moriarty in *On the Road,* Segal certainly seems to have a point.

Similarly, Simon Reynolds and Joy Press (1995) argue that there is a direct connection between rock's obsession with the virility of 'rebel males' and the 'angry young men' of the fifties. Under the disguise of rebellion and non-conformity, both are constructed in opposition to decent, straight masculinity. What looks like subversion and opposition towards the status quo is actually fear and loathing of the feminine. The argument is that the consumption of images of rebellion is more often the reassertion of masculine dominance than more unsettling forms of dissonance. Indeed, 'authentic' forms of rebellion are usually understood through overtly masculinist frameworks. The rock 'n' roll lifestyle of drugs, alcohol, violence and excess primarily invented in the sixties is actually the self-indulgence of the masculine playboy.

David Bowie is as much the product of the fifties and the sixties as rock 'n' roll and the moon landings. Like many of his generation, from the beat poets to the counter-culture, Bowie grew up in a generation that sought to question the rigidities of decent, straight masculinity (Reynolds and Press 1995; Segal 1995). However, Bowie was to become a different kind of rebel male. While much rock music of this period can indeed be understood as a masculine rejection of femininity and domesticity, this is only part of the Bowie story. For Bowie would go on to pervert the by now predictable tale of the rock 'n' roll self-indulgent lifestyle. If Bowie was to become a playboy, it was of a very different kind.

As a young consumer of popular music, it was Little Richard rather than Bill Haley and Buddy Holly who captured his imagination. Bowie would later claim that when he first heard Little Richard it changed his life for good. Unlike most rock stars of his era, Richard was both bisexual and black, but above all he was different. Indeed it was Bowie's interest in slightly different forms of art and music that were just off the 'mainstream' that would later underwrite his career in popular music. The experience of listening to Little Richard in the English suburbs would inspire Bowie to create his own identity. Bowie was attracted to the stars of the fifties and sixties who partially unfixed the gendered identities assumed by men and women.

These transformations paved the way for some of the enhanced forms of social and cultural experimentation in respect of the social identities that emerged in modern society. Indeed it was here that Bowie was able to make his mark. Such a view, as I hope to make plain throughout this book, dispenses with the idea that consumer culture is purely reactionary or progressive. The consumption of rebellious images and narratives may indeed enhance new forms of masculine control and domination, but equally it may not. Another one of Bowie's early heroes was the film star James Dean. James Dean's image as 'the first teenager' comes from his performance as Jim Stark, a misunderstood adolescent in *Rebel Without A Cause* (1955). According to this famous film, being a teenager is a troubled period, indeed 'a time when nothing seems to fit'. The film's narrative could easily be understood through a conservative lens where teenage confusion is the result of emasculated father figures, absent parents and families that lack social discipline. Dean's inner turmoil and confusion is largely shared by the other young people represented in the film who are all searching for something 'sincere' in a world where male authority has broken down. Seemingly it is the decline of social discipline and paternal control that has led to teenage unrest and confusion. Yet it is doubtful that this is the message that has been taken from the film by its many teenage viewers across the generations. Dean's troubled and uncertain masculinity coupled with his well-groomed image emphasizes his liquid eyes and soft hair and lips, giving him a feminine appearance. His ambiguous masculinity has constructed an enduring image of the moody and sensitive male. Dean offered an appearance of masculinity distinct from the clean-cut, patriotic, all-American boy that was the dominant norm of this period (Ehrenreich et al. 1991). The teenage culture of the fifties allowed for the visibility of new kinds of heterosexual masculinity. Dean, in respect of the film's title, embodies subtle forms of rebellion. Notably Dean offers an image of uncertainty and ambiguity rather than conformity or outright rebellion. It is this subversive culture of gender-bending and image manipulation that would pave the way for David Bowie.

The new sexual, consumer and ethical opportunities offered to young men by the invention of the teenager is explored in Colin MacInnes's (1980) London-based novel, *Absolute Beginners*. The title refers to the idea that along with the arrival of teenage identities comes the possibility of new opportunities. The hero of the novel embraces the teenage ideal with gusto as he turns his back on traditional family and class loyalties and adopts a more bohemian lifestyle in a less respectable part of the city. In an early part of the narrative the possibilities for new, heterosexual masculine scripts are indicated through an exchange between the 'absolute beginner' and his father. The father conveys to his son that while the son's life is marked by opportunity, his own youth was blighted by economic austerity, sexual repression and rigid forms of social hierarchy. The jubilant world of mass consumption and money-making opportunities is also marked in terms of the narrator's brother, Vernon, who suggests that teenagers are actually class traitors.

> 'You're dissolute!' he suddenly cried out, 'Immoral! That's what I say you teenagers all are!'
>
> I eyed the oaf, then spoke up slow. 'I'll tell you one thing about teenagers,' I said, 'compared with how I remember you ten years ago . . . which is we wash between our toes, and change our vests and pants occasionally, and don't keep empty bottles underneath our beds for the good reason we don't touch the stuff.' (MacInnes 1980: 38)

While the emergence of the teenager did not transcend class, it did temporarily displace it as a marker for social identity.

The new consumption and leisure opportunities suggested by 'the teenager' encouraged a myth of classlessness while helping promote new cultural forms that questioned the rigidities of the British class structure. David Bowie, who was to appear in Julien Temple's film version of *Absolute Beginners* in 1986, emerged into a climate where the undermining of rigid distinction between high and low culture meant that many people were coming to see popular music as a new artform. The ambivalence of the teenager then was that while it was good business, it also allowed for more fluid lifestyles and forms of cultural experimentation.

Changes within the mass production of lifestyle and leisure industries enhanced the commodification of everyday life. As I have already indicated, the new forms of identity that were made available to men and women in the fifties and sixties may be viewed as ambiguous in terms of their impact upon sexual identities. However, what is not to be underestimated is the extent to which these cultures were dependent upon the operation of a dominant capitalist economic system. The development of a commodity culture is as much about the ways in which subcultures and lifestyle groupings make culture as it is about capitalist concerns seeking to manufacture dreams and forms of identification. For a form of popular music, star image or product to become successful, it will need to be marketed, constructed and consumed. There is indeed much more to being a star of popular music than simply making good music. An image, a lifestyle or a point of identification will need to be constructed so that fans and public alike have something they might want to buy.

The dominance of the major labels can be traced back to the 1930s when, following the global economic slump, there was a collapse in the rise of smaller recording companies. By the end of the 1930s it was EMI and Decca who manufactured most of the music that was being consumed in Britain. Similarly, in America by 1938 American labels RCA and Decca produced three-quarters of all records that were sold (Frith 1988). During this period, radio began to replace record players in people's homes; this meant a shift in profits from records to performing rights and royalties. It was at this point that Decca discovered that advertising and promotion could be used both to increase sales and make fast profits. By the end of the Second World War, the basic structure of the music industry was in place. The emphasis of record companies upon the promotion of well-known stars under the control of a small number of companies remains the basis of the music industry today.

The focus of the music industry upon a few star performers is largely a product of the way songs become known to audiences through a process of progressive personalization. The music industry that emerged in the late nineteenth and early twentieth centuries relied upon performers in the music hall and theatres to sell sheet music. The technological development of radio and records meant that performers became identified with particular songs. In the fifties, Judy Garland singing 'Over the Rainbow' and Frank Sinatra's performance of 'My Way' promoted the idea of 'original' versions of these songs. Personal identification with the star was also enhanced once performers started to develop 'individual' performing and vocal styles. Again in the 1950s, Johnnie Ray was one of the first artists of popular music to use his body and voice to evoke a sense of individuality and sexuality in music. Stars of popular music are not only good for business but fit the increasing forms of individuality demanded by capitalist cultures of consumption (Marshall 1997).

The development of new technologies involved in the reproduction of sound enhanced the possibilities for creative innovation within popular music. During the fifties and sixties, new technological innovations such as recording tape, multiple track recorders and the availability of cheap record players all contributed towards a more sophisticated popular music. The key difference between sixties' rock and popular music and earlier stylistic innovations within British music like skiffle, R and B and jazz is that it was developed through the media of mass communication. Whereas these latter musical movements had initially developed amongst a minority of enthusiasts, rock music became the focus of television media, particularly through popular programmes like *Ready, Steady Go!* and *Juke Box Jury* in the mid sixties (Laing 1969). Large numbers of music fans were able to see visual representations of the artists who played the music they listened to; this enhanced the importance of star images in the selling of music. The mass commodification of music and its organization through a capitalist dominated music industry was a key component in the shaping of this new era.

Popular music, lifestyles and the sixties

Before David Jones's transformation into the global artist David Bowie, his early musical career in the sixties was less than success-ful. This is characterized in his appearance in a number of bands which failed to make much impression on the music scene. His first band was an R and B group called the Konrads where Jones changed his name to Dave Jay. Indeed it was not until 1966 that Jones finally adopted the stage name David Bowie. Previously he had released his first recording in 1964 with the King Bees (entitled 'Liza Jane'); later, in bands such as the Mannish Boys and the Lower Third, he would still fail to find a popular audi-ence. During this period David Jones was like any young singer or performer hoping to break into the popular music scene. His main hope of success was to have a hit single in the British Top 40. Given Britain's dominant position within the popular music charts of the sixties, young stars legitimately dreamed that this would propel them to more international forms of success. This was to elude Bowie until the release of 'Space Oddity' in 1969 which was his first chart success, reaching no. 5. Leading up to this period, Bowie was variously under the influence of the Beatles, then the Rolling Stones and the Who. While Britain was going through a revolution in popular music, Bowie sought success by imitating the leading bands of the time.

Despite the early impact of American style rock 'n' roll in the early sixties, it had not automatically swamped the teenage market. In fact a number of English, more family-orientated per-formers like Tommy Steele and Cliff Richard offered 'respectable' and 'toned down' versions of this music. Here popular music helped produce a masculinity that was 'scruffy and cheeky rather than menacing or sensual' (Laing 1969: 107). This softening of the overt masculine sexuality of early rock 'n' roll music (music that George Melly (1970: 36) described as 'screw and smash music') transformed it into popular entertainment. Notably both Tommy Steele and Cliff Richard released records, appeared in pantomimes and made feature films. In the early period of rock 'n' roll there had indeed been a transition from the 'teen lyrics' of acts like Bill Haley and the Comets to a brasher form of masculine heterosexuality evident in the music of Elvis Presley (Chambers 1985). As we shall see later, despite the 'mainstream' appeal of figures such as Tommy Steele and Cliff Richard, they were to be as important in the career of David Bowie as the more obvious influences of John Lennon of the Beatles and Mick Jagger of the Rolling Stones.

Beatlemania had reached its peak by the middle of the sixties. For just a few short years the so-called British invasion of the American charts meant that London was able to position itself as the world's music capital. While the focus of attention was soon to switch back to California, during the years 1965–7 swinging London became the centre of cultural innovation. The development of the counter-culture only later directly impacted on Bowie, and it is the impact of 'mod' during this period that is more easily discernible in his music. While neither the Beatles nor the Stones are usually directly associated with the mod movement, they were undoubtedly influenced by its cultural ripples. More crucially, according to the myth Bowie has constructed about himself and his friend and rival Marc Bolan, both could be found searching for mod gear in the bins of London's fashion district, Carnaby Street. Of all Bowie's bands, it was the Lower Third who adopted the most overtly mod image. Despite attracting a hard core following amongst London mods (especially at the Marquee club), their influence failed to spread. This lack of cultural impact and the adoption of a mod subcultural identity was an important point in the making of 'David Bowie'. The mod lifestyle that grew up around London in the early sixties offered a sense of stylishness that contrasted with the cruder masculinity of rockers. The mods fostered an image of stylish consumption, neat dress sense, Vespa scooters, green Parkas and coffee bars.

Mods were mostly of working- and lower middle-class origin, lived for the weekend and endured their employment as a means of engaging in visible consumption. Their dress sense confirmed a surface respectability, while their subversion came from the fact that they 'appeared' to conform to social norms. The mods seemingly engaged in a collective fantasy whereby the dream-like worlds of mass consumption could, if only in the imagination, transform the harsher realities of daily life. Mod signified the idea that new forms of identity could be fashioned out of 'ordinary' objects. The mods' obsession with small details of dress and appearance helped give them a feminine look. Hence mod culture, viewed more sociologically, interrupted the idea that masculinity was natural. By suggesting different heterosexual scripts from the dominant culture or the more overt masculinity of rock 'n' roll cultures, it offered a politics of stylistic innovation. In this respect, Bowie's later interest in bohemian artistic communities and subcultures like mod share a number of features in common. Both take pleasure in the displacement and partial destruction of existing forms of common sense. The radicalness of subcultures and more artistic/bohemian identifications comes from their ability to suggest alternatives to dominant definitions of 'normality' (Hebdige 1979).

Popular music and masculinity in the sixties

On 12 November 1964, David Jones appeared on BBC television as the President of the Society for the Prevention of Cruelty to Long-Haired Men. Interviewed by television journalist Cliff Michelmore, Jones complained of the remarks he had to suffer in respect of his long hair. These included 'Darlin'' and 'Can I carry your handbag?' David Jones's complaint was that young men could not have long hair without being accused of being homosexual. This, he said, had to stop.

David Jones evidently sought to use the media event as a publicity stunt to kick-start his musical career. In this easily forgotten television moment we have a microcosm of his later genius. By protesting against the ways the dominant culture polices the conduct of young men, Jones was practising an early form of cultural politics, whether or not he was playing his role in earnest (or more likely with his tongue firmly planted in his cheek). In making this move Bowie adopts the pose of the 'outsider'. This stance brings together, as we have seen, elements of beat culture, bohemianism, subculture and film star images that were offering different and more rebellious images of masculinity in the sixties.

The point here is not that mod culture was either overtly political or that it celebrated gayness. Popular music since the fifties and sixties has been a place where new sexualities have emerged and gained a foothold in public culture. To quote Jon Savage (1990: 160), fashionable and musical subcultures like mod 'took control of the "private" out of the hands of the dominant culture'. Mods did not so much provide an assault on dominant masculine norms but blurred questions of sexuality in ways that meant they were positioned both inside and outside the dominant culture. Many of those participating, and indeed influencing, the direction of the subculture were aware of the challenge mod posed to more traditional masculine sensibilities. Phil Lancaster, a former member of the moddish Lower Third, was resistant to some of the feminine features suggested by the mod look. He comments: 'I'd never known blokes put hair lacquer on. I said I wouldn't go – to me it was being queer' (Gillman 1986: 104–5).

Mod then sought to blur the distinction between gay culture and heterosexuality by suggesting new codes of conduct and self-presentation. If popular music in the sixties stopped some way short of advocating gayness, it certainly developed new modes of heterosexual masculinity.

These features can be brought into focus by looking at the two most influential groups of the sixties, the Beatles and the Stones. Both the Beatles and the Stones offered more androgynous forms of masculinity, but expressed them in different ways. Whereas the Beatles offered a soft masculinity of reciprocal communication, the performance of the Stones was more aggressive and brash. Much of the Beatles' image and lyrics offered an alternative to the dominant norms of tough masculinity. The cultivation of expressiveness, an ease with tenderness and the desire to communicate were features of many of their songs (Bromell 2000). The form of masculinity being performed here is a new form of heterosexuality that is learning to communicate with the feminine. Many Beatles' songs contain pleas for understanding ('Help'), fleeting erotic encounters ('Norwegian Wood') and an acceptance of equal relations between the sexes ('The Ballad of John and Yoko'). On the other hand, the Stones on record and in performance, while flirting with androgyny, symbolized a masculinized form of cock rock. Jagger's outrageous stage presence incorporated a strutting, dominating and boastful male sexuality.

The contrast is evident in the Stones' song 'Street Fighting Man' and the Beatles' 'Revolution'. Notably both songs were released as singles in 1968. This was the year of civil rights protests in America, the invasion of Czechoslovakia by Soviet troops and global protest against the war in Vietnam. 1968 is the year when the 'permissive society' finally arrived, along with a number of liberal reforms in terms of the regulation of personal conduct in areas such as homosexuality and artistic censorship (Green 1999). Popularly this is often understood as a time of freedom and autonomy when the constraints of the past were discarded in favour of new freedoms. Yet the cultural consequences of social and cultural change are communicated quite differently by the Beatles and the Stones. While Lennon's vocals in 'Revolution' warn against the excesses of violent and destructive masculinity, this is precisely what is celebrated by Jagger's strutting performance in 'Street Fighting Man'. 'Revolution' cautions against 'people with minds that hate', advocating 'freeing your mind instead'. The gentler masculinity of the Beatles suggests a different path to those who 'talk about destruction'. By comparison, Jagger's tone is more self-assured as he crows that 'Yes, I think the time is right for violent revolution.' What is important for the emergence of David Bowie is the extent to which popular music is unsettling codes of masculinity. The pluralization of masculinities made available by public cultures in the sixties paved the way for more radical forms of experimentation later (Whiteley 1997).

Englishness, Utopia and the lost Deram album

Despite the radical innovations taking place within popular music, Bowie's first album (released on the Deram label and called simply *David Bowie*) can be more easily connected to English popular entertainers like Tommy Steele than the stylistic innovations of sixties' popular music. Bowie's first album was released on 1 June 1967, the same day as the Beatles' ground-breaking album *Sgt Pepper's Lonely Hearts Club Band*. Yet it is easy to overlook the fact that the Beatles' avant-garde album included 'With a Little Help from My Friends' and 'When I'm Sixty-Four', both evoking a sense of cheerful entertainment. It is however the popularity of songs by Bernard Cribbins and Anthony Newley who evoked a working-class idiom by singing in cockney accents that more directly influenced Bowie's recording (Melly 1970: 67).

Many have seen Bowie's first album as an embarrassment. At first it is hard to believe that the Deram album is made by the same artist who would a few years later release *Ziggy Stardust*, *Aladdin Sane* and *Diamond Dogs*. It is not, as its detractors are aware, avant-garde pretension that marks out Bowie's first recording. The British music magazine, *New Musical Express*, commented: 'Here's a Cockney singer who reminds me of Anthony Newley and Tommy Steele, which can't be bad. He sings with a mild beat, about ordinary things like a Rubber Band, an Uncle Arthur, about a romance which started on Sunday and he promised to Love You Till Tuesday' (Pitt 1983: 75). The album at first listening exemplifies a quirky English sensibility containing a number of novelty or comic recordings like 'The Laughing Gnome', 'Uncle Arthur' and 'Please Mr Gravedigger'. Under the guidance of his then manager, Kenneth Pitt, the record positioned Bowie as the next popular entertainer to exploit the transformation of rock 'n' roll into innocent teenage pop.

To dismiss the record in this way is to misunderstand Bowie's aesthetic sensibility. First, viewed through the lens of Bowie's later recordings, a number of his most prominent themes are evident on this record. 'She's Got Medals' is a cheeky tale of a woman originally named Mary who changes her name to Tommy to join the army, and then becomes Eileen on settling down in London. Bowie's interest in cross-dressing and gender transformation is given early recognition. 'We are Hungry Men' concerns the prospect of global ecological collapse due to over-population, with Bowie cast in the role of fascist messiah leading the people into the promised land. However, more important than the words is the way in which these songs are sung and performed. These songs need to be understood as tongue-in-cheek narratives which are sung in character rather than auto-biographical expressions of Bowie's own beliefs. There are good reasons to avoid reading Bowie's songs as an expression of his deep inner self. There is a strong British tradition of the 'charac-ter' song which connects recording artists like the Kinks, Elvis Costello and Blur across the generations (Frith 1996). Bowie remains part of this popular tradition. Finally, whatever Bowie's later avant-garde pretensions, he remains a popular entertainer. Bowie's theatricality has been heavily influenced by an English music hall tradition that is especially evident on his earliest recordings.

Bowie's first long-playing recording emphasizes a pronounced sense of Englishness under threat and in decline. Rather than celebrating the modernity of London's swinging sixties, Bowie's first album articulates a number of outsiders ('Uncle Arthur', 'She's Got Medals', 'Little Bombardier') who display an inabil-ity to fit into conventional roles and identities including gender and matrimony. This is the voice of an 'old England' which, having lost its empire and been ravaged by two World Wars, is caught in a downward spiral. In this, it is the horror of England's wartime past that is never far from the surface, constructing a sense of misery and eccentricity. The album's cultural English-ness and quirkiness gives it an overwhelmingly suburban feel. The world of the city is seen as a space of corruption, vanity, squalor and exploitation. The album is less a celebration of what the Who called 'My Generation' and more a cynical commentary on new metropolitan lifestyles. Unlike many popular musicians and teenagers connected to subcultural movements, Bowie fails to evoke any sense of generational difference. Bowie's characters are curiously out of step with his own recent past, articulating a cynical reading of new subcultural lifestyles in 'The London Boys' ('you take the pills too much') and 'Join the Gang' ('it's a big illusion, but at least you are in') that distances the narrator from the pleasures of youthful styles. It is a decaying suburban Englishness that takes centre stage. This is evoked through a need to escape into another less corrupt world, evident most powerfully in the infamous last track, 'Please Mr Gravedigger'. From the sound of bombs dropping in the background to the chiming church bells, it resonates with a sense of a disappearing England. An England of small churches, gravediggers, loneliness and child murders is powerfully articulated on one of Bowie's most eccentric tracks. In English popular music, it is probably the Smiths in the 1980s who most consistently revisit this territory.

Viewed in terms of Bowie's later career, the two most important songs on the Deram album are 'When I Live My Dream' and 'There is a Happy Land'. This is not because they are radical in form or content but because they represent a suburban utopianism. Questions of utopia and dystopia are periodic concerns in Bowie's music. By utopian I do not mean that Bowie sketches a fully worked-out 'other' world like the writers Thomas More or William Morris. Bowie's utopianism, at this point, is distinct from the radical constructions of counter-cultural movements. As the cultural critic Richard Dyer (1992: 18) notes, utopia in an entertainment context is more a case of 'the feelings it embodies' rather than 'how it would be organised'. Such is the importance of conceptions of utopia in Bowie's music that we will be returning to this concept later. For now, the utopia conjured up by the two songs in question have their roots in a conservative politics. Both 'When I Live My Dream' and 'There is a Happy Land' represent the need to disappear into a fairy-tale world. Bowie sings that 'there is a happy land where only children live'. This is a world where the rigid conformity required by suburban modes of living can only be escaped by regressing into childhood. The utopian impulse does not so much promise a better tomorrow as it does within more radical art, but offers seductive forms of escape. The world of childhood is returned to in order to escape a broken heart or flee from the corruption of grown-ups. Englishness has been corrupted by the ravages of war and the modern economy but it remains preserved in fantasy. This is a suburban solution to a political question. If redemption cannot be discovered by recovering a more urbane politics, then we can only hope to escape from the present. This is a deeply conservative cultural politics. The unsettling influence of the city is rejected by stealing a brief visit to the fantasy land of childhood. Perhaps what is key at this point is that Bowie affirms he is a 'dreaming kind of guy'. Whatever the context, we could argue, the utopian impulse does at least open the possibility for something different to be imagined. At this point, however, it is an English cultural nationalism that appears to be dominant.

Whereas Bowie's later stylistic innovations would seek to escape suburbia through a bohemian sensibility, here the exit route leads back to childhood. If Bowie's music of the early seventies offers a utopian form of individualism, it is less radical and more suburban motifs that are offered on his first recording. Notably the single 'Rubber Band' (first released in December 1966) tells the story of a man who loses his 'sweetheart' due to the First World War; similarly 'Little Bombardier' narrates a post-war tale of unemployment, loneliness and finally exile.

The structure of feeling of a suburban Englishness about to be eclipsed shares a number of sentiments with George Orwell's ([1939] 1990) character George Bowling in his novel *Coming Up for Air*. George or 'Fatty' Bowling is a middle-aged married man with children from the London suburbs who temporarily seeks to escape his life of drab respectability by disappearing into the land of his childhood. He runs away from his 'nagging' wife, demanding children, creeping commercialism and middle-class conformity. For George Bowling, 'the basic trouble with people like us, I said to myself, is that we all imagine we've something to lose' (Orwell [1939] 1990: 11). His over-regulated life as an insurance salesman and the threat of impending war sends George into daydreams about his childhood. George's imagination is captured by images of Sunday dress, church halls, village greens and fishing by the river. These images of pastoral Englishness are shattered when he finds that the Lower Binfield of his childhood is actually populated by unfriendly strangers, mass housing projects and industrial civilization. On discovering that a pond where he had fished as a boy had become a rubbish dump, George flies into a rage: 'they'd filled my pool up with tin cans. God rot and bust them! Say what you like – call it silly, childish, anything – but doesn't it make you puke sometimes to see what they're doing to England, with their bird-baths and their plastic gnomes, and their pixies and tin cans, where the beech woods used to be?' (Orwell [1939] 1990: 229).

Bowie's first album and Orwell's novel seemingly share a number of features in common. The idea of Englishness in decline, the utopian fantasy and hope offered by a retreat into childhood, and finally a sense of a dream shattered by the impossibility of returning to more innocent and less tainted times. These are indeed the fantasies of English suburbia. Overall the sound of the album evokes a sense of English eccentricity. Produced by Mike Vernon, it mixes the usual fare of popular music (guitar, piano, drums) with music hall (tuba and trumpet) and more random sound effects. Despite biographer David Buckley's (1999) accurate perception that Bowie had taken his first steps towards merging the worlds of theatre and popular music, it seems that his art had already reached a dead end.

The project of converting Bowie into a mainstream star at this stage failed. This undoubtedly had as much to do with the dated quality of the music as it did with Deram's failure to promote the album. Over the next few years Bowie's music would undergo a dramatic change of direction. The aim of becoming a cabaret star would gradually be replaced by the allure of rock and popular music. Perhaps more significantly, Bowie would switch his musical orientations into a closer relationship with the sixties' counter-culture.

Space Oddity, Dylan and the counter-culture

The narrative recounted by many of the biographies is that Bowie's new direction can be located within a change of lifestyle.

At the time of recording his first album Bowie was sharing living space with his then manager, Kenneth Pitt. While the nature of the relationship is contested, Pitt seemed to play the role of a substitute father. Pitt, by most accounts, was a closet homosexual who sought to guide and substantially subsidize Bowie's career in its early stages. Given the long period before Bowie's image and music found resonance with a mass audience, it is probably true to say he would not have become a star without Pitt's help. Pitt not only materially supported Bowie, but sought to give him an education in the arts, theatre and modern literature. Bowie's avowed bookishness found an outlet in Pitt who introduced the young artist to the works of radical and gay writers from Oscar Wilde to James Baldwin. Like many gay and bisexual men of this period, Bowie was attracted to theatrical and artistic high culture as it allowed 'queerness' at least some recognition.

Pitt's role in Bowie's development as an artist is illustrated in a letter he received from John Jones. Bowie's father writes to Pitt:

> Rather belatedly I am writing to thank you for the various doc-
> uments, copies of letters and pieces of information concerning
> David you have so kindly sent from time to time. My wife and I
> are grateful to you for sending us a copy of the album – this was
> indeed a kind thought. This seems to be the first major break-
> through and we both have every confidence that with your help
> and guidance David will in due course achieve the success his
> ability and hard work deserve. (28 June 1967, Pitt 1983: 80)

The formal and financial tone of the letter implies Pitt is a guardian figure. However, the relationship between Pitt and Bowie has been represented by many as holding back Bowie's development, and as being largely responsible for his inferior output before he discovered the liberating potential of the counter-culture. This is at best an overstatement, and at worst a disguised form of homophobia. Pitt's sensibilities were undoubtedly those of a man from a different generation, and yet it is likely that he considerably broadened Bowie's cultural horizons while offering him financial support.

It is during this period that Bowie met a number of other people who were to have an important impact on his artistic development. This resulted in a power struggle between Kenneth Pitt and others, while Bowie reflected on the future direction of his career. Still under Pitt's protection, Bowie began to associate himself with more overtly bohemian influences. Indeed it has been Bowie's lifelong capacity to bridge the worlds of popular entertainment, bohemia and the high arts that best explains his early creative roots. During the lead-up to Bowie's next album he experimented with mime, folk music and Buddhism while developing an interest in UFOs and American popular culture. It is out of this cultural mixture that Bowie's best known music was born.

Bowie's participation in the counter-culture involved him in the Beckenham Arts Lab which supported a hybrid mix of folk music, mime, poetry and art. Here the emphasis was placed upon authentic forms of self-expression within a supportive community. During this period Bowie helped edit an arts-based newsletter called *Growth* which held that 'Growth is people, Growth is revolution, Growth grows at its own speed, expands according to the energy input it receives, is open to all, but closed to old ideas, clichés, destructive elements and grey thoughts' (Sandford 1996). The ideas and discourses associated with folk rock articulated an anti-commercialism that sought to espouse less tainted modes of cultural expression.

It is also during this period that Bowie studied mime under the tutelage of the artist and performer Lindsay Kemp. Bowie was to say of Kemp later: 'He lived on his emotions, he was a wonderful influence. His day-to-day life was the most theatrical thing I have seen, ever. It was everything I thought Bohemia probably was. I joined the circus' (Buckley 1999: 45).

Bowie performed with Kemp in a production called *Pierrot in Turquoise* during 1967. Joining 'the circus', as Bowie put it, would later enable him to bring elements of theatre and performance into popular music. Kemp, a bohemian gay man, offered a set of influences very different from those of folk music. He was a larger-than-life figure who combined flamboyance, eccentricity and artistry. The idea of bohemia offered a refuge where the young Bowie (and those like him) could explore experiences other than those sanctioned by 'mainstream' society. Kemp's life was given over to the idea of dedicated performance. Both Kemp and his boyfriend Orlando were shaved bald and outrageously camp. Kemp's lack of artistic success did not prevent him from viewing his life and art with the utmost seriousness. It is here that Bowie encountered the idea of the artist as rebel, seeking to stretch the limits of the possible. Many of Bowie's biographers have underestimated the importance of this cultural involvement, as they did the earlier Deram album. This is largely because mime is not considered by many to be a 'proper' art form. More to the point was the way the idea of bohemia became a haven for a number of artistic practices that were to receive neither mass appreciation nor academic credibility. This allowed artistic experimentation in the sixties which sought to break with dominant forms of contemporary experience. The other cultural space that aided Bowie's development was the counter-culture.

The counter-culture was particularly critical of the masculinity of the productivist worker. There was a widespread desire to uncover different forms of experience and rationality that had been subsumed under the needs of a repressive capitalist system. This provided the focus for a different form of radical politics that did not just emphasize the needs of minorities. The sixties was a time when a number of social movements from gay politics to feminism and from black civil rights to working-class trade unionists were beginning to make themselves heard. We have already seen how in the field of popular music and entertainment previously excluded identities were emerging. Yet the counter-culture also offered definitions of 'unfreedom' that attracted millions of white middle-class people into its ranks. The politics of liberation was not exclusively a concern of the culturally marginalized and the materially downtrodden.

One of the most prominent philosophers of the sixties was Herbert Marcuse. In a number of publications, Marcuse (1968, 1969) argued that Western societies suffered from what he called 'surplus repression'. The capitalist system, he said, required an alienated worker and a 'happy' consumer to the detriment of more authentic forms of human development. Radical politics should be, in Marcuse's terms, about the expansion of human happiness. It was the release of repressed energies through more libidinous forms of sexuality, playful work and artistic creativity that could deliver a new era of authentic freedom and fulfilment. Society was based upon the repression of the instincts and the promotion of aggression. According to the historian of the sixties, David Pichaske (1989: 12), this was popularly translated as 'let's let the machines do the work, and let's get loaded, sing, dance and screw'. The sixties-based counter-culture was centrally concerned with a revolution of the self against established forms of authority and tradition. Indeed the importance of the popular music of the Beatles, the Stones and Bob Dylan is that they communicated this revolution to a mass audience. This is a further indication of how the left/right polarity of the sixties does not map onto the more culturally ambivalent features of the decade. Rightist arguments about moral decay and leftist concerns about revolutionary possibilities fail to connect with the idea that the sixties more popularly can be understood as an individual and collective experiment in new forms of lifestyle and self-expression.

The shift into new forms of creativity evident within popular music is what Beatles expert Ian MacDonald (1995) calls 'a revolution in the head'. By this he means that the lasting historical legacy of the sixties was the rise of popular individualism. It is the inward turn and search for personal forms of liberation that connect the concerns of authenticity and personal expression, giving rise to both folk music and gay politics. Both of these social and aesthetic movements in their early phases valued the natural and the spontaneous as opposed to the dominant values of technocratic civilization. These different social and cultural movements sought to enhance 'authentic' cultural expression 'repressed' by contemporary capitalism. These perspectives, like the ones we hold today, are the product of a particular time and place. That Bowie was exploring new forms of artistic expression through music, religion and mime simply meant that as ever he was a man of his time. This is a time when experiments with the self were linked to a form of political utopianism whereby a politics of the imagination was connected to the possibility of a future without repression. If sexuality and creative self-expression were actively disallowed by the system then a new society needed to be created. The recognition of polymorphous sexuality, aspects of experience seemingly beyond Western rationality and a greater emphasis upon play all created cultural waves beyond their source.

These aspects undoubtedly form the background to the recording of Bowie's second album, confusingly like the first also called *David Bowie*, but this time with the subtitle *Man of Words, Man of Music*. This was released in Britain on the Philips label right at the end of the sixties in November 1969. The record was to emerge in a cultural climate that caught artists and commercial institutions within a complex set of contradictions. A poster which sought to advertise the album *David Bowie* (1969) read: 'Go straight to your nearest friendly together neighborhood record dealer and ask for a new Philips album called David Bowie (or SBL7912, if that's the way you feel). He'll have some bread off you. But what's that if it gets you a headful of DAVID BOWIE at his best.' This exemplifies the problem for musicians who were both part of the counter-culture while utilizing commercial institutions to disseminate their work. If, in Marcuse's terms, capitalism perpetuates itself through the creation of false needs, then how do popular musicians maintain their 'credibility' and 'authenticity' while working within the 'system'? It is the satisfaction of these false needs through the development of commercial television and advertising that is preventing the development of a more authentic society. Musicians sympathetic to the counter-culture would have been trapped between the desire to reach a wide audience (thereby implicating themselves in the capitalist music industry) and the need to connect with less commercially oriented values.

This ambivalence has given rise to some of the most powerful myths of contemporary music. The distinction between popular music and rock music has arisen from these contradictions. Rock is defined through the rejection of music that is characterized as soft, trivial, overly commercial and worthless. These features are seen as being characteristic of pop; whereas rock is concerned with authentic forms of rebellion, freedom, technical musicianship and uniqueness. The development of rock and the counter-culture in the sixties sought to provide new ways of valuing popular music. Many critics have noted how this distinction is similar to that used to map the difference between high and popular culture. High culture is the preserve of the educated whereas mass culture is cheap, unsubstantial and consumable. From our point of view it is also important to note the gendered nature of the opposition between rock and pop (Keightly 2001). Rock culture is engaged in a taste war in favour of the 'tough' and 'muscular' as opposed to the merely 'decorative' forms of cultural production engaged in by 'pop' musicians. The problem the counter-culture sought to correct was that adult 'straight' society promoted ephemeral popular music. The refusal of the mainstream was sustained through the production of a cultural space that was 'outside' of consumer culture. Rock's seriousness and rebelliousness distinguished it from pop. The result was the displacement of everything that was 'bad' about music into the domain of the popular. This meant that 'rock' was able to gain respectability while appearing to be above the commercialism of the dominant society. That rock music uses similar means of promotion, selling techniques and commodification to popular music is of course obscured by this logic.

The opposition between rock and pop will prove to be important for our study. It is precisely these oppositions that Bowie seeks to deconstruct within his image and his music. However, at the close of the sixties, it is these contours that Bowie is working within. The seriousness of rock and the counter-culture was in the search for a more rebellious 'true self' that might point the way beyond 'mainstream' society. Like many other performers in the sixties, Bowie emphasizes his authenticity by positioning himself as a singer-songwriter. This was an important way of establishing credibility with an audience. The 'authenticity' of an artist was established by expressing a disdain for glamour and the material rewards of stardom. For the counter-culture such rewards hindered the pursuit of art and self-expression. By the time Bowie came to work on his new album, much of the optimistic rhetoric of the counter-culture was beginning to fade. The idea of developing an alternative society on the principles of freedom and love were dealt a severe blow at the free

Rolling Stones concert at Altamont Speedway in December 1969. The concert was interrupted by the violent behaviour of Hell's Angels who killed one of the few black men in the audience.

The decline of the counter-culture can be traced through the career of Bob Dylan. Dylan and his music are important in our context given his influence on Bowie's music of this period and his significance for the counter-culture. Much has been written on Dylan's importance in respect of the American Folk Revival. In America the folk revival had reached its height in the summer of 1963 at the Newport Folk Festival. The festival ended with the communal singing of Dylan's 'Blowin' in the Wind' and the Baptist hymn which had become the anthem of the civil rights movement, 'We Shall Overcome'. Folk culture has its own distinctive rituals and performance rites that need to be understood. Folk values naturalness, anti-commercialism and is suspicious of glamour. Joan Baez (who regularly appeared with Dylan and was rumoured to have been his lover) is a good representative of a folk performer in that she wore little make-up, simple clothes and often performed barefoot. Above all, folk seeks to questions the division between art and life where communal gatherings take priority over the status of well-known stars (Frith 1996). It is this movement that many of Dylan's followers at the time perceived him to have betrayed by turning electric. Dylan's transition from a folk singer writing songs to further a social movement into an individual artist was a painful one. His music shifted from overtly social concerns to more individual poetic dimensions. The release of *Highway 61 Revisited* (1965) and *Blonde on Blonde* (1966) and his tour of Britain during this time attracted a good deal of public controversy. The British tour of 1965–6 was in stark contrast to his previous tour in 1964 where he had been mobbed by enthusiastic fans. This time he was met by the anger and frustration of a number of his followers who felt he had turned his back on them (MacDonald 2003; Marcus 1997). This culminated in a single infamous event on 17 May 1966 at the Manchester Free Trade Hall when a fan shouted out 'Judas' to which Dylan replied 'I don't believe you. You're a liar!' The perception was that Dylan had betrayed a social movement in favour of rock star arrogance. Yet what is important for our purpose is that Dylan's music in this period abounds with disillusionment and cynicism. It evokes not the warm communalism of the civil rights movement but the expression of both individual and social disaffection. His poetic masterpiece, 'Desolation Row' (from *Highway 61 Revisited*), strikes a tone of wistful resignation that offers little sense of social redemption. 'Desolation Row' is peopled with a surreal collection of broken heroes including Dr Filth, Ophelia, Cinderella, Einstein, Ezra Pound and T. S. Eliot. The song is delivered through gritted teeth and, while it articulates sympathy for the oppressed, it defies and is critical of the counter-culture.

This digression is important, given the prominence of Dylan within Bowie's musical imagination. Bowie is reported to have burst into tears when Kenneth Pitt pointed out that his new record sounded like an impersonation of his new hero. In contrast to Dylan's music, however, Bowie's critique of 'the new society' is less guarded and more clearly articulated. This is probably due to their different positions and status in respect of the counter-culture: Dylan was a major voice and influence whereas Bowie was still seeking to make his name. Due to Dylan's renown as a significant figure within the folk revival, his social concerns had to be more heavily disguised than Bowie's.

Bowie's second album, while undoubtedly influenced by Dylan, is not simply an expression of Dylan's poetic cynicism. If anything it moves between utopianism (this time inspired by the counter-culture), cultural cynicism and more 'personal' forms of pain. These different contradictory positions are not resolved within the album, and give grounds to the argument that Bowie's flirtation with folk rock was to be a brief affair.

The loss of his father, John Jones, while Bowie was working on the recording and the break up with his then partner, Hermione Lee, were to deeply affect the young artist. A growing sense of ambivalence towards his substitute 'father', Kenneth Pitt, meant that Bowie was experiencing an ongoing period of dislocation and change. It is during this period that Bowie met two people who were to become significant figures in shaping his personal life and professional career. These were his friend and fellow musician, Tony Visconti, who was to produce Bowie's current album and much of his best work over the years, and the woman he was later to marry, Angela Barnett (or Angie). Both Visconti and Angie helped pull Bowie in more counter-cultural directions and were significant figures during the recording of *David Bowie: Man of Words, Man of Music*.

Bowie's sense of personal loss is most evident on 'Letter to Hermione'. The song evokes confusion and bewilderment at the end of a love affair with the injured party clinging to the past. Given that Bowie during this period is under the influence of folk rock, his music has a more intensely autobiographical frame of reference than much of his later writing. While the music, even during this period, is never just a reflection of his experience, it is possible with this particular song to trace connections between Bowie the artist and the life of David Jones. It is precisely this presumed link, as we shall see, that becomes more difficult (although not impossible) to make as his career progresses. Part of the mythology of folk rock was to create a sense of the artist writing about their own inner and outer experiences. While the pose of the folk-rock musician is no less pronounced than some of Bowie's more overtly invented characters, the music expresses a concrete relation between life and cultural expressions. The relationship between some of Bowie's later cultural creations, including Ziggy Stardust, seeks if anything to challenge these connections. The 'Cygnet Committee' offers a bitter and disillusioned interpretation of the counter-culture. Bowie predicts the end of the counter-culture: 'the road is coming to its end'. The narrative moves on to warn against easily worn slogans like 'love is all you need' or 'kick out the jams'('Cygnet Committee', 1969). Bowie delivers the song as an anguished cry as though trying to hold onto radical ideals in a context where they are fast disappearing. Unlike Bowie's earlier observations on the counter-culture, this one is made by an insider rather than an outsider. Yet the perspective of the outsider re-emerges through a sense of disconnection from those who have become corrupted by 'business cesspools'. The sense of the corruption of the counter-culture needs to be opposed to its ongoing potential most evident on 'Memory of a Free Festival'. 'Memory of a Free Festival' was written to commemorate Bowie's own participation in the Beckenham Free Festival held on 16 August 1969. The song describes an afternoon of peace, drug-induced psychedelia and love as Bowie played 'songs and felt the London sky'. Many of his biographers unearth a different memory of the afternoon which recalls David being upset by some of the festival supporters' attempts to make money (Gillman and Gillman 1986: 178, Sandford 1996: 57). The album, later retitled *Space Oddity*, is also notable for being Bowie's first collaboration with his long-term friend and producer, Tony Visconti. In fact the album does not sound out of place next to much of the guitar-based folk and rock music of this period. Bowie at this time was running with rather than against or ahead of the dominant styles in popular music.

Bowie was a product of sixties' culture. Yet if the music we have described so far encompassed his total output it is unlikely I would be writing this book. Until the end of the sixties, Bowie was still searching for his own voice. While I have sought to describe the ways that music and society work through one another, we cannot ignore the spark of individual creativity offered by the artist himself. It is possible to overstate the extent to which we are manufactured by our history and culture and this chapter should end with the event that changed everything. This was the release in July 1969 of Bowie's breakthrough single 'Space Oddity'.

'Space Oddity' remains one of Bowie's most played and popular songs. Like all music that embeds itself in our consciousness, the reasons for this are often complex. Popular music is a multi-layered phenomenon that gives rise to diverse and often contradictory forms of understanding. Indeed writers on black American music have long been aware that popular music can exhibit a 'double consciousness' (Gilroy 1993). This concept seeks to unravel the extent to which black people and black cultures have been produced in a situation where they are both inside and outside the West. The history of black people is one of movement across borders, intercultural dialogue and aesthetics, and the suffering of discrimination and racism. The historian of black popular music, Craig Werner (2000), has argued that black popular music has generally made a better case for politi-

cal change than political manifestos. Sometimes this was communicated directly, for instance by Aretha Franklin demanding
'Respect' in 1967 or, more ambiguously, by Martha Reeves and
the Vandellas partially documenting a race riot in 'Dancing in
the Street'. The racialized meanings of these songs were understood by many among the black audiences of the time.

What does this have to do with Bowie? In order to capture the
meaning of the song, we need to explore its initial context. 'Space
Oddity' has often been interpreted as a song about the space
race and the consequences of living in a civilization increasingly
driven by science and technology and the sense of alienation that
this produces. Indeed, many of Bowie's contemporaries saw the
single as an attempt to 'cash in' on the space race and the popular
fascination with outer space and Stanley Kubrick's film *2001: A
Space Odyssey*. In this respect, the record has a chequered history.
Despite Kenneth Pitt's attempts to buy the song into the charts, it
was initially banned by the BBC. The Apollo mission had not yet
returned from its trip to the moon and the disc failed to make it
onto radio playlists. However, one of the reasons the song continues to have resonance within our culture is its connection with
a utopian politics of the self that was being promoted by new
social movements. Bowie as a bisexual male would have existed
both within and outside the structures of Western modernity.
The song evokes the possibility of breaking free of earthly constraints and becoming the star of your own life. This resonates
with the ambition of gay politics at the close of the sixties to
realize the self as opposed to succumbing to the dominant society
that sought to hide homosexuality in a closet. Gay liberation
displays a family resemblance to the counter-culture's desire to
liberate human nature from the constraints of the system. The
desire to move beyond existing social and sexual realities is
both liberating and potentially troubling. The metaphor of space
travel is recurrent within Bowie's work and cannot simply be
dismissed as a reference to the landings on the moon.

Viewed in the context of other songs of this period (like the
Beatles' 'Lucy in the Sky with Diamonds'), the song undoubtedly
also refers to the experience of drug taking. However, again, I
would resist the idea that 'Space Oddity' can be reductively

understood as a response to either chemical reaction or the space race. Popular music is always a cultural invention and never merely a consequence of other processes. The song continues to strike a chord with our own times as it suggests the possibility of reinventing the self. Such reinvention has to take place in outer space where we are less constrained by existing realities. Not surprisingly, for many in the gay liberation movement, the idea of escaping the dominant heterosexist society would appear to be a utopian one in a cruel and discriminating society. As Bowie sings, 'I am floating in the most peculiar way' ('Space Oddity', 1969). Not for the last time in the context of a pop song Bowie explores the possibility of becoming something different. We all need hope and aesthetic experiences that allow us to dream of the (im)possible. Bowie, it seems, was just discovering the power of this logic. The song itself begins with an acoustic guitar solo and drums gradually build it into a more orchestrated sound (strings, flute, cello). This track was produced by Gus Dudgeon rather than Tony Visconti and is also remembered for Rick Wakeman playing the mellotron. While the production gives the song a technological sound that complements the narrative, it is Bowie's voice that really stands out. Despite, as I have argued, Bowie being influenced by Dylan at this point, his voice here is already distinctively his own. Neither overtly masculine nor feminine, it depicts perfectly controlled emotion moving from warning to resignation as he narrates the drama of an ill-fated space flight.

Yet Bowie remains a figure of such intense contradiction that he cannot be understood by relating him purely to potentially progressive causes. In an interview with journalist Kate Simpson for the music paper 'Music Now!', Bowie introduces a theme with which many of his sympathetic followers would struggle. Here he speaks at length about his frustration with the counter-culture:

> You have to do your own 'thing', and if you haven't got that awareness then you are not the kind of person who is going to be able to run your own life. Unless of course you are in a certain state where you are happy to follow other people. You can't analyse it.

We've been trying for two thousand years. This country is crying out for a leader. God knows what it is looking for, but if it's not careful it's going to end up with a Hitler. This place is ready to be picked up by anybody who has a strong enough personality to lead. The only person who is coming through with any strength is Enoch Powell. He is the only one with a following. (Simpson 1969)

Bowie's political consciousness pulls him in opposite directions. The first is a reaction against both the communalism of the counter-culture and the dominant forms of reality sanctioned by the system. This search will ultimately involve him in the radical gay and artistic movements coming out of America in the late sixties and early seventies. Yet, as we shall see, as Bowie discovers the language of the artistic avant-garde, he becomes even further entrapped in its contradictions. Bowie's desire to shock through arresting images and cultural associations is simultaneously radical and reactionary. This perhaps also demonstrates how cultural movements can be both radical and exclusive. The defence of the right-wing and racist politician, Enoch Powell, as we shall see later offers an authoritarian context to the understanding of Bowie's music. It also amply demonstrates how the new 'freedoms' of the self embodied in popular music can be articulated in a number of ways.

three

POSTMODERN BOWIE

Bowie, I have argued, emerged out of the engagements and tensions of the sixties. As a result of the impact of popular music, social movements and the media of mass communication, society witnessed a collective experiment in 'becoming'. The era of the sixties lives on in the modern imagination due to the fact that it introduced for the first time the possibility of people working on their identity in response to a society that was flooded with images, information and new ideas and perspectives. This cultural change for good or ill cannot be cynically dismissed as rampant commercialism or mourned as the passing of a well-ordered society but has to be viewed as a truly mass project. What to become and how to be are the central questions for an age where everything that was fixed and solid is now seemingly open to question. Here we see the emergence of a new kind of politics – the politics of identity.

If the personal becomes political then how we make ourselves becomes every bit as crucial as the more traditional concerns of who gets what. If what we might become is open to question, this inevitably dissolves the comfort of certainty. The politicization of self-identity both opens new possibilities as well as being fraught with existential anxiety. If we can 'shop around' for an identity, we are partially free to make and unmake identities. Or at least so it seems. However, viewed more carefully, what becomes evident at the end of the sixties is a society that continues to regulate and police the production of identity. As most critics of identity politics fully recognize, even during times where human societies are expanding their cultural repertoires of identities they might seek to inhabit, powerful cultural norms continue to rule in and rule out different kinds of identity. There is then no identity that is not policed, checked over and sanctioned. If you like, since the sixties we are what we make ourselves, but we are so as a result of certain pressures and opportunities. The kinds of experimentation engaged in by stars, icons and celebrities can indeed lead to more expanded and open repertoires on the part of ordinary people. But, as we shall see, how this is translated into popular experience is a different story.

Whatever our politics, we need to recognize that at the end of the sixties for increasing numbers of people identity was not so much experienced as a given but conceived of as a task. If the cracks in the regulation of identity had started to emerge in the fifties, by the sixties they were becoming huge social and cultural transformations. While society remained heavily regulated by divisions of gender, race and class, the possibility of escaping these 'facts of nature' – if just for a moment – was becoming increasingly apparent. The popular music and commercial culture of the seventies offered the chance to escape into a different world where it was possible to shape a 'new you', to metamorphose into a different kind of human being. What emerges from the sixties, after the decline of the counter-culture, is the possibility of remaking the self under new directions and influences.

To say that Bowie was at the forefront of these changes is an exaggeration. However, to argue that he instinctively understood and tapped into these dimensions takes us to the heart of his genius. But there is a crucial difference from the sixties in terms of the politics of identity. If the counter-culture sought to find the 'real me' that was submerged beneath the 'false needs' imposed by mainstream society, such ideas at the turn of the decade were coming to look more like restriction than liberation. What, many were beginning to ask, if there were no 'real me' waiting to be discovered? What indeed are we to make of ourselves if commercial and image cultures are drawn upon as a resource in the making of the self? If 'the rules' as to how we assemble ourselves are increasingly open to question, then which direction 'should' we take? This, as we shall see, is the ground upon which Bowie's images and musical narratives work and disturb. Letting go of the idea of the 'deep self' is just a further step in proclaiming our identities as something we can endlessly refashion and remake. There are of course deep dangers in this process. Such a process, as we will see, is as likely to end up with new forms of artistic experimentation as with increasingly shallow forms of consumer narcissism. The sixties won new freedoms as to how we might fashion the self, but this 'freedom' can be used in a number of different ways. In this chapter I want to concentrate upon the generative side of the argument and engage in what I have called 'the possibility' of identity.

Reinventing the self in pop

The end of the sixties and the collapse of the counter-culture led many at the dawn of the new decade to start searching for new political and artistic opportunities. Indeed, the revolutionary possibilities of aesthetic and social experimentation were soon to witness political retreat with a popular reaction against the perceived excesses of the sixties. The summer of love of 1967 had quickly become a distant memory, the cultural landscape becoming increasingly coloured by those who sought to distance themselves from the perceived immorality of the counter-culture. Here conservative campaigners, on both sides of the Atlantic, began to concern themselves with bad language, the display of sexuality and the widespread perception of the perversion of morals. However, no culture completely changes or disappears overnight. In terms of popular music, the early seventies were characterized by musical forms that were clearly rooted in the sixties. The mutual development of both progressive rock and teen pop inevitably grew out of a desire to provide 'educated' music as well as to entertain. Progressive rock was male-dominated and mainly enjoyed by the same college audiences who had been caught up with the counter-culture. Teen pop, on the other hand, was overwhelmingly aimed at working-class girls. Perhaps what is interesting about Bowie is that, unlike any other major star of this period (with the possible exception of

Marc Bolan), he moved between both audiences. Yet he was only able to do so with considerable ambivalence. For example, Bob Harris, the television presenter of the BBC's *Old Grey Whistle Test* (an evening show on the 'serious' BBC2 that dealt with mostly progressive rock in the early seventies), viewed art rock artists like David Bowie, Roxy Music and Marc Bolan with extreme suspicion, given their desire to break out of the mould fashioned by the rock 'establishment'. Yet Bowie's strangeness was more easily welcomed by the teen-pop press. An interview conducted with Bowie in the 1973 *Popswop Annual* features him along with other stars of the day including Rod Stewart, Elton John and Marc Bolan. The interview highlights 'the amazing Mr David Bowie's' love of art, music and mime. The intimate portrait of David treats him as though he is a potential boyfriend for the readers. At no point does Bowie's ambiguous sexuality become an issue. His perceived femininity then was potentially more troubling for the guardians of progressive rock than it was for an audience of pre-teenage and teenage girls.

At the turn of the seventies it was the music of the progressive rock band Pink Floyd and their main creative force Syd Barrett, the Velvet Underground and the sound of Iggy Pop and the Stooges that most influenced Bowie. These influences are evident on Bowie's own progressive rock effort, *The Man Who Sold the World*, released in 1970. In many respects the album marks the end of sixties' optimism, dealing for the most part with the darker side of human identity. While I want to deal with some of these features in the next chapter, listening to the recording today it is the music's dystopian sound which is most evident punctured by grinding guitars, doom-laden drumbeats and Bowie's chilling vocals. Like Neil Young's *After the Gold Rush* (1970) and John Lennon's *Plastic Ono Band* (1970), Bowie's album seeks to address the cultural void created by the decline of the counter-culture. However, unlike these two landmark records, Bowie's stance is less mournful of the collapse of utopian optimism. Instead, he is more concerned to point his audience in a direction informed by the occult, playful sexual ambiguity and Nietzschean individualism. The political thinker Hannah Arendt (1969) argued at the time that many young people were burdened not so much with a sense of radical possibility but instead with a sense of time running out. The idea that Western civilization is built upon progress was becoming increasingly open to question during this period. It was the concern of many of Bowie's generation that the threat of nuclear destruction and ecological collapse was indeed what the world was facing. This was the period that began increasingly to focus on ecological concerns such as overpopulation, the threat of nuclear war and the destruction of the environment more generally. The sense of imminent collapse was in terms of Bowie's recording both an ever-present danger but was also coupled with the possibility of reinventing ourselves. If the music of Lennon and Young during this time finds them searching for new radical directions within the self, Bowie offers a more strident if no less ambivalent view of human future. Whereas Lennon and Young voice the possibility of recovering a more authentic self against the 'empty' promises of the counter-culture, Bowie seemingly ditches notions of 'authenticity' altogether. David Bowie's own particular brand of 'becoming' simply suggests possibilities, not a 'real' point of departure or arrival. How does this work? Bowie's particular passage through the disintegration of the counter-culture is not really about the rejection of falseness; while this was admittedly in evidence on his previous recording, on this later album a more prominent theme is the idea that we might play or indeed experiment with human identity. This does not lead to the 'real' human being beneath the surface of contemporary culture but just to more surfaces and further possibilities of invention. *The Man Who Sold the World* (1970) is his first postmodern recording. By this I mean that Bowie's music aims to demonstrate the extent to which culture and the self is an invention. Instead of the search for 'authenticity' that was so evident within the counter-culture, Bowie offers a more playful encounter with human becoming. Indeed, as we shall see, the question as to who 'I' might become is evident from this point to the present day. In particular, the Nietzschean themes of how to invent oneself in a universe that lacks the central ordering feature of a God or single divine creator is referenced by many of the songs. Indeed Bowie takes a central Nietzschean theme by linking the threat of human catastrophe with the possible emergence of a new kind of human being. If the earth is under threat then this offers both opportunity as well as suffering. Bowie, like Nietzsche, attempts to offer a new image of what human beings could become in the face of cultural change. To be modern, Bowie seems to suggest, is to enter the ebb and flow of contemporary culture while reinventing ourselves.

During this period Bowie and his wife Angie were living at what became known as Haddon Hall (nicknamed 'Hard-on Hall'). This large Victorian house in Beckenham not only periodically housed musicians like Mick Ronson and John Cambridge and producer and lifelong collaborator Tony Visconti, but gained a reputation for being a place of sexual and bohemian experimentation. According to Angie the house became a focal point for a whole band of people who experienced themselves as 'outside' mainstream society. Angie captures some of this atmosphere in her autobiography:

Bit by bit, Haddon Hall came up in the world. David did the living room in a dark green and painted scarlet the woodwork on the gothic chairs I'd had reupholstered in crushed velvet, and I dyed twenty-six lace curtains the same brilliant red (that's the room you see on the cover of *The Man Who Sold the World*). Our antiques and David's growing collection of Art Nouveau and Deco pieces really popped in their new settings, and our guests lounged and frolicked in luxury. Yes: high style, getting higher; a salon of distinction, a setting fit for a star. (Bowie 1993: 99)

The idea of the house being a bohemian salon is an instructive one. It was, if the descriptions and the myths are to be believed, a place where organic food was eaten, a variety of drugs taken, various sexual practices performed and of course a host of ideas debated. Haddon Hall was a place where most of the alternative ideologies and perspectives of the time (no matter how weird) would have been encountered. This was in part the continuation of the sixties with its emphasis upon whatever the so-called 'mainstream' found unacceptable but also an attempt to find something new at the decade's close. It is perhaps in the cultural laboratory of Haddon Hall that Bowie begins to fuse together a sexually ambiguous persona and the idea that the end of the sixties would see the emergence of a new kind of human being.

This aspect of Bowie's performance is most memorably captured on the cover of *The Man Who Sold the World*. For many artists of this time the album cover became the key focus of the artist's image. How artists were seen in an age where questions of identity were coming to the fore was increasingly significant. Stars were becoming important not only because they dramatized the search for an identity but because they could draw upon new codes and conventions. For many of their followers and fans they were at the forefront of the exploration of what we might become. Such was the power of the stars that they could temporarily suspend everyday reality and introduce new possibilities into the human imagination. Stars were more than role models; they were expanding the realm of the possible. The cover of the record displays Bowie in one of his most famous visual poses. Draped across a covered couch the long-haired Bowie is pictured wearing a blue-and-white patterned dress, holding the king of diamonds playing card between his fingers. The scattered cards on the floor and Bowie's gaze, straight into the camera, signify not so much an effeminate masculinity as an alluring bohemianism. As Richard Dyer (1992) has commented, it is notable that within popular culture women are often pictured looking away from the camera whereas men catch the gaze of the viewer. This conveys the idea that women may be regarded and stared at in ways not deemed appropriate for men. Had Bowie positioned his gaze away from the camera this would have converted him into an object to be looked at. Hence the ambivalence of the image is that even while Bowie is pictured wearing a dress, he does so in a way that retains his masculinity. This is an important point which will become more apparent in the discussion below of the imagery and cultural codes utilized by Bowie to suggest different masculine possibilities for gay and straight men.

Despite the decadent image on the record cover very little of its content actually deals with issues of gender or sexuality. Perhaps more important is how Bowie understood the idea of 'performance' needed to connect his stage presence with the images that became associated with his music and star interviews. Indeed the radical effect of the recording lies in the tension between the cover and the progressive rock of the sound. Again produced by Tony Visconti (who also plays on the album), this time Bowie was accompanied by Mick Ronson (guitar) and Mick Woodmansey (drums, percussion) who would prove important in helping Bowie produce some of his most popular music. Evidently influenced by the hard guitar rock of contemporary bands like Black Sabbath, most of the songs feature Mick Ronson's guitar. Listened to today, it is also the sound of the synthesizer and sinister percussion (particularly on 'The Man Who Sold the World') that distinguishes the album from its contemporaries. The sound achieved here has also been employed by more contemporary bands like the Cure and Siouxsie and the Banshees due to its gothic and futuristic quality.

In his first major interview, for the American publication *Rolling Stone* magazine, Bowie extended his use of shock tactics. Getting yourself noticed and selling records meant bending some of the conventions of the time. In the interview much is made of Bowie's flamboyant appearance and his previous life as a 'shaven-headed transvestite' (Mendelssohn 1971). Bowie, as is well known amongst his fans, used interviews in the seventies to propagate wild exaggerations and blatant untruths as well as the outrageous and the shocking. This is as much part of his art and cultural production as any of his other more musical performances. Here Bowie is attacking the culture of authenticity so beloved by the counter-culture and the culture industry. The identity being constructed by Bowie out of the bricolage of the present is intended to get him noticed. Bowie ends the interview with the typically provocative one-liner: 'Tell your readers that they can make up their minds about me when I begin getting adverse publicity: when I'm found in bed with Raquel Welch's husband' (Mendelssohn 1971). As I have indicated, however, the lyrical and musical content of the album is concerned with a different kind of decadence. The counter-culture has been eclipsed to make way for a form of human identity that has reached its limit. As Bowie sings mournfully, 'man is an obstacle, sad as the clown' ('After All' 1970). The idea of the end of Man, and his potential rebirth, is evident in much of the counter-culture and social philosophy of this period. That we are 'nobody's children' suggests we are living in a world of rampant individualism. In such a world what was beginning to be shaken up were the old ties to community, place and class location. Increasingly individuals were thrown back upon their own resources and compelled to construct their biographies out of the values, ideas and fragments of commercial culture they had ready to hand. Yet in this world, according to social theorist Zygmunt Bauman (2004: 32), 'identities are mixed blessings. They vacillate between a dream and a nightmare, and there is no telling when one will turn into the other.' The nightmare of identity is having to live without clear guidelines on how to script the self, and the threat that the self will become subject to control and manipulation rather than autonomy. Thus in terms of Bowie's record the threat to identity is evident in madness ('All the Madmen'), violence ('Running Gun Blues'), totalitarian forms of manipulation ('Saviour Machine') and finally the manipulation of a lover ('She Shook Me Cold'). It is however 'the possibility of identity' that was to become Bowie's dominant theme. Questions of identity threat and breakdown are never far beneath the surface. This motif is most evident on the album where Bowie borrows directly from Nietzsche on the final song, 'The Supermen'. The first few lines of the song draw directly upon one of Nietzsche's (1961) most famous books, *Thus Spake Zarathustra*. For Bowie, 'The supermen would walk in file, guardians of a loveless isle' ('The Supermen' 1970). In the myth of the Superman, Nietzsche suggests that human beings might learn to live by very different values. We might indeed invent a new set of codes and values, while also seeking to live dangerously at the edge of a new morality. While there is much controversy as to what Nietzsche meant by these pronouncements, the young Bowie undoubtedly takes this as a call to invent new images, iconic representations and a sense of self in the age of mass culture. To give life meaning, Bowie suggests, one must invent the self out of the fragments of commercial culture. Meaning is not something you discover but create. This is a theme, I will argue, not just of this record, but of Bowie's art. We shall see how the possibility of identity and the need to overcome the ways in which we have been constituted by society connects much of Bowie's artistic production in the seventies and later periods. There is a more negative side to this particular legacy as I explore in the following chapters. However, for now, we can see that what Bowie does is to take Nietzsche, or at least certain motifs of his work, and apply them in a context where new possibilities are being opened by the emergence of Pop Art, gay politics and glam rock. It is to these themes I shall now turn. The argument is that it is important to appreciate these cultural phenomena in order to begin to understand the artistic context for some of Bowie's most exciting cultural productions.

Glam, pop, gay: adventures in postmodern art

What becomes apparent in Bowie's art in the seventies is the mutual interconnection between Pop Art and glam rock. Indeed it was the influence of these two (at first very different) artistic and popular cultural formations that gave Bowie the tag of postmodern. Yet Bowie comes to Pop Art rather late, given that the Beatles can be credited for bringing art into pop as early as 1965 with the recording of *Rubber Soul*. What was initially exciting about Pop Art was its ability to close the gap between the art world and commercial forms of culture. However, Bowie's interest in Pop Art comes more through Andy Warhol and the music of the Velvet Underground than the Beatles. It is Bowie's fascination with Andy Warhol that becomes evident during the seventies. In 1971, Bowie made a trip to America to visit Warhol at the Factory. While the meeting was not personally successful (Warhol was unimpressed by Bowie's song about him), it nonetheless solidified Bowie's interest in the Pop Art project. Indeed the meeting between Warhol and Bowie was only salvaged once the famous artist became fascinated with the would-be star of popular music's shoes. On a number of different levels, it is this meeting that fused Bowie's interest in art and pop.

The artistic movement, Pop Art, still excites considerable passion within the academy. Cultural studies and the political left remain divided over its cultural significance as an artistic movement. For some, Pop Art is a form of betrayal, as it is the moment that the aesthetic dimension is finally dissolved into the networks of late capitalism. Pop Art completes Theodor Adorno's (1991) predictions about the cultural industry, where art becomes another commodity like Coca-Cola to be bought and sold on the market place. Pop Art delivers a world where artists lose their autonomy and become just another product. Others, more influenced by Walter Benjamin's (1973) critique of Adorno, were excited by Pop Art's ability to democratize art, bringing it out of the gallery and down to street level. Rather than viewing art as a substitute for religion, Benjamin argued that technological forms of reproduction potentially deconstruct the divisions between high and popular culture. The work of art becomes democratized through its reproducibility, thereby undermining the presence of the original. In a world where anyone can potentially become an artist (through the availability of technology) and where art is no longer confined to the gallery (art prints are used to decorate ordinary living and working spaces), society can be said to have moved beyond 'a theology of art' (Benjamin 1973: 218). In Benjamin's vision art becomes 'profane, concrete and suitable for mass reception' (Huyssen 1973: 143). Benjamin argues that it is the cultural potential within the decline of aura of the individual genius or original work of art that effectively democratizes artistic production and reception.

These cultural dispositions are similar to those that can be associated with the development of glam rock. As rock critic Barney Hoskyns (1998: 6) comments: 'The genius of glam was that it was all about stardom. It said flaunt it if you've got it, and if you haven't got it make it up with make-up, cover your face with stardust, re-invent yourself as a Martian androgyny. Glam was prefab, anti-craft, allied to artifice and the trash aesthetic.' Whereas folk music attempts to hide or deny the commercial setting and the industry's growing reliance upon a star system, glam embraces such processes. The cultural production of image, star profiles and fashionability have their roots in glam's reaction against the sixties' counter-culture. Through glam's focus upon certain visual dynamics, style (over substance) and spectacle, it brought to the fore questions of commodification and individualism. This point was missed by a number of sociologists at the time who saw glam rock purely in terms of the commodification of music and leisure cultures, thereby displacing the political protests associated with the counter-culture. For example, Ian Taylor and David Wall (1976) argued that glam had effectively nullified the liberatory potential of sixties' youth culture. Further, glam was undermining more traditional working-class pursuits like football and replacing them with 'classless' pop products. They argued that according to their interviews with young people aged between twelve and eighteen, Bowie was the most prominent star of his generation. In this analysis Bowie was the greatest exponent of the culture of 'political nihilism' which offered young people 'one-dimensional' forms of consumption (Taylor and Wall 1976: 121). In this view, Pop Art and glam had not only turned culture into a commodity, they had nullified prospects for political change. These are perhaps heavy charges to lay against popular music and are more indicative of the disappointment felt by many radicals than an informed appreciation of Bowie's art.

These concerns not only misunderstand glam's own internal contradictions (incorporating the anti-utopianism of Iggy Pop and the camp of Gary Glitter) but fail to appreciate that glam's radicalism lay within questions of sexuality and consumption rather than class. As Dick Hebdige (1979) has argued, viewed more sympathetically, glam offered a critique of both the puritanism of much hippy culture and challenged some of the chauvinism associated with working-class parent culture. To put the point bluntly, from William Burroughs Bowie borrowed the 'cut up' technique he used to write his lyrics, from Jean Genet the ability to be able to live 'in style' and from Andy Warhol an interest in Pop Art. These influences which shaped the 'structure of feeling' of Bowie's work could also be placed alongside his more obviously musical influences and friendships, including Marc Bolan, Lou Reed and perhaps most crucially Iggy Pop. However, in this context, it remains Bowie's relationship with

Andy Warhol (whom he later played in the film *Basquiat*, 1996) that is most crucial.

Bowie's 1971 album *Hunky Dory* contains three songs dedicated to his heroes; these included 'Song for Bob Dylan' (whose influence was beginning to fade), 'Queen Bitch' (written for Lou Reed) and 'Andy Warhol'. The *Hunky Dory* album is also musically significant as it began to map out a different direction within Bowie's art, marking his transformation from folk and progressive rock to the pop of glam. The culture of glam and Pop Art put aside the elitist anti-commercialism of the established art world and the counter-culture, while engaging in commercial and popular culture as a means of being creative. Both glam rock and Pop Art deal in the sexy, sensational and saleable.

Through its development in the fifties and the sixties, Pop Art dramatized the impact of the commodity form and the urbanity of the city. Emerging out of the twin centres of New York and London, Pop Art sought to reverse an aesthetics of distance from everyday life promoted by more established schools of art. The key move here was to debunk the idea that 'real art' is necessarily non-commercial. Part of Warhol's radical effect was to turn the elitism of the art world on its head by suggesting that what's good is what sells. This opened up the possibility of musicians like David Bowie, Bryan Ferry and Brian Eno bringing art into pop (Frith and Horne 1987). The idea was that art was inevitably caught up in a commercial setting, implying that cultural producers should seek to develop an aesthetic of mass consumption. This meant that artists could both draw aesthetic lessons from mass culture while seeking to work within commercial media.

Pop Art encourages the artist to abandon the romantic idea of his or her self as the authentic source of the work of art. For example, Warhol in developing his studio (the Factory) sought to make it a site of automation and productivity, reducing his own personal touch to a minimum. Warhol sought to dissolve notions of originality through the production of art as commerce in respect of Campbell's soup tins and screen prints of Elvis Presley and Marilyn Monroe. The dispensing of notions of depth and the aura of the artist brings Pop Art into the arena of postmodernism. Art need not be an expression of the 'deep self', but could be about the ironic play of identity. Pop Art was more concerned with making an impact through the media than becoming a new religion. Pop Art's cultural politics can be found in its attack on the 'seriousness' of the established art world. It appealed to many as it claimed that culture could be fun and was not the exclusive preserve of an elite.

Finally, such processes open up certain possibilities in respect of the democratization of glamour, art and culture. As Peter Wollen (1993: 163) comments, 'Warhol's rationalisation of the work process was half serious, half theatrical.' Pop Art enabled art to be playful, kitsch and performative; it presumed a camp style which allowed for the aestheticization of everyday life. Posters, the packaging of music, stage performances, postcards and fashion could all become as much part of art as more traditional arenas such as galleries. Despite much of the pessimism that either sees postmodernism in terms of commodification or irrationality, these reflections offer consumers the possibility of being artists themselves. To view Pop Art simply through the prism of commodification misses the ways it served to develop new artistic productions and sensibilities. Here we might point to Pop Art's connection with a camp sensibility and forms of ideological interruption that can be associated with subcultures. Camp exhibits a relish for exaggeration, artifice and androgyny. It depends upon a playful rather than a serious disposition as well as the 'victory of "style" over "content", "aesthetics" over "morality", of irony over tragedy' (Sontag 1994: 287). By championing the witty and the decorative, it punctured the high seriousness of bourgeois art, allowing for the development of 'creativity' within a number of popular forms from music to photography.

We need to be careful not to push this argument too far. It remains the case that Pop Art's and above all Warhol's embrace of capitalism cancels a certain degree of critical potential within art. Art that simply samples and rearranges images from the past is indeed an attack on high seriousness. However, as we shall see, particularly with Bowie's cultural production in the mid eighties, art that merely revels in the market can lose much of its critical potential. These artistic developments allowed figures like Bowie to call themselves artists working in a mass media age. Bowie (1980: 24), virtually parroting Warhol, would comment: 'I'm really just a Photostat machine'. In postmodern terms, what Bowie means is: don't look into my 'personality' to find the meaning of my work. If I am obsessed with image, style and surface, look at contemporary capitalism and the culture that it manufactures. Secondly, this culture of the pop (and rock) world is as commodified as the art world. Indeed both the cultures of teen pop and progressive rock are the result of processes of marketing and commodification, the only difference being they are usually made with different audiences in mind. Finally, if the artist is not a 'special' genius but simply someone who buys and sells work in a market place, what is to stop other people doing the same? Such claims on Bowie's part are obviously part pose, part outrageous bluff, but also part of the culture within which he moves. If we view the distinctively different images and personas adopted by Bowie as central to his art, then it is perhaps easy to understand his interest in notions of change. What fascinates Pop Art is 'nowness' and 'immediacy', not the ability to work within a historically defined tradition. Bowie's cultural inventions – including Ziggy Stardust, Aladdin Sane and The Thin White Duke – are not so much direct expressions of his personality but commodified and arresting images designed to be displayed in the public arena. This process is prefigured in one of Bowie's most popular songs, 'Changes' (1971). Here Bowie, not for the last time, can be observed playing with images of change and fabrication. With ironic intent he sings of being a 'faker', always on the move, 'too fast' for his critics and imitators. Bowie articulates in this song a camp sensibility that maintains a playful disposition towards issues connected to image manipulation.

We need to add one more ingredient into the mix, which is the connection between Pop Art and the birth of radical gay politics. This is particularly evident in the birth of 'camp' at the end of the sixties. Camp is largely an invention of gay men. There is undoubtedly a link between the rise of gay liberation at the end of the sixties and the emergence of camp as a cultural sensibility. Richard Dyer (2002: 52) describes camp as 'a way of prising the form of something away from its content, of revelling in style while dismissing the content as trivial'. We have already seen that Andy Warhol's camp was bent (excuse the pun) on mocking the pretensions of the art establishment, whereas Bowie sought a similar role for himself in respect of the 'high seriousness' that had begun to be connected to rock music. At the end of the sixties, there were basically two kinds of camp and Bowie and Warhol had a foot in each of them. There was the pop camp of television serials like *The Adventures of Batman and Robin*, fictional hero James Bond and the 1968 film, *Barbarella*. This version of camp is, more or less, 'so bad it's good'. There was also sex camp which largely developed through a gay subculture of androgyny and gender blurring and included film stars such as Judy Garland, Bette Davis, Greta Garbo, Marlene Dietrich and Joan Crawford. These stars are all important as they defy the film conventions of the male as hero and the female as passive sex object. It is here that we find camp's cultural politics (Ross 1989). Camp aims to unsettle and disrupt the boundaries of taste by challenging the naturalness of gender, the construction of sexuality and the dominance of 'established' views of art. It does so through the subversive means of wit and parody. The utilization of mimicry, simulation and artifice challenges the established categories of culture. It is perhaps not hard to understand how such a cultural sensibility was the invention of gay men. Camp was not only a way of subverting the established categories of gender like heterosexuality but, by emphasizing the surface and style of visual codes, it picks on gay men's often-pronounced eye for appearance. This, it should be added, is not an essential feature of gay men, but more something they had to be good at to pass as 'normal' in a prejudiced society. Some cultural theorists like David Halpern (1995) argue that camp is essentially a form of resistance for gay men, given its ability to parody the 'normal' and invite us to view it as being as constructed as anything else.

The camp sensibility of David Bowie is most evident in his most famous creation, Ziggy Stardust. However, the release of the album, *Hunky Dory*, in December 1971 (a mere six or seven months after *The Man Who Sold the World*) also captures the spirit of camp. As a disciple of Andy Warhol, Bowie was interested in the different ways stardom could be fabricated by the images, discourses and narratives of popular culture. This fascination with stardom is evident on the album's cover. Borrowing a pose from Hollywood in the 1920s–1930s, Bowie is pictured in soft focus, eyes to one side, brushing his hair back, with the viewer's gaze being invited to fall on the side of his face. This time Bowie's pose is more feminine, given that his eyes do not meet those of the viewer. In more traditional rock terms the obviously constructed nature of the image simply indicates the inauthenticity of Bowie's pose and image. Like Warhol, Bowie's fabricated image is deliberately pointing to the fact that all popular music in our society is both an art object as well as a commodity.

By intentionally borrowing a set of stylistic conventions from a previous era, the album cover invites the viewer to recognize all images of popular music as constructed. Bowie's film star image suggests that all star images, no matter how 'authentic', are actually constructed. This is undoubtedly the 'effect' Warhol was trying to generate by reproducing images of stars such as Marilyn Monroe, James Dean and Elvis Presley. This has the postmodern effect I mentioned earlier of de-naturalizing the dominant, taken-for-granted assumptions of everyday life and popular culture. Bowie presses this further by playing with icons from a past Hollywood era in that it both feminizes his image and unsettles the established masculine conventions of the period. What is radical about Bowie is his grasp that his music was likely to be read through his image and not the other way round. The meaning of 'David Bowie', as hopefully I am demonstrating, is not dependent upon a particular song or interview, but is largely constructed through his image. Just as the image of Warhol as the bohemian painter of mass culture helped sell his visual art, so Bowie's image helped bring him to a broader mainstream recognition. Many fans of David Bowie might find such a claim scandalous. Let us be clear. I am not suggesting that Bowie's music is not worthy of consideration. However, what I am pressing is that much popular music is understood through the construction of star images. Obviously if a band is well packaged and the music fails to hit the mark, it is unlikely to be successful. However, during the seventies, Bowie understood the power of images in selling music and getting noticed. Popular music is about the imagination and not the appreciation of sounds in the abstract. Bowie was way ahead of most people in appreciating this aspect of contemporary culture.

Having said this, the album *Hunky Dory* (1971) adopts a far more obviously commercial sound than *The Man Who Sold the World*. This is not so much a rock album as one with a pronounced pop sensibility. Less emphasis is placed on Mick Ronson's guitar playing with more room in the mix for orchestration and, notably, for Rick Wakeman's piano playing. In many respects, the sound recalls Bowie's first album in that it represents an attempt to capture a more accessible style of music. For example, 'Kooks' and 'Fill Your Heart' are both quirky songs that would not be out of place alongside 'The Laughing Gnome'. In this respect, *Hunky Dory* suggests that Bowie sought to move his music in a more 'mainstream' direction while maintaining a bohemian image. What is also clear in comparison with *The Man Who Sold the World* is that the songs on *Hunky Dory* more explicitly feature Bowie's voice. The lyrics are more easily discernible, less crowded by layers of sound. Bowie's crisp delivery focuses the listener's attention on the individuality of the star performer, an effect strengthened by the sleeve illustration.

Perhaps the most important connection between Bowie and Warhol is that Warhol was the producer of *The Velvet Underground and Nico* released in 1967. In interviews and reportage, Bowie often mentions this particular record as a personal favourite. The Velvet's album is famous for the bright yellow plastic banana on the cover (constructed by Warhol), and for Lou Reed and John Cale's songs about the underbelly of life in New York at the end of the sixties. The first long player by the Velvets is rarely out of the lists regularly produced by music magazines, proclaiming it one of the most influential of all time. Notably, unlike a lot of other music being produced at the height of the counter-culture, its cutting edge is less its utopian optimism than the matter-of-fact way it deals with drugs, sexual obsession and street life. What was important for those influenced by the recording was not that they wanted to be New York hustlers but that they could identify with the origins of the songs (Gilbert 1999). The narratives are from the point of view of someone in an urban setting. The observer, if you like, invites you to understand everyday life as an outsider. Bowie would use this cultural device to great effect on his next album (notably on 'Five Years'). Like much of Bowie's best music, it acts as a commentary upon aspects of urban culture rather than a reflection of the personality of the 'author'. The best place to explore these is of course through Bowie's creation, Ziggy Stardust.

Deconstructing rock: Ziggy, fame and sexuality

Central to what Ian Chambers (1985) has called Bowie's construction of the 'sensationalist aesthetic of the strange' is the idea of the artist/individual who reconstructs themselves through culture. These features are most apparent in David Bowie's 1972 album *The Rise and Fall of Ziggy Stardust and the Spiders from Mars*. Here Bowie invents the myth of a rock star who literally 'falls to earth' and forms a successful band before descending into a destructive cycle of inflated egos and suicide. The album itself does not follow a conventional narrative structure despite the availability of titles such as 'Starman', 'Star', 'Ziggy Stardust' and 'Rock 'n' Roll Suicide' whose theatricality outlines the pleasures, sufferings, projections and dangers of stardom. The album sleeve famously pictures Bowie in a decaying urban setting, red hair, blue jump-suit and guitar under his arm. Ziggy Stardust was not just the title of a song or album but was a character who could be presented on stage. Bowie's interest in mime and theatre brought about the idea of inventing personae to be projected in popular music. Ziggy Stardust is constructed from a multitude of sources. To mention a few, these are as diverse as the film *Clockwork Orange*, Japanese kabuki theatre, science pulp fiction, Jimi Hendrix, and (Z)Iggy Pop amongst others. The debates rage on fans' websites and in popular music journalism on the 'connotations and superimpositions' that reveal Ziggy Stardust's constructed nature (Barthes 1974: 122). While these questions are of obvious interest, they bypass the most central aspect of the invention of Ziggy Stardust – that he is crucially concerned with how to live with stardom. The myth of Ziggy Stardust draws its power from the highs and lows of this particular dream. Part of the fascination with this period in Bowie's career is that he acted like a star before he was one; the overriding theme of the album concerns his 'transformation as a rock and roll star' ('Star' 1972). The album's endurance is centred on the fact that it plays through the myth of stardom as fun, as excitement and finally as breakdown.

The final song on the Ziggy album and at the concerts was 'Rock 'n' Roll Suicide' which represents our hero in theatrical despair. The theatricality of the Ziggy myth was noted at the time by rock journalist Ray Coleman (1972) who wrote that Bowie has 'a detached love affair with his audience, wooing them, yet never surrendering that final aloofness that makes him slightly untouchable'. This is the key to Ziggy's continued resonance. The spectacle of the concerts was not just concerned with Bowie's own performance, but with the audience's ability to participate through fashion and fantasy. Many of the fans who went to Bowie concerts dressed in an outrageous manner. By doing this they were not merely copying a distant star but had perhaps begun the process of transforming themselves. Just as Warhol sought to convert previously anonymous members of the public into stars through his films, so Bowie handed his audience the tools for aesthetic self-creation. Bowie himself later reflected on this:

> I took the idea of fabrication and how it snowballed in popular culture. Realism and honesty had become boring to many jaded people in the early seventies. I think the band only half under-stood what I meant, but I thought it would be such great fun to fabricate something so totally unearthly and unreal and have it as a living icon. So the story of Ziggy came out of that thinking. A lot of it came out of my own problems. It was a way of creating myself. (Welch 1999: 44)

That Bowie, albeit temporarily, became caught in a myth of his own making has become a central concern to many of his biographers. Despite Pop Art's attempt to sever works of art from the biography of the artist, in the final analysis this does not seem possible. Part of the drama of this stage of Bowie's career is the way that Bowie himself became Ziggy Stardust. In performance and in 'real-life', Bowie would become a burnt-out rock star struggling with drugs, questions of identity and self-hatred. Here perhaps we have the beginnings of modern celebrity culture. The current fascination with artists like Eminem is the seamless quality of their performances on stage and the way their private lives are played through the media. Ziggy Stardust may have started life as a cultural invention, but soon neither Bowie, his audiences nor the media would be able to tell where this particular invention began and ended. For now what Ziggy offered his audience was a utopian personality that suggested transformation lived as hope and tragedy. His championing of artifice offered both a critique of naturalism and authenticity, while offering the possibility of a new identity.

The exchange between Ziggy and his audience was founded on this opportunity to be different. This difference might only last as long as an evening's performance, until the lights went up and people made their way home. But in a culture that was heavily gendered (with men and women's roles being tightly scripted) and still fearful of gayness, Bowie was able to offer a form of 'difference' that could be explored through the imagination. By stepping inside a Bowie concert the audience could, for a few hours, put to one side the confines and limits of the ways in which they were regulated in everyday life. Culturally, Ziggy Stardust articulates a point of ambivalence between the claims of cultural supremacists and ethnic nationalists by demonstrating that cultures cannot be boxed off from one another. Inevitably they provide zones of contact, repulsion, interrogation and jouissance. Not surprisingly, the performances of Ziggy had an exhilarating effect upon the audience. One fan remembers:

I was at the Hammersmith Odeon when Bowie killed off Ziggy in '73. I got trampled to death! A lot of men were throwing off their underwear and showing their cocks all over the place. A lot of fluid was flying about. One girl was actually sucking someone at the same time as trying to listen to what was going on. I thought it was extraordinary because nobody had any inhibitions. (Vermorel and Vermorel 1985: 182–3)

Such an intense experience of sexual and emotional release is echoed by others. As one fan reports from amidst the crowd at Ziggy's final concert:

I'm quite sure that Bowie was completely off his head because his eyes would roll occasionally and the sweat was pouring. He was so excited. He was so pushed to the limit, to the very edge. And everyone around me was trying to see this and of course I got terribly squashed. But the sweat and the smell was really horrible. Some poor people were sweating and others were wanking themselves off. It wasn't very pleasant but I was absolutely stuck where I was and I couldn't move. I had to keep watching him. I had a really good seat right at the front and I'd gone with another girl who was a Bowie fanatic and she was crying. Then she passed out and the St John Ambulance men had to take her away. She was in a state of hypnotism almost, just gone. There was hysteria, particularly on the left-hand aisle because people were going wild when he reached down to the audience. They were crying and screaming. They'd try and touch him. And he'd tease them terribly. He was a right provocative little sod. (Vermorel and Vermorel 1985: 105)

Ziggy's appeal should be situated in a context that recognizes the rigidly sexual and gendered codes operating in the late sixties and early seventies. The open expression of sexuality and desire in a public place gave the concert a carnival-type atmosphere. This sense of 'release' from the usual rules of appropriate behaviour can be explored through the cultural theorist Mikhail Bakhtin's (1968) notion of the carnivalesque. Bakhtin originally used this idea to explain the folk festivals of the Middle Ages. These festivals had a utopian dimension as they offered a temporary liberation from the established order. The usual markings of rank and order were put to one side, and the time of carnival became a celebration of community, abundance and laughter. The world was, if only temporarily, turned upside down. The carnival (or in our case a Ziggy concert) symbolized the suspension of what passed for normality. The audience could let themselves go in the intense atmosphere it generated. By stepping inside a Bowie performance, his audience was, if just for an evening, being invited to leave the pressures, confines and limits of everyday life behind.

David Bowie's creation should be located within the context of the feminist and gay liberation movements. Between 1969 and 1973, a number of gay liberation theorists sought to reject the idea that a progressive sexual politics should embrace assimilation. The aim of gay liberation was to abolish a gender system that privileged heterosexuality. Bowie's utopianism came from the discursive unfixing of oppositions between straight and gay, natural and artificial, masculine and feminine (Seidman 1997). Bowie temporarily expanded the possibilities available within a largely conservative sexual culture. Research on the 'visibility' of British gay men in urban contexts further emphasizes Bowie's importance. In the fifties and sixties, gay men often lived in fear of blackmail and arrest. Not surprisingly many sought to conform to the styles of heterosexual men, while carefully displaying small signs (a ring or cravat) to indicate sexual difference. In terms of the transformation of gay men's styles of dress (like Pop Art), it is the connection between Britain and America that is important. Many British gay men, including Bowie himself, visited America after the Stonewall riots in 1969, bringing back ideas about gay politics and lifestyle (Cole 1999). In this context, Bowie's 'utopian difference' has important political as well as social and cultural implications.

The emphasis on the transformation of identity in the radical gay politics of this period is mirrored in the images drawn upon by Bowie. For example, in Bowie's home city of London, the Gay Liberation Front published a manifesto in 1971. The idea behind 'gay liberation' was to confront the ways in which gays had been stereotyped and oppressed. The manifesto states that gays are: 'characterised as scandalous, obscene perverts; as rampant, wild sex monsters; as pathetic doomed and compulsive degenerates, while the truth is blanketed under a conspiracy of silence' (London Gay Liberation Front Manifesto 1971: 119). 'Gay liberation' was an attempt to build upon the liberal legal reforms that had partially decriminalized homosexuality while creating a wider culture that was receptive to sexual difference. What was interesting was how important symbols and cultural signs became to this social movement. For example, the Gay Liberation Front held protests by dressing up in drag (men dressed as women and women dressed as men) and then entering a bar or public house and waiting to be served. Notable here is the idea of subverting image and using symbolism to demolish the ways in which the dominant society negatively constructed the identity of gay people. Whereas the closet makes gay people invisible, radical gay politics aimed at both interrupting the dominant images of heterosexuality and producing different sexual meanings and possibilities. It is in this context that Ziggy Stardust makes his impact.

Specifically, how did Bowie achieve this? Primarily by breaking with the traditional discourses of rock and heterosexuality and by drawing attention to performativity. Rock music usually trades upon notions of individuality, eccentricity and above all authenticity which becomes confined and finally defeated by commercialism. The ideological tie between heterosexuality and rock is evident in 'cock rock', which connects aggressive masculine sexuality with the 'othering' of women (Frith and McRobbie 1990). The 'authenticity' of rock presumes a masculine sensibility, a 'being with the boys' and macho posturing. By exploiting the myth of rock music within a single album or concert, Bowie actually reveals its constructed nature. Within this format, Bowie's cultural production (like that of Warhol) simultaneously enacts and destroys the symbolic economy of rock. While rock music continues to reinforce the polarity between authenticity and commerce, Bowie subverts this division by performing it as camp tragedy. Since the fifties and sixties, popular music has bought new sexualities to public recognition. While stopping short of affirming gayness, hippies and mods introduced more ambiguous codes of male sexuality (Savage 1990). David Bowie's cultural achievement was not to reverse rock's phallocentric norms but to disrupt gendered and sexual binaries from within. This went beyond much of glam rock of the early seventies which played with gender coding to signify 'outrageousness' or 'decadence' (Denski and Sholle 1992). By revealing rock to be a performance, Bowie questioned the dominance of masculine and heterosexual norms (Butler 1990). However, these features, at this stage, were more a matter of image manipulation than of musical innovation. The music was a continuation of the melodious commercial sound of *Hunky Dory*, although this time played more as theatrical rock. Both *Hunky Dory* and *Ziggy Stardust* feature Mick Ronson on guitar, Trevor Bolder on bass, Mick Woodmansey on drums and were produced by Ken Scott. While Bowie's performativity meant that his music sounded different from the glam rock of the time, its distinctiveness came more from the way it was performed and imagined.

Finally, Bowie's deliberate manipulation of religious themes and icons is also worthy of note. Bowie's image in the seventies was dependent upon Christian themes evident in science fiction, literature and cinema. The idea of the 'alien messiah' is common in science fiction films and literature and a key concept for the understanding of David Bowie. In the context of science fiction, the 'alien messiah' functions as an inspirational figure for a threatened humanity whose supra-human qualities offer solace to a troubled world. These features are evident in *The Rise and Fall of Ziggy Stardust and the Spiders From Mars* (1972) and the film *The Man Who Fell to Earth* (1976). The Ziggy album begins with the warning that humanity has five years to survive ('Five Years'), and ends with the possibility of being saved by Ziggy ('Rock 'n' Roll Suicide'). Indeed, the power of the final song on the album comes from the fact that 'the kids' had already turned their back on Ziggy, and yet he is able to use his special powers to save a desperate individual. As an allegory of the life of Jesus (who died so that we might be saved), this requires little by way of interpretation. Similarly, David Bowie's first major film role positions him as an alien outsider who has come both to save his own people on the planet of Anthea and to offer a warning in respect of the earth's path towards destruction. The film is faithfully based on an earlier novel where Mr Newton (Bowie's character) is represented as queer, alien and Christ-like (Tevis 1963/1999). Both Ziggy and Mr Newton seek to rescue humanity through a kind of divine intervention. Indeed we shall see later how many of Bowie's own fans employ the language of the sacred to express their devotion to their favourite star.

On 22 January 1972, *Melody Maker* (then Britain's leading music magazine) under the headline 'Oh You Pretty Thing' declared Bowie to be gay. While the article proposed that Bowie had little time for gay politics, it articulated the would-be star as a bisexual bohemian who pontificated on the use of drag, Nietzschean supermen and the destruction of the planet (Watts 1972). Despite Bowie's declared lack of interest in sexual liberation, this did not stop *Gay News* from championing him as the leading star within 'Gay Rock' (Holmes 1972). That Bowie was married to his wife Angie while living with their son Zowie seemingly only amplified popular interest in his sexuality. Despite gaining a no. 5 single in the UK charts with 'Space Oddity' in 1969, it was Bowie's performance on *Top of the Pops* on 5 July 1972 that brought him to mass attention. Bowie's appearance that night was to stick in the memory of and influence a later generation of pop gender-benders, including Boy George, Marc Almond and Billy MacKenzie (George 1995; Almond 1999; Doyle 1998). Bowie's orange hair, blue and green jump suit, camp demeanour and arm draped around guitarist Mick Ronson's shoulder brought him to the attention of a 'mainstream' audience. It was the visual impact of this performance that most overtly broke with the prevailing norms of male heterosexual rock music. Bowie's cultural politics is emphasized by his embrace of theatricality, make-up and sexual ambivalence, all of which introduce the mystery of otherness into the practice of stardom.

Despite the popular impact of glam rock, most of the images that dominated British and American society were of straight, laddish masculinity. Images of playboys (Jason King, Simon Templar), stars of popular music (Rod Stewart) or football (Rodney Marsh and George Best) exemplified an ordinary heterosexual masculinity. Indeed, most of the glam rock stars popular in Britain (like Sweet and Slade) were careful to maintain a heterosexual identity despite the fact that they were wearing glitter and platform shoes (Hunt 1998). It is in this cultural context that Bowie putting his arm around guitarist Mick Ronson on *Top of the*

Pops could seem so subversive. The ordinary space of people's living rooms during a mainstream chart show might seem an unlikely place to make history. Viewed today, this particular clip of pop history looks relatively banal. In terms of the early seventies, the simple act of Bowie touching Ronson was the stuff of which revolutions are made. After this event it seemed to many that the world would never be the same. But, just as quickly as Ziggy was born, Bowie killed him off, although there would be another album before this happened.

The album *Aladdin Sane*, released in April 1973, is really a companion piece to Ziggy. While the Ziggy myth is continued, the album is also a serious attempt to become successful in America. In British popular music there is an established tradition going back to the fifties and sixties where acts can only be said to have 'made it' if their success is repeated in the United States. Becoming a major star in the seventies (as today) meant 'breaking' the North American market. In this respect, *Aladdin Sane* was at least partially successful reaching a creditable no. 17 in the American charts. Not surprisingly many in the music press chose to view the album through the 'Ziggy goes to America' optic. The singles associated with the album – 'The Jean Genie' and 'Drive In Saturday' – further emphasized Bowie's ambivalent sexuality, but also sought to press home the theatricality of his image. Musically, the album is much more of a mixture than the Ziggy album in that it moves between moments of avant-garde jazz ('Aladdin Sane'), the driving rock 'n' roll of the Stones ('Watch That Man') and a beautiful closing ballad ('Lady Grinning Soul'). Despite the continuation with the theatrical rock of the Ziggy album, it is the introduction of Mike Garson's jazz piano-playing on 'Aladdin Sane', 'Time' and 'Lady Grinning Soul' that gives the recording its most innovative moments. Further Mick Ronson's guitar sound is less restrained and contributes to a more overtly dissonant quality. If the *Ziggy Stardust* album is explicitly concerned with the rise and fall of stardom, *Aladdin Sane* is more explicitly connected with the simulation of stardom and the fragmentation of the self. Bowie (1980: 32–3) comments on his creation: 'I don't think that Aladdin is as clearly cut and defined a character as Ziggy was. Ziggy was meant to be clearly cut and well defined with areas for interplay, whereas Aladdin is pretty ephemeral. He's also a situation as opposed to being an individual. I think he encompasses situations as well as just being a personality.'

The lack of firm definition given to *Aladdin Sane* works in a number of ways. The image of *Aladdin Sane* is best known to Bowie fans and lovers of popular music as presented on the front of the album. Bowie is pictured facing the camera with his eyes closed. His red, carrot-top haircut and the bolt of red and blue lightning across his face make this a striking pose. On the back cover of the album, along with the track listing, there is the outline of Bowie's image that appeared on the front. Bowie has evaporated. Turning again to the cover image, it has a plastic and unreal quality. It is as if the image is asking you to guess where the 'real' Bowie begins and where the fabricated image ends. This is analogous with the invention of Ziggy Stardust; yet this time Bowie takes the process a step further. What is striking is the definite nature of this image: it has no background or context, instead focusing the viewer's eyes intensely upon Bowie's creation. The cultural theorist Paul Virilio (1994) has argued that modern forms of representation actually reduce the complexity of the visual field by getting us to focus upon specific images. These 'phatic images' are so powerful that we concentrate on them to the detriment of the surrounding features. For Virilio such a process is evident in Chaplin's silhouette or Marilyn Monroe's red lips. Such is their power, and here we might include *Aladdin Sane*, that when one scrutinizes them 'the context disappears into a blur' (Virilio 1994: 14). It is no longer Bowie as the leader of the band metamorphosized into Ziggy that holds our attention, but Bowie as Bowie. While popular music is always a collective production, it is Bowie's image that has taken centre stage. While Ziggy is positioned inside a loose narrative, Aladdin Sane acts as a postmodern image floating free of surrounding context. This obviously allows a good deal of space for the inventions and projections of many of Bowie's followers and fans. They are free in the context of their everyday lives to make of Aladdin Sane what they will.

Many of the lyrics of *Aladdin Sane* are a celebration of the pleasures of American popular and visual culture. The power of the image is continually invoked, drawing attention to 'Che Guevara' ('Panic in Detroit') and 'Jagger's eyes' ('Drive In Saturday' 1973). Bowie is plundering America's fragmented popular culture and reflecting it back to his audience, but through the singular power of his own image. Bowie, we are left to imagine, has become his self-creation. For many of his fans, as we shall see later, it was Bowie's ability to control his own image that was to become a source of considerable fascination. Yet off stage he was under increasing amounts of personal strain. Since the success of Ziggy in 1972, Bowie had been touring Britain, America and Japan without a break. At this point, Bowie pulled his most dramatic publicity stunt yet; he broke up the band. Seemingly without discussing it with anyone else, Bowie announced on 12 May 1973 at London's Earls Court that the Spiders had played their final concert. Bowie, the focus of so much attention, no longer needed the Spiders. In the best traditions of popular theatre, he kept everyone in suspense about what might follow.

Bowie and Burroughs

The retirement of Ziggy and the Spiders caused a considerable amount of public controversy. Was this the end of Bowie, or just his invented characters? An expectant public were soon to receive their answer with the interim album, *PinUps*. This collection of sixties' cover versions kept the fans interested until Bowie's next big project. Bowie had mastered the art of using bisexuality and his alluring 'otherness' to become the global star of popular music in the early seventies. From this point, Bowie's music and image in respect of gender and sexual politics was to become a good deal more ambiguous. So far I have only concentrated upon the way that Bowie's images and representations disrupt the dominant image cultures of the early seventies. Here I shall argue that the postmodern cultural politics of Bowie's music and image both replicates dominant assumptions about gender and sexuality, while simultaneously deconstructing them

(Walser 1993). This is evident if we consider the impact that the literary work of William Burroughs had upon Bowie.

Burroughs is an interesting literary figure in that many popular and rock musicians from Patti Smith to Richard Hell claim to have been influenced by him. Bowie's album *Diamond Dogs* is often thought to have been inspired by George Orwell's novel *1984*, and yet it is Burroughs's influence arguably that looms larger. Admittedly, the album includes songs like '1984' and 'Big Brother' (obviously referencing Orwell's novel) yet the dystopian world of *Diamond Dogs* can be more closely associated with the literary fictions of Burroughs than that of Orwell. Just as Bowie was interested in 'queering' rock, he sought to 'queer' literary influences to aid him in this process.

Bowie first met Burroughs in person on 17 November 1973 at his home in London. Evidently Bowie had only recently discovered Burroughs's work but was keen to explore their shared artistic contexts. The conversation included a lively mix of topics from love to science fiction and from sexuality to Genet's play 'The Maids' (Copetas 1974). After the meeting Bowie is reported to have read extracts from Burroughs's novel *The Wild Boys* (1971) to some of his concert audiences. However, Burroughs's influence upon Bowie goes beyond his reading preferences.

In writing and recording the 1974 album *Diamond Dogs*, Bowie began to experiment with Burroughs's cut-up technique. Jamie Russell (2001) argues that by using cut-up technique, Burroughs was searching for a literary weapon that could free the individual from external control. In this respect, Burroughs's homosexual identity is central in that he sought, through cut-up technique, a way of disrupting the regulation of his identity beyond normative heterosexual codes and assumptions. In particular, in developing cut-up, Burroughs sought to shatter the popular conception of the homosexual as effeminate. For Burroughs, being a gay male in the late twentieth century meant being subjected to a form of social and cultural repression. By literally cutting up newspapers, magazines and medical journals, Burroughs sought to fracture the dominant culture of control and create new meanings and existential possibilities. Despite Samuel Beckett's famous charge in respect of Burroughs's literary pro-

duction, 'that's not writing, it's plumbing', this technique captured Bowie's imagination (Russell 2001: 61).

The cover of *Diamond Dogs* literally displays a cut-up human
being with Bowie posing as half human and half dog. He is
accompanied by two other creatures who lack his overt sexual
presence, but who are similarly part canine and part human.
While their sexual identity is ambiguous, Bowie's thrusting masculinity is displayed through a pose that reveals his genitals.
Bowie as a dog-like creature, is lying on what looks like a stage in
front of the words 'The Strangest Living Curiosities'. Just inside
the cover, Bowie is depicted as a street hustler wearing leather
boots, fedora hat and exquisite waitcoast, seated in front of a
cityscape. Bowie's masculine sexuality is alluded to in that he is
pictured coolly restraining a mad dog. In reading this image it
is perhaps accurate to say that it cuts two ways. Given Bowie's
status as a gay and bisexual superstar, the image resists the way
mainstream seventies' culture viewed more ambivalent forms
of male sexuality as exclusively feminine. This image is also a
representation of a dominant male sexuality where manliness
is equated with the ability to be able to control an aggressive
sexuality. The representation of Bowie as dog-like suggests a
view of masculine sexuality as essentially 'animal', needing to
be trained and commanded.

The cover of the album bears a close relationship to
Burroughs's (1969) own description of a Penny Arcade Peep
Show in his aforementioned novel, *The Wild Boys*. The arcade
is located in a funfair and is populated by decadent young
men who wear 'rainbow jock straps' and 'loincloths'. Inside the
Peep Show, Burroughs introduces the reader to a world of both
explicit and surreal homosexual encounter. The freakishness of
the utopian and dystopian worlds of Bowie and Burroughs is
intended to undermine dominant ideas of homosexuality and
introduce alternative masculine sexual pleasures. The freak
show has a long history as a form of troubling and disruptive
sexual fantasy. In the nineteenth century, freak shows were inex-
pensive but spectacular forms of entertainment that challenged
conventional boundaries between animals and humans, men
and women and the sexual and the sexless (Gamson 1998). More

so than Burroughs, Bowie's art like that of the freak show is of low cultural value, offending traditional bourgeois categories of taste and refinement. The effect of Bowie's sexual explicitness is potentially far greater in a popular domain, and has to be judged in the context of the culture of the time.

Both Bowie and Burroughs are welcoming us to a carnival-esque freak show. Arguably both in different ways are asking us to imagine a new queer utopia where femininity is permanently displaced and an aggressive male sexuality affirmed. These features move gay men away from victim status but end up championing a masculine misogyny. The broken narrative of *Diamond Dogs* displays a world of emotionless sexual encounter between men, as well as between men and women. It is a society built upon coolness, cruelty and ultimately the victory of state repression. 'Hunger City' is seemingly overrun with dog-like people who have little regard for one another beyond brisk forms of sexual exchange. Musically the album is close to the kind of raw rock 'n' roll influenced by the Rolling Stones. Despite Mick Ronson's absence, it is the muscular soaring guitar that catches the ear. In many respects, then, the album's sound is a continuation of the guitar rock of *Aladdin Sane*. Yet pianist Mike Garson described the music as having 'a different vibe; it felt heavier, it was on the dark side' (Pegg 2000: 217). These features are also reflected in the characters Bowie invents on the album. On the title track, Bowie introduces a 'scavenger' and a 'cool cat' called Halloween Jack whose girlfriend is a 'little Hussy' with a 'Dali brooch'. Similar metaphors for hypermasculine cool recur throughout the album.

Perhaps the most important track on the 1974 release is 'Sweet Thing'. The song has a more uncertain opening than most of the other tracks and, while it has its rock moments, it also utilizes the softer sound of piano and saxophone. Here Bowie's voice alternates between a high falsetto of anguish and celebration and a masculine tone that suggests warning and concern. The music suggests sexual confusion with Bowie moving between brash rock 'n' roll and more gentle or tender moments. Indeed, despite the fact it has never been released as a single, many of the fans I interviewed have picked it out as a favourite

Bowie song. The song signifies the loneliness, emptiness and relations of dominance in a sexual encounter based upon traditional forms of masculinity. Not only does the masculine subject relate to himself as an object ('if you want it'), but also the 'other' in this relationship is diminished ('pain in a stranger') ('Sweet Thing', 1974).

Recent psychoanalytic thinking on gender identity has tried to account for how masculine forms of sexuality develop. In patriarchal families, the nurturing, holding mother and the liberating, exciting father are expressed as polar opposites. Such opposing roles mean that masculinity springs from the need to deny identification with the mother. Hence central to the cultural achievement of masculinity is the repression of emotional attunement, the fragility of the body and empathetic understanding. These are all cast off because of their dangerous associations with femininity. Feminine traits are experienced as a threat to the developing male's identity. Little boys identify with their fathers so as to fend off the threat of being absorbed by their mothers, and to achieve instead their sense of autonomy. The idea of autonomous individuality becomes a masculine and thereby hegemonic ideal. As Jessica Benjamin (1990: 172) comments, the ideal of the 'self-sufficient individual continues to dominate our discourse'. It is the emphasis upon individual self-reliance and the rejection of dependence that ensures male dominance. Through identification with images and narratives of independence many (men as well as women) learn to banish more difficult feelings of helplessness and dependency. Masculinity, returning to the forms of desire evident within *Diamond Dogs*, emphasizes separation over connection, self-sufficiency over dependency and autonomy over concern for the 'other'. It is possible then for so-called postmodern texts such as *Diamond Dogs* to subvert the language of heterosexuality while remaining hypermasculine. Indeed, we might add a rider here, that the culture of disconnected individualism also has a more than passing resemblance to the culture required of late capitalism. However, I want to explore these questions more fully in the next chapter.

Bowie and identity after glam

David Bowie's constructed utopian self sought to go beyond the straitjacket of the normalization offered by mainstream rock culture. We have begun to unravel some of the contradictions evident in Bowie's cultural productions in respect of their commodification and masculinism. Yet the 'Ziggy myth' seemingly had a number of disastrous personal consequences for David Bowie. As I indicated earlier, Bowie has suggested in many of his interviews that he himself became trapped by his own creation. Talking some years after the *Ziggy Stardust* album, Bowie commented:

> About two years ago, I realized I had become a total product of my concept character Ziggy Stardust. So I set out on a very successful crusade to re-establish my own identity. I stripped myself down and took myself apart, layer by layer. I used to sit in bed and pick on one thing a week that I either didn't like or couldn't understand. And during the course of the week, I'd try to kill it off. (Bowie 1980: 24–6).

During the mid seventies, Bowie was caught up in contractual disputes with his record company, a widely reported interest in UFOs and the occult, a failing marriage with his wife Angie and numerous drug and alcohol problems (Tremlett 1996). His latest project, *Young Americans*, which Bowie described as 'plastic soul', was recorded at a time when he was 'absolutely infuriated' to be still 'in rock 'n' roll' (Welch 1999: 83). Musically, the record broke new ground for Bowie, given that he was one of the first white artists to attempt to record soul. While many read Bowie's engagement with black soul music as further evidence of his Americanization, this rubric offers a poor understanding of Bowie's endless mutability. Cultural critic Jonathan Dollimore (1991) notes that many gay artists have sought to escape the confines of 'mainstream' culture by engaging with subordinate cultures of difference. This was a further attempt on the part of Bowie to disturb the 'mainstream' orientations of heterosexual rock. He tried to bring the 'marginal' into the 'mainstream' by engaging both with black soul music and later electronic avant-garde music. The album was recorded at Sigma Sound studio, home of the Philadelphia International label whose artists included the Three Degrees, the O'Jays and the Stylistics. While *Young Americans* was produced by Tony Visconti, the inclusion of guitarist Carlos Alomar (who had previously worked with James Brown and Ben E. King) was important in trying to capture the soul sound. Overall, the sound on *Young Americans* has a lush, melancholic feel with the exception of the album's stand-out track 'Fame'. This was recorded and co-written with John Lennon, and gave Bowie his first US number no. 1 single. Compared with the rest of *Young Americans*, the track 'Fame' sounds harsh, discordant and disconnected. This is matched by Bowie's staccato-like delivery. If the figure of Ziggy Stardust enthusiastically moved within the ambivalence of fame and stardom, the song 'Fame' expresses something unrelenting, severe and cold about the condition. It is indeed the hollowness and emptiness of celebrity that is articulated by one of Bowie's best-known songs. It seems that his quickly changing masks were hiding a great deal of personal suffering. Bowie needed to find a way of reinventing not just his public self. It was time to escape temporarily from the narcissistic world of celebrity.

There would of course be one final creation before Bowie made this move. The Thin White Duke acted as a death mask from which Bowie would flee to Berlin. After the recording of *Station to Station* (1976), Bowie began a three-album collaboration with Brian Eno, *Low* (1977), *'Heroes'* (1977) and *Lodger* (1979), and moved out of the Los Angeles celebrity scene. In an interview with Charles Shaar Murray (1991: 234), Bowie comments on his need to move away, saying that '*Low* was a reaction to having gone through that peculiar dull greeny-grey limelight of American rock and roll and its repercussions.' Bowie's decision to move out of the media spotlight and 'escape' to the divided city of Berlin meant he was able to adopt a more self-consciously 'low profile'. This connects with his expressed desire to 'kill' Ziggy and move in a different artistic direction. About this period Bowie comments, 'I wanted to move out of the area of narrative and character. I wanted, generally to re-evaluate what I was doing' (Jones 1977). While *Low* is now widely considered to be amongst Bowie's best work, RCA at the time threatened not to release it, given its experimental nature and lack of obvious commercial appeal. Despite this, the title track of *'Heroes'* (the companion recording with *Low*) is widely hailed as Bowie's most popular song. Indeed, despite Bowie's ability to engage in the avant-garde, he always kept a keen eye on commercial success. Although the single version of '"Heroes"' did not achieve immediate chart success, it has subsequently generated a public and commercial resonance that has not been achieved by many other pieces of music. Bowie claims that the song was inspired by a couple (man and woman) whom he would watch by the Berlin Wall each day. The Hansa studio in Berlin overlooked the wall from where Bowie could view the couple conduct what he assumed was an affair. Bowie mused that this was an act of heroism in that there seemed to be something clandestine about their meetings (Murray 1991). The song's power comes from the filmic quality of its narrative and the resonance of the music. Perhaps the most remarkable feature of this song is Bowie's vocal. The song begins with the sound of synthesizer and guitar with Bowie almost whispering. His voice gets progressively louder until the introduction of what Tony Visconti calls 'a clanging metallic sound' at the song's mid-point (Pegg 2000: 69). At this point the vocal literally takes off, utilizing what Bowie would sometimes call his histrionics.

'Heroes' does not so much refer to the untouchability and other-worldliness of fame and celebrity, but instead looks to ways in which everyday life can be heroic. These are opportunities for heroism the song suggests, that are both open to everyone and are by their nature fleeting. These are often moments that could well double as shots from a film. Indeed many of the fans that I interviewed reported similar epiphanies. Such moments might include winning a competition, falling in love or even (as we shall see) going to see Bowie for the first time. Stardom is magical when it is able to add sparkle and glamour to everyday life. Notably, Bowie's concern with more earthly themes was a result of his time in Berlin. During this period, Bowie literally 'fell to earth'. The importance of Berlin to Bowie's biography meant that he had temporarily stepped off the rollercoaster of fame and tried to become (as far as is possible) an ordinary person again.

While Bowie was finding himself, the music industry was being challenged by a new cultural movement called punk. Punk upheld an amateurish ethic that sought to blur the distinction between the performers and the audience (Rowe 1995). This was obviously a challenge to the stars of Bowie's generation. At the time punk was widely seen to be putting up two fingers to established stars and celebrities. This – albeit temporarily – threatened many existing stars in the music industry until punk itself was also converted into a commodity. In fact Bowie detected some deep dangers in some of punk's egalitarian ethics. It seemed to Bowie that the adoption of a rigid, classifiable identity with attendant rules was the opposite of the more explorative approach that he brought to his own art (Murray 1991). For Bowie the world of mediated fame and celebrity was a world of ambivalence. The complex dilemmas facing an artist who is loved and hated by critics and fans alike was not to be resolved by the psychological security offered by attachment to a 'movement' like punk. Bowie's own prioritization of the individual capacity for aesthetic reflexivity in a media-dominated age was enough to make him suspicious of some of punk's absolute claims. Despite the inevitable ambivalence of an established star who risks becoming yesterday's news because of the fluctuations in fashion, Bowie and punk had a good deal in common. Many punks cited Bowie's capacity to work on questions of identity in order to produce something 'abnormal' or 'strange' as influential (Frith 1989). This, it seems, did not prevent Bowie from viewing punk critically.

In the middle of a period dominated by punk, Bowie made one of his most underrated albums of all time. *Lodger* was released in May 1979, reaching no. 4 in the UK charts and a respectable no. 20 in the US. If Bowie in part sought to disappear during the making of *Low* and *'Heroes'*, he established himself centre-stage again with *Lodger*. Speaking after the recording of *'Heroes'*, Bowie once again returned to the importance of remaking identity in the context of change:

> 'My role as an artist in rock,' he says, 'is rather different to most. I encapsulate things very quickly, in a very short space of time. Over two or three months usually. And generally my policy has been that as soon as a system or a process works, it's out of date. I move to another area. Another piece of time.' (Jones 1977)

The need of an individual to keep moving and changing is a key motif of this and other Bowie work. At this point, Bowie's art progresses from mobility to a commitment to a journey without end. The album cover pictures Bowie as a hanging man strung up in a bathroom. If you open the gatefold sleeve on the original record (this effect does not quite work on the CD), you will notice that the sleeve is designed as a postcard to be sent to his record company. As ever, Bowie's image suggests no definite meaning but presents a number of interpretative possibilities. The image is playful; this is not a 'serious' cry for help. On the inside cover, Bowie is pictured with a make-up artist, drawing attention to the fact that this image is a construction. However, viewed differently this image may resemble a puppet – Bowie is the performing artist or clown working for the amusement of his fans and the record industry. The dangling man is also a performer to be worked by the industry, his fans and of course Bowie himself. Bowie seems to be saying 'Yes, I am just a mask (or an image I "lodge" in for a while)' but the effect of this process can be catastrophic. Bowie's postmodern politics recognize the ambiguity of an image that can never be finally tied down or interpreted. A process that began with *Aladdin Sane* starts to seep into Bowie's own biography. The mask is still performative but now it hints at Bowie's personal troubles. His emotional trauma and pain were well known to his fan base during this time. His temporary 'escape' to Berlin, his problems with his marriage and widely reported issues of drug addiction are at least partially signified by an ironic image of suicide.

Lodger's opening track beautifully illustrates much of this. The 'fantastic voyage' is the voyage of the self. Our identities are fragile and are increasingly put under pressure in 'this criminal world' ('Fantastic Voyage' 1977). The self articulated in the song is both uncertain and searching. If our identities have no definite anchoring in culture, then of course this could not be otherwise. However, while our own selves are fragile all we need is our 'dignity' and a sense of the value of life. Indeed if the identities that we have are only what we 'perform', then we are all potentially adrift. The cultural theorist Judith Butler (1990) has perhaps gone furthest in recognizing the implications of this ontological condition. If all our identities are indeed a performance, this means that in a world of images all we can do is continually experiment with new ways of being, without any final point of arrival. We are all, to refer back to the earlier metaphor, 'dangling men' or 'puppets'. Such a position has radical possibilities in the quest to reveal the performative nature of identity but offers little guidance as to what we should become. These themes are revisited on 'Boys Keep Swinging'. The intended irony of the title both refers to a self that can be constantly reinvented and to the pleasures of 'straight' masculinity. However, the irony of the song is that if masculinity is indeed a cultural invention, then such 'pleasures' are open to everyone. The mocking tone of the song, and of course the video that accompanied the single release, suggest that such pleasures are more a matter of culture than nature. The video presents Bowie in drag and in three different feminine poses. Our identities are like markings in the sand that can easily be washed away by the tide of history and culture.

David Bowie's first album of the new decade, *Scary Monsters (and Super Creeps)* (1980), further develops these themes. Artistically this remains one of Bowie's most complex and genuinely popular works. It is the album that makes the most concerted attempt to deal publicly with Bowie's own position as a popular icon. The record arrived after the demise of punk when Bowie was attracting a new wave of followers. Bowie's interest in fame, glamour and electronic dance music was ideally suited for the 'New Romantic' phenomenon. Recorded at the Power Station studios in New York, Bowie broke off his three-album collaboration with Brian Eno. However, he continued to employ a number of other musicians and guitarists like Carlos Alomar and Robert Fripp (who had also worked on *'Heroes'*). With Tony Visconti producing the album it is probably Bowie's finest attempt to merge art rock with pop. On release it was hailed by many music critics as an instant Bowie classic, with *Billboard* magazine correctly predicting that 'this should be the most accessible and commercially successful Bowie LP in years' (Pegg 2000: 236). The sleeve illustration is a torn picture of Bowie dressed in a Pierrot costume that has been ripped at the collar. The artwork is by Edward Bell who designed a series of paintings used for a Bowie calendar entitled *Glamour*. The figure of the clown – which appeared on the video for the single 'Ashes to Ashes' (1980) – refers to Bowie's past. In 1971 Bowie was widely quoted as saying, 'I think rock should be tarted up, made into a prostitute, a parody of itself. It should be the clown, the Pierrot medium' (Hoskyns 1998: 21). Similarly in 1973, Bowie commented 'What do they want from me? That's the joke of it. But then again people need figures like me, the clowns' (Rock 2000: 31–2). Alberto Melucci (1996) has argued that the figure of the clown represents the loss of mystery and wonder in late modern culture. The clown stands for the 'other' in a culture driven by rationalization, prediction and control. By emphasizing exaggeration, mimicry and otherness, the clown draws our attention to that which escapes our understanding. This perhaps partially explains the fascination with Bowie. Whereas Bowie's clowning in the early seventies had sought to dramatize the complexities of stardom, by the early eighties he was also concerned to express a more redemptive attitude to his own past.

While Bowie remains self-referential about the processes of pop stardom, the album has concerns that move beyond a surface preoccupation with glamour. In this respect, the hugely successful single 'Ashes to Ashes' refers back to Major Tom on his first British hit single 'Space Oddity' (1969) only to tell us he's 'a junkie'. Further, 'Fashion' and 'Teenage Wildlife' offer warnings about the risks, dangers and ambivalences of being famous. If 'Fashion' mockingly points to the consumer culture's ability to foster 'goon squads', 'Teenage Wildlife' relates how Bowie 'feels like a group of one'. These allusions were widely recognized at the time and invited fans and critics alike to participate in spotting intertextual clues to Bowie's troubled personal life. As with Ziggy, Bowie's success in converting himself into a 'writerly' text resonated with his followers. This much is well documented; however, what concerns me is that the album again addresses the necessity of self-creation in an increasingly fragmented consumer culture.

The flip side of the album sleeve pictured stills from his recent albums *Low*, *'Heroes'* and *Lodger*, teasing the reader into trying to decide which is the 'real' David Bowie. Again, Bowie is playing the postmodern game of pointing out ways in which contemporary culture is constructed – but this time with a difference. The question that dominates the album, and one we are invited to ponder, is who am I? What does it mean to be a self in a world of fluid identities? This question is most heavily referenced in the album's fourth (and least commercially successful) single, 'Up The Hill Backwards' (1980). Bowie's voice evokes a jaded resignation referring to 'the vacuum created by the arrival of freedom'. This offers 'possibilities' but few actual guidelines and signposts. Modern culture poses a number of different ways of 'becoming' without being able to resolve the question as to which identity we should choose. As Bowie put it, it's got nothing to do with 'you'. That is, the answer to these questions of identity does not lie within the self. Whereas for *Ziggy Stardust* this situation seemed to offer potential, by the end of the decade Bowie has adopted a more melancholic pose. Bowie's criticisms of punk imply that such questions cannot be resolved by adopting a regressive communalism. However, and as Bowie's numerous self-inventions demonstrate, there is no simple answer. The very openness of issues of identity is a matter of both opportunity and ambivalence. Further, as I have already indicated, Bowie believes that this is not something that his fans can expect him to resolve for them. Following the French philosopher Michel Foucault (1997) (and to some degree David Bowie himself), we might argue that our shared quest is to 'take care of the self' rather than to 'know the self'. The question is not so much who I am (as I might become many things) but how ought I to live. This is not so much discovering ourselves in our essence but

learning to live out our many possibilities artfully and ethi-
cally. The self is always a cultural invention. In this respect, we
should be wary of instant solutions to questions of identity or
of hard and fast rules that inhibit the invention of the self. We
are then each of us responsible for the ways in which we evolve.
David Bowie is encouraging us to explore the dangers and possibilities of selfhood. Yet his life and music also resonate with
the awareness that such questions could be resolved by many
of his followers attempting to become him, rather than carrying
out their own experiments. This much is consistent with Bowie's
Ziggy period. Yet increasingly, as I have sought to demonstrate,
Bowie's inventions are becoming less strident and (for now) less
overtly masculine in nature. His theatricality evokes a sense of
the tragic and the fragility of the man behind the mask. On *Scary
Monsters* Bowie plays out these possibilities in a form of camp
tragedy. In 'Scream Like A Baby', Bowie stutters 'I'm learning
to be an integrated part of society'. It is therefore not just the
self-respect of non-conformity that Bowie dramatizes but our
shared capacity for extraordinary self-invention. While on *Scary
Monsters* Bowie plays the part beautifully of the bruised star of
popular music, it is not clear where he will go next. Bowie, the
wounded survivor, will undoubtedly continue but with over ten
years of outstanding popular music behind him there is, for the
first time, a sense that he is running out of fresh ideas.

The last of the postmodern dreamers?

Bowie would indeed lose his way in the eighties. Here Bowie's
narrative became less about postmodern playfulness than the
logic of the culture industry and the loss of creativity. This is a
complex story and the subject of the next chapter. In more recent
times, Bowie has returned to many of the questions he initially
posed in the late seventies and early eighties on the album *hours*
(1999). The two most prominent themes on the recording are
reconciliation and the necessity of dreaming. This strikes a contrast with *Scary Monsters*, given the prevailing sense of tragedy
and the impossibility of choosing the self. With the release of

hours, it is not the different ways of realizing the self that are explored but the need to form a deeper connection with the self's own individual narrative. Reconciliation is implied on the cover where Bowie is pictured comforting a previous incarnation (Major Tom?) of himself, his new self taking care of his former self. Songs such as ' Something in the Air', 'Thursday's Child' and 'Survive' articulate a sense of coming to terms with personal limitations and failed relationships.

While the album can hardly be described as autobiographical (many of Bowie's songs are explicitly 'in character'), it does something different to *Scary Monsters*. It is as though Bowie moved beyond an exclusive focus upon image into a more ethical space. The question is no longer 'who might I become?' but 'how might I live with uncertainty and with who I used to be?' This is a different set of issues. Such a sensibility is most evident on 'What's Really Happening?' where Bowie suggests that 'now it's time to face the lie'.

These images are no less theatrical than the Bowie of *Changes* but they offer a different sense of identity to that of postmodern playfulness. Within this new set of articulations, Bowie maintains the importance of the imagination and of dreaming. Such a possibility is now disconnected from explicit concerns with gender and sexual politics. Rather, Bowie affirms the role of the artist who maintains a sense of 'otherness' through aesthetic rather than sexual or gender transformation. While the 'dreaming' alluded to on a number of the album's tracks refers to the capacity to be 'creative', it offers no final salvation. In particular, the closing song on the album, 'The Dreamers', refers to the emptiness but also to the necessity of self-creation. Given Bowie's rise through the glam rock of the seventies, his survival of punk, his status among the New Romantics and the stadium rock of the eighties, perhaps 'the last of the dreamers' is a fitting epitaph ('The Dreamers', 1999). While *hours* (1999) articulates fame as injury, the album remains alive to the need to keep dreaming. Despite his own changes, Bowie has been able to sustain a self that dreams of a better tomorrow. Now much of that old restlessness has gone; it is not as though his former questions have been resolved, but he can now live with a sense of openness towards the future and without seeking to deny who he used to be. If anything, it is his ability to survive the turbulence of a long career in popular music that is being celebrated. Bowie's youthful image, toned body and fashionable dress-sense powerfully communicate the sense of someone who has literally 'survived' the wounds of an unforgiving industry where performers quickly become yesterday's news. His durability seems to say that while the stars of his generation have imploded, disappeared or become stuck in endless cycles of repetition, he continues to refashion himself. This may not be achieved with the vigour of youth, but this time he can communicate a sense of the possible without seeking to detach himself from his past. In terms of who he is, this remains an unanswered question, the difference being that he no longer needs to escape his past. It is, then, no surprise that Bowie has retained a loyal group of fans over the years. The sheer uncertainty of modern life is an experience shared by celebrities and their fans alike the world over.

———— four ————

COMMODIFYING BOWIE

In the previous two chapters, I focused upon the reflexive aspects of Bowie's celebrity during the sixties and seventies. In this respect, I emphasized Bowie's ability to pull together artistic ideas from creative workers such as Andy Warhol and William Burroughs in order to develop a new aesthetic in popular music. To this end I connected an analysis of Bowie's performances to a critical culture of fame, sexuality and gender. Here I argued that Bowie should be viewed as a postmodern performer because of how he sought to unsettle the categories of identity. It has been these features that many who wish to claim Bowie as a radical figure within popular music tend to focus upon. Here Bowie acts as a postmodern artist de-naturalizing rock music and heterosexual masculinity, while drawing together high and low cultural forms. All claims to Bowie's radicalness as a popular performer have to begin with these aspects.

Tracing Bowie's career through the eighties and nineties means revising such arguments. During these decades, Bowie made more money than ever before and yet creatively he went into decline. It is in the eighties that Bowie became a genuinely global superstar while simultaneously producing art which was less interesting but more commercial than his previous work. With the benefit of hindsight, I think we can readdress some of Bowie's earlier cultural creations and re-evaluate them in the context of commodification. David Bowie at this juncture does not to so much embody radical individualism as a kind of marketized individualism. In political terms, if the self articulated by Bowie in the sixties and seventies draws inspiration from counter-cultural and subcultural movements, in the eighties he moves closer to more 'mainstream' aspects of society. The eighties has become known as the decade which saw the rise of the New Right on both sides of the Atlantic. Many have labelled this period as the 'me-decade', the rise of the 'selfish society', or simply as the time when shopping was prioritized over politics. The British Conservative prime minister Margaret Thatcher's famous remark 'there is no such thing as society' is often quoted to sum up the cultural politics of the decade. The eighties was the time that saw huge cultural industries (the film and recording industry, the conglomeration of newspapers and television) increasing their market share and the global visibility of their products. It was the decade when public utilities were privatized, society became more individualistic and competitive and culture was increasingly dominated by capitalism. This is not to argue that in decades previous to the eighties, such cultural products were necessarily more 'alternative' or less commercially driven. As we have seen in previous chapters, music, art and culture have to make their impact in an overwhelmingly commercial setting. Instead my argument is about the *intensification* and increasingly *commercial* focus of our culture due to economic and ideological changes that came about in the eighties. In this chapter, I want to argue that during the eighties David Bowie increasingly resembled a commodity to be bought and sold on the market. His more experimental music behind him (for the time being at least), this was a time to make lots of money.

Here, one might object, why should any of this concern me? So what if Bowie became a commodity like toothpaste or soap powder? I just like his image and his music. Of course, all popular music in our society takes the form of a commodity. From the music we listen to on the radio to the compact discs we play on our home stereos, the music industry is centrally involved in selection, recording and relentless promotion. Just think of the different ways that Bowie has been repackaged over the years. As fans we have been asked to buy a number of greatest hits collections, re-mastered recordings of old favourites and newly presented versions of his back catalogue, sometimes with extra tracks or new artwork. As a major star, Bowie is automatically big business. Indeed, as outlined in the previous chapter, Pop Art is the merging of business and art. We need to ask however what this does to the critical potential of music and performance. We might be forgiven for thinking that on one level the impact is very limited in an industry able to support performers as diverse as the Beatles, David Bowie and Kylie Minogue. Maybe. Yet many have argued otherwise. For example, the critical theorist Theodor Adorno (1991) claims that, rather than being spontaneously created, it matters greatly if our art and culture are relentlessly promoted by an industry oriented towards profit. The critical potential of art and culture, he reasons, is damaged if it becomes a mass spectacle aimed at appealing to millions of people across the globe, rather than something that invites critical reflection. Undoubtedly Adorno overstates the dichotomy between commerce and art. Yet Adorno is quite correct in his insistence that we should consider the extent to which Bowie's art has been complicit with the dominant strategies of the culture industry. In other words, has Bowie always made critical and valuable music? How are we to account for periods when he made music that sold well but in retrospect is limited and sometimes disappointing?

Inevitably this marks out Bowie as a less than perfect figure within popular culture. However, this book aims to be a multifaceted appreciation of David Bowie rather than an uncritical fan account. Even Bowie's most overtly commercial phase poses interesting questions. At his most 'mainstream', Bowie is someone whose output is worthy of more serious critical analysis.

Bowie into the eighties

In the previous chapter I sought to emphasize that Bowie represented a form of individualism which encouraged ordinary people to experience their identities as reflexive projects. The unsettling of the markers of class, community and gendered and racial identity led many in the late sixties and early seventies to adopt an experimental attitude in this respect. For the most part I have argued that such an attitude resulted in the partial unfixing of traditional male, female and sexual scripts. This created imaginative opportunities for those who wished to fashion new or different identities. In particular, I claimed that Bowie's embrace of a form of Nietzschean individualism was progressive in that it sought to invent other possibilities in the face of traditional features of society.

Here I want to argue that there are some negative aspects that perhaps inevitably accompany these features. Let us return to Bowie's discovery of Nietzsche on *The Man Who Sold the World* (1971). We might start by arguing that Bowie's individualism is not only overtly masculinist but has more than a passing connection to the dominant culture of capitalist society. The modern consumerist dream is one that emphasizes the desires of the individual as opposed to responsibilities and obligations towards other people. Indeed, the late cultural theorist Raymond Williams (1989) argued that avant-garde artistic movements and commercial cultures often promote very similar ideas and feelings. Williams warned that the Nietzchean politics of many artistic cultural movements end up prioritizing the creativity of certain radical individuals over that of the community. The creativity of a few radical individuals is highlighted against the so-called apathy of the masses who need to be shocked, mocked and derided into action. In this setting, it was the artist who took on the role of 'genius' or 'superman' in relation to the ignorant masses. Whereas most artists inspired by this vision have adopted anti-commercialism, Bowie took these features into mass culture.

As we have seen, it was Pop Art that allowed Bowie to handle this contradiction. Bowie embraced the commercial setting of his performances while at the same time seeking to destabilize some of rock's more established myths. What happens to this matrix if Bowie's work becomes less experimental? The tensions between art and capitalism collapse as Bowie seemingly becomes a stadium status mega-star of the music industry. If previously some of Bowie's inventions had sought to warn against the empty narcissism of the consumer culture, he was to become a shining example of it. For example, the album *Aladdin Sane* seeks to both abnormalize the process of making stars while promoting Bowie as one of the key figures of the early seventies. This is not so much empty commodification as reflexive commodification. Arguably Bowie offers a contradictory collection encompassing a celebration of American style consumerism ('Drive In Saturday'), subcultural cool ('The Jean Genie') and the avant-gardist experimentation ('Aladdin Sane (1913–1938–197?'). For example, the song 'Cracked Actor' hints not only at a more troubled relationship with stardom than was previously evident on the *Ziggy Stardust* album, but of the emptiness of commodification and perils of the culture industry. 'Forget that I'm fifty, cause you just got paid' ('Cracked Actor', 1973). Here fame and celebrity mask bodily decline and personal misfortune. This image of the culture industry selling dreams of fulfilment and hedonism papering over the relations of profiteering and exploitation has been central to the way many people seek to understand popular culture. Bowie's song emphasizes the capacity of culture to act more like industry in its capacity to recycle the old as if it were new. The added twist here is that this image is being offered by one of the main stars of the culture industry. The dominant image culture of our society is based less upon artistic experimentation than upon the ruthless pursuit of profit and the endless repackaging of images and icons. Bowie's exploration of the world of faded film stars is, it seems, pointing to some of the more toxic features of commodification. For all of Bowie's sexual ambiguity and gender disruption, he is reminding us that he is, after all, a commodity to be bought and sold on the market place. Bowie is caught up in the genuine contradiction of disrupting the dominant images and representations of our culture while reinforcing the norms of consumer society.

We need to remember that above all Bowie maintains his position in our culture because he has been successfully marketed as a product. This is particularly evident during the eighties but is also apparent in the emphasis he places on the liberation that is achieved by constant change, which of course is designed to keep the cash tills ringing. Bowie plays into the imperatives of the market and consumer identities by suggesting that a 'new you' can be purchased ready-made from the supermarket.

Arguably Bowie paves the way for a number of artists such as Madonna, Prince and Michael Jackson, all of whom took centre stage during the 1980s. By privileging image, Bowie (along with these other artists) is a product of mainstream society while also being critical of some of its features.

The more destructive side of Bowie's identity politics suggests that the 'lad insane' might do well to discover a new identity through the imperatives of the fashion and consumer industries. This is the point where identity politics plays into commodification. Indeed, if Bowie's radicalism of the early seventies served to deconstruct the categories of the 'serious' and the 'popular', it did so without concern for the wider impacts of capitalism.

While these features were most evident in Bowie's cultural production during the eighties, they were also apparent in the seventies, the difference being that the music-texts produced by Bowie during this period are generally more internally contradictory and move between a number of different locations. It is Bowie's ability, if you like, to bring together aspects of commercial culture, subculture, postmodernism, the avant-garde and gay culture that adds to the complexity of his cultural performances. These aspects seemed to disappear in the eighties.

Previously I discussed Bowie's album *Lodger* as being interesting because of the images of alienation and detachment that it articulates. We can appreciate many of these features in various ways. The idea of the changing and moving self is most obviously signified on the track 'Move On' (1979). The need to move on – to the next island, relationship or artistic project – becomes part of an experience of travelling through the different cultural features of everyday life. Here Bowie uses the metaphor of travel to communicate his own and our culture's continual restlessness and desire for change. Occupying a world of flickering and restless images can leave us with a sense that our identities have little substance. In this respect, we become 'like a shadow' or 'a leaf' ('Move On', 1979). Part of Bowie's distinctiveness as an artist who works within popular culture is the emphasis he places upon change. Bowie just keeps moving on. At this point these discordant features have a radical effect that is also communicated through the music. While the production was left to Bowie and Visconti, Brian Eno brought his own innovative way of working to this album. For instance, some of the distorted guitar sound is produced by Adrien Belew. On arriving in the studio he was simply instructed 'to play accidentally' without being allowed to hear any of the music they had recorded in the previous sessions. However, the imperative to 'move on' also mimics a wider consumer culture where our identities, passions and interests are *required* to be endlessly dissatisfied. By this I mean that a capitalist economy is dependent upon our desires remaining unfulfilled. If we had already bought all the music worth listening to, there would be no need for us to keep trying out new music. Capitalism not only demands that consumers consume, we are literally required to do so. Read more cynically than I would want, you could argue that Bowie acts as the perfect celebrity-as-commodity. Continually changing his form, adopting new guises, he always offers the fans 'something new' to keep them consuming. These features are only part of Bowie's make-up before the early eighties. Indeed, part of Bowie's project, as I have argued at length, is the exploration of stardom and celebrity by immersing himself in its contradictions, passions and repetitiveness. Such a project would of course only be realized if Bowie were able to convert himself into a big star at the beginning of the eighties. This means it is pointless to complain that Bowie 'sold out'. It is not that Bowie simply becomes part of corporate rock, more that his exploration of the cultures of fame and celebrity becomes less defined by features that are distinctive. Perhaps more to the point is that, moving into the eighties, Bowie allied himself less with subcultural politics and more with the politics of the commodity and the spectacle.

Let's Dance

Bowie's previous outing, *Scary Monsters (and Super Creeps)*, had seen him connect with the subcultural movement, the New Romantics. Bowie, having been absent in Berlin during the punk scene, was back at the creative edge of popular culture. For the

New Romantics, Bowie was the key icon, suggesting that you could experiment with gender, sexuality and consumption while seeking to develop a certain 'look'. New Romantics were largely college-educated young people who enjoyed experimenting with second-hand clothes and make-up while practising the art of gender-bending. Building on the art school origins of punk, New Romantics were more concerned with dressing up than social protest. If punk had – similarly to rock music – sought to insist upon music's authenticity and to some extent anti-capitalist values, then New Romantics were more concerned with a politics of style and dressing up. New Romantics were the expression of the bored suburbs rather than the anger of the inner city. These contradictions contain an echo of the tensions that had previously existed between the sixties' counter-culture and glam rock. Punk's championing of independent record labels, anti-authoritarian politics and 'authentic' street culture were a bridge too far for an established artist of the record industry like David Bowie. The rise of independent labels caused much concern in the music industry in the late seventies. By 1982 Britain's independents had expanded to 18 per cent of British record sales. While this challenge to the established majors like EMI, CBS and Polygram was to prove to be short-lived, punk was relatively successful in connecting a politics of protest, new aesthetic styles and new forms of economic control. Punk aimed to combine more local forms of economic power against the global reach of the major labels. In terms of its own identity, punk set the immediacy of three easily learnt chords against the technological sophistication of more mainstream rock (Rowe 1995).

The major players in the popular music industry would soon react to reassert their dominance. They did this in the early eighties by heavily investing in major stars. The branding of David Bowie in this respect was part of a broader economic and political strategy to re-establish control over cultural and musical production. Indeed, according to sociologist Simon Frith (1997), one of the primary ways in which the industry aims to keep control of sales is through the development of a star system. The great majority of any major label's profits comes not from new artists but established big names like the Beatles, Bob Marley and of course David Bowie. This is obviously a key feature in an industry where 90 per cent of releases fail to make a profit.

These economic rather than cultural features perhaps explain why EMI were so keen to sign David Bowie from RCA. In 1979, EMI had been the global distributor of popular music dominating 20 per cent of the singles market and 22 per cent of albums. By 1983, this position was occupied by CBS, but due to the rise of independent labels they could only distribute 16 per cent of the world's albums and 15 per cent of its singles (Rowe 1995). EMI gave Bowie an advance of 20 million dollars against the future earnings of Bowie's next five albums (Sandford 1996). It has been estimated that in 1983 alone Bowie would have made a pre-tax profit of approximately 50 million dollars (Tremlett 1996). Not surprisingly, Bowie often jokingly referred to his *Let's Dance* album and tour as his pension plan! Despite having been one of the most prominent stars of the seventies, Bowie entered the new decade claiming to be broke. This was largely a result of the contractual arrangements entered into by Bowie once he left his old manager Kenneth Pitt for Tony DeFries in 1970. The difference between the men was that if Pitt represented a theatrical tradition, DeFries was a cutting-edge entrepreneur hoping to carve his way in the entertainment business. Such was Bowie's desire to be famous it is unlikely he read his new contract with DeFries closely. The basic result of the deal was that David Bowie became an employee of MainMan (a company created in part by DeFries). All of Bowie's earnings during this period went to MainMan with Bowie receiving an allowance for expenses. Given that these expenses had to cover many of Bowie's entourage, including the excesses of Iggy Pop, it is not always clear that MainMan profited from what was an exploitative arrangement. Despite Bowie's drug dependence during the early part of the seventies, it was only a matter of time before he would try and get himself out of this contract. In 1975 Bowie finally broke rank with Tony DeFries. MainMan continued to be entitled to 50 per cent of earnings from *Hunky Dory* to *David Live* and 16 per cent of future earnings up until 1982. Further, in 1981, Bowie applied for and received a tax exemption certificate that as a Swiss resident would help him make the most of his future earnings. This signalled the end of his contract with RCA, clearing the way for the mega-deal with EMI. Bowie, finally free from MainMan, paying little in the way of taxes and financed by one of the world's largest entertainment conglomerates, was ready to become a global superstar. He was now a fully paid-up member of the super-rich. At this point in the early eighties he joined the relatively small ranks of global music stars including Michael Jackson, Phil Collins and Queen. It is, however, primarily these financial arrangements that helped make the *Let's Dance* album the commercial success it would become.

Undoubtedly Bowie needed a big hit to start his contract with EMI. He recorded *Let's Dance* with producer Nile Rodgers at the Power Station studios in New York in late 1982. Nile Rodgers turned out to be an inspired choice of producer, working with Bowie for the first time and chosen due to his chart success with his band, Chic. Whatever the meanings that might be read into the music, perhaps most important is the big sound that was created by Rodgers. The album's sound is accessible, dance-orientated and above all commercial. It is music that is designed not only for chart success but also for playing in large open-air venues. Bowie would later describe the music as 'warm, optimistic and funky' (Pegg 2000: 238). In order to capture this sound he employed Chic's drummer Tony Thompson and bassist Bernard Edwards, along with other session players rather than musicians like Carlos Alomar who had originally been booked to play on the album. *Let's Dance* was released by EMI in April 1983. The record company quickly reported that it was their fastest selling album since the Beatles' *Sgt Pepper's* album. Indeed, to stimulate interest amongst the record-buying public, EMI issued over a million souvenir badges with the motif: 'Bowie Is Back'. This proved to be the case: the album *Let's Dance* went to no. 1 in the UK, spending 58 weeks in the charts, and achieved a no. 4 in America where it stayed in the charts 68 weeks. Just as significant, the success of *Let's Dance* reignited popular interest in Bowie's back catalogue – ten of his albums were in the UK top 100 during July 1983.

The spectacle that was the Serious Moonlight global tour took in the cities of Munich, Paris and London, finishing in

Hong Kong, the culmination of 98 concerts playing to 2.5 million concert-goers across four continents. All tickets were sold well in advance. Such was the popularity amongst the general public that the *New Musical Express* reported that tickets for the shows in London and Birmingham had been sold out in under 24 hours. The demand was intense, so much so that the *Birmingham Evening Post* ran a story claiming tickets retailing for £9.80 were being sold by ticket touts for more than five times their value. Once inside the respective venues, Bowie fans were offered further opportunities to purchase tour merchandise, including concert programmes, T-shirts, sweatshirts, tiepins and badges alongside more traditional produce like albums. People attending the concerts would have been entertained by Bowie showcasing his most ear-catching songs on *Let's Dance* and of some of his best-known songs of the past. Many of the Bowie fans that I interviewed were aware that he was attracting a different kind of fan base, a mass rather than a subcultural audience. The large scale of these concerts obviously allowed many people their first experience of David Bowie and his music. It is not then surprising that in Bowie's own estimation 1983 secured his personal financial future.

Enough of economics we might say, what of *Let's Dance*'s cultural impact? My contention here is that *Let's Dance* is the point at which David Bowie becomes more about economics than culture, or where culture and economics become so interchangeable it is difficult to pull them apart. Culturally, *Let's Dance* is mostly about the accumulation of capital. If we were talking about a movie we would be discussing a blockbuster. Just as the blockbuster was a creation of the 1980s, so was stadium rock. Like a blockbuster, the mega-music event needs to open 'big', be relatively undemanding (concentrating on well-known songs), expensive to produce and part of a 'must-see' phenomenon. Part of *Let's Dance*'s dramatic impact are the stories which tell of its rapid rise up the charts, the overwhelming demand for tickets, its eye-catching videos and its huge venues for thousands of people. Big money has to make a big impact. This is indeed the world that philosophers like Adorno (1991) feared would arrive where the price of the ticket becomes more important than the performance. Culture and capitalism mirror one another. The image on the front of the album which was replayed in the tour brochure and numerous other publicity pictures is Bowie the boxer. The eye is drawn to Bowie's tanned and well-defined body. Bowie seems to be 'up for the fight' but this time the challenge is global domination and the amassing of wealth.

Let's Dance was about the accumulation of capital and the sheer scale and spectacle of the tour as it moved across the globe. It also featured Bowie adopting a normalized image. Gone is the image of the 'outsider' and its unsettling representations seeking to de-naturalize aspects of gender and sexuality. Throughout the Serious Moonlight tour, Bowie played the straight man in a suit flanked by booming drums and a lot of macho guitar play from the boys in the band. All of this from the man who sought to pervert rock 'n' roll. It is notable that Bowie's new heterosexual image had no room for any of the songs from the *Ziggy Stardust* album, despite the tour's focus on crowd-pleasing numbers. Bowie's adoption of the new mega-star persona had, it seems, little time for the performativity of his earlier alter ego. If anything, Bowie adopts the cool appearance of an eighties' yuppie. The videos for 'Modern Love' and 'Cat People' feature concert footage of a blonde-haired Bowie backed by men in pin-stripe suits. This would undoubtedly have served to remind concert-goers of the spectacle of the concerts, and perhaps have prompted them to buy the single as a memento. The tour and the album, while easy to listen to and affecting, are about the politics of mass entertainment.

Yet Bowie is far too reflexive a star to leave things there. In many of the images, interviews and musical productions that accompanied the tour and album, Bowie articulated a concern about questions of cultural imperialism. This is a subordinate narrative to the one of mass entertainment I described above, but is curious in this setting. The cultural theorist Edward Said (1993: 8) argues that the study of cultural imperialism involves 'the practice, the theory, and the attitudes of the dominating metropolitan centre ruling a distant territory'. In keeping with this definition, many have understood cultural imperialism to be the global penetration of American values and consumerist lifestyles over indigenous cultures and experiences. Cultural imperialism is where commercial Western cultures become 'the' culture. In terms of popular music many critics have been concerned about what happens to the practice of 'other' music and traditions once they have been exposed to Western music. These global perceptions certainly have their critics, but what is interesting in our context is that such concerns were shared by a number of musicians like Peter Gabriel and Paul Simon in the early eighties. Such features can also be linked to the marketing and development of world music, which was also a feature of the eighties. While many sought to incorporate music from different parts of the world into their music, Bowie's concerns about this question never really altered his musical style. Instead it was in interviews and some video images that such concerns were articulated. Why, we might ask, would this become a concern of Bowie's at this point? One issue could be guilt over some of Bowie's earlier proclamations in respect of race and Nazism which we will look at more closely in the next chapter. There is no doubt that since the late seventies Bowie has adopted a more 'responsible' and 'liberal' position on these subjects. However, in this context, I think that his concern with the global spread of Western consumerism has to be linked to his own position as a global mega-star and can be understood either as guilt because of his new found wealth, or as ambivalence at being marketed as a global celebrity to audiences all over the world.

The place where these concerns are most evident is on the video for the album's title track and global smash single, *Let's Dance*. As I remember, during 1983 and much of 1984, this video seemed to be an almost ever-present feature of everyday life. During the early eighties, music videos became increasingly important in the promotion of popular music, so much so that there was a growing concern that consumers were buying music more for the visual images than the music. Bowie's video features a narrative that aims to warn of the dangers for indigenous people of Western lifestyles and consumerism. It is set in the Australian outback and features the plight of two young Aborigines trying to make their way in a hostile world. The video moves from Bowie singing in a bar to a young Aboriginal woman putting on a pair of red shoes who learns how to 'dance' to the tune of Western capitalism. Later in the video, the young woman's boyfriend is represented working in a factory, while she scrubs the streets so that they might buy an engagement ring or enjoy a meal out. Consumer items, it seems, come at a very high cost for native peoples. The final frames of the video show the girl kicking off the shoes as a means of retaining her integrity and cultural identity.

The politics of these concerns often lead Bowie into contradictory territory. In an interview, Bowie argues that celebrity and politics forge very uneasy relations. Notably these comments were made after the completion of the Let's Dance tour. He comments:

> What one ends up doing, I think, is charity work, which is very interesting. I think it's because you start doing things quietly and low-profile rather than doing something excessive in one's writing. It's because I'm terrified of all forms of musical writing in the popular music idiom just getting crunched within days of release in terms of any political significance or any social statement they might make. It just becomes a T-shirt too fast. I often adore and appreciate the sentiment, but I'm just so unsure of myself in that area. I'm never sure how much real, physical manifest good it can do, whereas I know if I can do this for such and such a charity then that's a physical accomplishment. (quoted in Murray 1984: 40)

Later in the same interview, Bowie develops a similar point when he says:

> In song writing, I feel all at sea with that; I'm not sure where my place is with all of that. My writing for so long has been to do with the surreal that I don't know whether I could take myself seriously as a writer of didactic statements . . . I think unless one has a penetrating understanding of the social issues of the time it's very dangerous to get involved in other areas where one might be misled by forces that would take you off the path. It's very important not to be led, and in political issues I think it's very dodgy for a lot of artists – including myself – who have

only an understanding of the top soil of the political and social system to declare themselves under a political banner. (quoted in Murray 1984: 40–1)

How are we to understand these sentiments? For some this is precisely the kind of non-commitment one would expect from a rich superstar. As is well known, the early eighties witnessed a great deal of politically committed music from the Style Council to the Specials and from the Beat to Bruce Springsteen. Much of this popular music was inspired by some of the political themes of the eighties including the British miners' strike, the imprisonment of Nelson Mandela, the escalation of nuclear weapons and the dominance of the New Right. As Bowie points out, much of this music dates quickly and, as Springsteen was to experience in respect of the title track of his 1984 album *Born in the USA*, it could easily become co-opted by your political opponents. Indeed the charity work Bowie is probably referring to is the concert he played at the Hammersmith Odeon for the Brixton Neighbourhood Community Association. Bowie also appeared at the Live Aid concert at Wembley arena in 1985. This mass charity event included most of the Western hemisphere's global stars of popular music such as Madonna, Queen, Status Quo and the Rolling Stones. The idea was to both raise money and awareness of the famine in Ethiopia. Undoubtedly this shows that Bowie during this period is willing to use his celebrity to promote what he feels are worthy causes. Yet for a performer who is more aware than many of the politics of the image, these are curious statements. Indeed I think these views are best understood as part of the process of normalization I mentioned earlier. In place of experimentation, Bowie embraces showmanship and giving the audience a good time. Gone, it seems, for the moment is his desire to shock or indeed challenge his audience. If Bowie is keen during this period to jettison any hint of sexual ambiguity, he is also promoting an image of himself as the rock star who means business and as the businessman who rocks. He could indeed be experiencing a sense of embarrassment about the lack of fit between being a multi-million dollar stadium status rock star and someone who is concerned with the Westernization of indigenous cultures. However, I think we could equally claim that he is merely expressing his reluctance to get involved in politics after his flirtation with the far right. For now Bowie, for all his liberal sentiments, was doing what he does best – that is, entertaining.

On another level, Bowie's reflections are an acute observation of the sheer difficulty of combining mass entertainment and political causes. We have good reason to be cynical about the 'effects' that radical lyrics or the support of political causes actually has on people's willingness to join political struggles. For example, I can remember dancing to the Special AKA single 'Nelson Mandela' (1984) and wondering how many people in the club I was in had any idea who he was. Many have also been critical of Live Aid for failing to puncture easily consumable stereotypes about generous Westerners and an African continent blighted by drought. The politics of starvation would need to include a concern about questions of debt, global inequality and the lack of democracy evident in the African context. Bowie's own experience will have told him that the act of putting his arm around Mick Ronson's shoulder on BBC television's *Top of the Pops* in 1972 had a far greater impact than the combined effect of most the 'radical' political music of the eighties. For culture to become politics, it has to find a deep resonance within people's sensibilities. This is of course not to denounce movements like punk that sought in the seven-inch single a form of agit prop, but that its radicalness was probably less from its lyric content and more about an 'attitude' which challenged authority and the status quo.

My argument is that if Bowie was centrally concerned with a reflexive engagement with fame and celebrity, then of course he was going to become a stadium rock star. In this context, Bowie's brief flirtation with a different kind of political engagement was always going to come second best to the trappings of mass entertainment. Indeed Bowie's politics at this time are more determined by questions of commodification and normalization than they are by any of the causes he may have chosen to support.

The mask of normality in the eighties

During the eighties Bowie maintained a frenetic work rate. This included eight new albums (including the *Tin Machine* project), performances in seven feature-length films including *Merry Christmas Mr Lawrence* and *Absolute Beginners*, the introduction to the children's classic *The Snowman* and his stage appearance in the Broadway production of *The Elephant Man*. To the mix we should add the 1987 Glass Spider tour as well as the previously mentioned Let's Dance tour, along with Bowie's role in producing Iggy Pop's 1986 comeback album, *Blah Blah Blah*. Bowie's productivity during this period is remarkable. His films, videos, singles and albums kept him constantly in the public eye. Bowie's consistently high profile allowed his record companies to release a variety of greatest hits packages. These included *ChangesTwoBowie* (1981), *Sound+Vision* (four CD box set, 1989) and *ChangesBowie* (1990) at the beginning of the new decade. Even for a man who liked to work quickly, Bowie during the eighties was constantly on the move. Whether on tour, recording, or on the film set, he rapidly moved from one cultural project to the next. It was during this period of hyperproductivity that Bowie arguably went into creative decline. If the stadium status music of *Let's Dance* could be viewed as an experiment in mass appeal, such a notion was difficult to maintain by the end of the decade. Bowie may well have adopted a more normalized image designed to appeal to a wide public; however, except for one or two songs and a few interesting films, it did very little to enhance his artistic credibility. If the seventies had delivered an embarrassment of riches from the inventive populism of *Ziggy Stardust* and *Hunky Dory* to the strange genius of *Low* and *'Heroes'*, the eighties would make Bowie look a spent force.

Bowie during this period is an artist who has lost his creative direction. After so much challenging and vibrant modern music came a period where the more Bowie became visible, the less he seemed to matter culturally. Bowie the simulacrum was endlessly reproduced in an image-dominated media and yet those images lacked the vibrant energy of his earlier work. The star that had built his career on change and challenging image rarely rose above the mediocre during the eighties. At this time Bowie's filofax was full of dates to be kept and new projects to embark upon, yet his was a career in artistic if not commercial decline.

There are of course many explanations that can be levelled at this state of affairs. Many believe Bowie simply burnt himself out. The messy divorce from Angie and the battle for custody of his son, his relentless work schedule, the effects of the drugs and the constant touring had taken their personal toll. David Bowie would not be the first to experience a period of relative decline after an earlier bout of creative and commercial success. Yet while many stars of rock and popular music of the early seventies, such as Bowie's own friends Lou Reed and Iggy Pop, increasingly found themselves without an audience, the same could not be said of Bowie. Here we might look to the death of Bowie's friend and collaborator, John Lennon, in 1980. His murder at the hands of a fan had a considerable effect on stars of popular music everywhere. Bowie was in New York performing in *The Elephant Man* when news of Lennon's death broke. He visited Lennon's widow Yoko Ono and former lover May Pang before winding up his critically acclaimed stage role as John Merrick. Bowie was to spend the next year in Switzerland removed from any immediate artistic ventures.

Bowie's first creative effort after this period of exile was the single 'Under Pressure' recorded with Queen's Freddie Mercury. This duet (like the *Peace on Earth/Little Drummer Boy* recorded with Bing Crosby) is often quickly dismissed by Bowie fans, despite being a UK no. 1 single during the Christmas period of 1981. It was during the recording sessions at Montreux that Bowie was to learn of Freddie Mercury's lucrative deal with EMI and perhaps most clearly articulate some of the vulnerabilities of celebrity. Previously, Valerie Solanas had shot Bowie's own hero, Andy Warhol, on 3 June 1968. Indeed, many have sought to chart Warhol's own creative decline in the aftermath of a shooting he was lucky to survive (Koestenbaum 2001). These incidents aside, it is not surprising that Bowie and Mercury, two superstars of ambiguous sexuality, would have felt themselves to be quite literally 'under pressure' following Lennon's death. This, perhaps partially at least, explains Bowie's decision to move his music and career in a more overtly commercial direction. Money in rich capitalist societies does not only signify status but a commodity perhaps even more precious – security. The EMI contract provided an opportunity to live a more protected existence. This would not only have given Bowie long-term financial security but an enhanced capacity to live at a remote distance from the general public. Whatever the impact on Bowie's own creativity, the huge personal fortune that was made possible by the deal with EMI secured the long-term future of his three homes in Switzerland, New York and London. Not surprisingly after Lennon's death, Bowie became increasingly adept at maintaining both his public image and private withdrawal.

Finally, the connection between Bowie's adoption of a more normalized image and his increasingly commercial output should be viewed in the context of the AIDS crisis. The AIDS crisis first emerged in the summer of 1981 when the single 'Under Pressure' was being recorded. Stars such as Bowie and Mercury who had been associated with homosexuality and bisexuality had to ride a wave of rising public hostility towards sexual minorities. At first stories began to appear in medical journals and sections of the gay press which provoked an awakening sense of crisis. This was mostly confined to large American cities, but as well-heeled cosmopolitans it is likely that both Bowie and Mercury would have been aware of the growing concern. When the single was recorded, the 'pressure' signified in the title may well have arisen from a sense of personal risk; this is particularly pertinent given that Freddie Mercury was to die of AIDS in 1991. By 1982, burgeoning public concern was converted into a full-scale moral panic with public anxieties targeting a marginalized group. This was a period of popular hysteria. Many right-wing political and religious organizations in America viewed AIDS as God's judgement on the moral decay associated with the rise of the permissive society. During this period, many in the entertainment industry refused to work with gay artists. While the New Right championed the individual consumer, it sought to roll back rights that had been won by gay campaigners in the sixties. In this rhetoric, AIDS was seen as a 'gay plague', threatening normal and decent society from within (Weeks 1981). Such was the ferocity of this attack, it is hard to perceive how someone in Bowie's position could not be affected by its poison. For example, gender-bender Boy George (who often claimed David Bowie as his hero) after an initial period of popularity encountered intense press hostility once details of his homosexual identity had become apparent in 1983 (Savage 1997). If the time was right for Bowie's provocative art in the seventies, the same could not be said in the early eighties. The rise of the New Right was a victory for the free market and those who wished to demonize alternative sexual practices. Perhaps not surprisingly, Bowie's normalized yuppie image has to be seen as both a product of the time and, perhaps most crucially, as yet another mask to hide behind. His 'normality' in this respect was a cultural invention to ensure his continued personal success and to protect his personal life from unwanted scrutiny. The unwritten bargain he seems to have struck with the mainstream media was that as long as he didn't 'flaunt it' in public they would leave him alone. Whatever the necessity of Bowie reining in his inclination to be provocative, it undoubtedly had a negative effect on his creative output.

Such decline in creative energy was evident in the first genuinely disappointing musical contribution to his career. The *Tonight* (1984) album was recorded just a few months after the Serious Moonlight tour. What is most noticeable about the album and recording sessions was that it included little new material, and much written by other people: 'Don't Look Down' (Iggy Pop/James Williamson), 'God Only Knows' (Brian Wilson/Tony Asher) and 'I Keep Forgettin' (Jerry Leiber and Mike Stroller). Bowie also included 'Tonight' and 'Neighbourhood Threat' that he had written with Iggy Pop during the late seventies. While we need to be careful not to stretch the point too far, so many cover versions and old songs leave Bowie's creative involvement open to question. This is apparent in an interview in which Bowie is asked whether he actually played on the album. Bowie's response is instructive:

'No, I didn't. Not at all. I very much left everybody else to it. I must say, I just came in with the songs and the ideas and how they should be played and then watched them put it all together. It was great!' He chuckles to himself. 'I didn't work very hard in those terms. I feel very guilty about it! I did five or six pieces of writing and I sing a lot, and Hugh Padgham (the engineer) and Derek put the sound together between them. It was nice not to be involved in that way.' (quoted in Murray 1984: 39)

As Bowie went into what I am describing as creative decline, his actual presence in the recording process diminished. It is true that Bowie has always worked quickly and been happy to collaborate with others. However, this is different from simply handing over artistic responsibility. Again there is a parallel with the career of Andy Warhol. Warhol's proclamation that the greatest artist achieves the widest circulation and his desire to convert himself into a machine meant he had progressively to give up the role of a non-conformist. Both Warhol and Bowie from the late sixties onwards attacked the idea of the work of art expressing the uniqueness of the author. What happens in this process is that art loses its autonomy and becomes a commodity. In other words, if David Bowie is simply a cultural creation and a simulation of the popular music industry, then why not hand over creative control to others? Just as Warhol turned into a publicity machine towards the end of his career, the same is increasingly true of David Bowie. Bowie's light touch becomes a mere trace flickering on the surface of his many productions.

David Bowie's next proper album on his EMI contract is quite possibly the worst of his long career. It was recorded after his famous duet with Mick Jagger on *Dancing in the Street*, some music composition for the film *Absolute Beginners* and his role in Jim Henson's film, *Labyrinth*. It seems that Bowie just moved from one project to the next, making sure that his diary was kept full and that his face was permanently in the spotlight. The recording of the 1987 album, *Never Let Me Down*, has little to distinguish it from a host of other eighties' pop albums. Bowie later commented: 'What, for me, was a bitter disappointment was the way it turned out. It wasn't played with any conviction . . . It was "studio-fied" to such an extent that, halfway through the sessions, I was just going out to lunch and leaving it to everyone' (Sandford 1996: 264). This statement can of course be understood as a later attempt by Bowie to distance himself from a disappointing album. Yet it remains consistent with the overall sense that Bowie had become disconnected from his own cultural production. Throughout the eighties, the image of the straight yuppie connects a number of seeming disconnected projects. Julien Temple's video of Bowie's 1986 hit single, 'Absolute Beginners', features Bowie dressed in a long white rain coat and pork pie hat, wandering lonely, stylish and looking for love in London's streets. Similarly, on the video accompanying the title track from the unexceptional *Never Let Me Down*, Bowie appears as a crooner in a suit in front of a band while beautiful young people compete with one another in a dance marathon. The videos that accompany this period are essentially promotional material. Whereas *Absolute Beginners* offers us stills from the film of the same title to prompt us to go and see the film, 'Never Let Me Down' merely showcases the single. For any other musical artist of this period, such visual material would barely be worthy of comment. However, given that Bowie's creative genius lies in the ways he is able to connect visual images to music, it seems as though something is missing from the performance. This is culture reduced to its economic function. David Bowie's celebrity is traded upon to publicize his latest film or record. This is a period when the cultural products associated with Bowie seem devoid of any deep content. The images and music simply reflect the dominant culture of the narcissistic straight eighties.

Tin Machine and straight masculinity

Such a situation was unlikely to last for long. Indeed Bowie's next move was one of the most unexpected of all; he formed a band called Tin Machine. This was a bid to find a musical direction that had more conviction. In late 1988, Bowie had just finished the greatest-hits inspired Glass Spider tour and met a relatively unknown guitarist and friend, Reeves Gabrels, in a

Turkish restaurant in Switzerland. During this period, Bowie was increasingly dismayed by his lack of sales but was even more haunted by his loss of artistic direction and vision. The hyperproductivity of the eighties merely disguised Bowie's growing sense of unease. This resulted in Bowie disposing of so-called chequebook musicians and forming a band. Many have read this move, regardless of the quality of the music, as a break with the production of 'mainstream' pop and a move in a more progressive and rock-oriented direction. The truth, however, is inevitably more complicated. The band included Bowie as chief songwriter and lead singer, Reeves Gabrels on lead guitar and a rhythm section comprised of two brothers, drummer Hunt Sales and bassist Tony Sales, who had previously worked with Bowie on Iggy Pop's 1977 *Lust for Life* album. Critical opinion has been sharply divided between those who saw Tin Machine as a further waste of Bowie's talent and others who enjoyed the harder, more rock-oriented music that they produced. On one level, Bowie's band successfully picked up on a rock subculture that included the likes of the Pixies and Sonic Youth and brought them into the mainstream. This is a strategy that has served Bowie well throughout his career. More critically the band could be accused of simply 'borrowing' from the already popular metal music of Bon Jovi and Guns N' Roses.

Tin Machine blended Bowie's yuppie image with more hard-rock credentials. The first Tin Machine album, called simply *Tin Machine*, pictures the band against a white background in thoughtful poses wearing suits. Indeed it was guitarist Reeves Gabrels who most accurately summed up the subsequent sound and image of Tin Machine in the motif 'Pinstripes and Purple Haze' (Deevoy 1989: 33). The sound of Tin Machine was a form of fast rock 'n' roll. This is indeed a long way from Bowie's more experimental recordings of the late seventies. Whatever the 'quality' of the music, through the invention of Tin Machine David Bowie adopted a much harder, more macho heterosexual image than had been in evidence during the eighties. Previously Bowie had adopted a variety of images from the circus artist that appeared on the cover of *Never Let Me Down* to a colourful Lord

Byron in the *Blue Jean* video. Now it seemed, in the most clichéd rock discourse of Bowie's career, it was time to 'get real'.

Bowie playing the straight, tough guy while claiming to have found the musical direction he was looking for in fast rock music obviously requires some explanation. Some have seen this turn as simply another mask adopted by Bowie. On this reading, Tin Machine reinvents rock inauthenticity after its deconstruction. Such a view certainly makes sense in terms of Bowie's career as a whole, but I think it takes too much for granted. On this understanding Bowie, who adopted a more normalized image both to give his music a wider commercial appeal and as a response to the AIDS crisis, is assumed to be adopting a similarly playful attitude to identity as he did in the seventies. My argument is that Bowie indeed adopted the mask of normality in the eighties, but he did so not as postmodern strategy but as a form of protection. He did so both to make money and to survive the public ambivalence towards openly gay and bisexual performers. To this end it worked. Yet Bowie, the media manipulator of the seventies, seemed to become aware he had become increasingly domesticated by a conservative culture industry. His original aim to be both successful as well as arresting had become unbalanced. Bowie's so-called 'new course' actually strengthened his attempt to 'pass' himself off as a normal heterosexual. Given what was widely known about Bowie's public and private performances, such a strategy was unlikely to convince many of the people who followed his career over the years. Bowie's performance as a regular straight guy might have saved him from the stigma levelled at openly gay stars during the eighties, but did little by way of developing new creative resources for his music.

In an interview with *Q* music magazine about Tin Machine's first album, Bowie is asked what he would have done if the project had not been successful. Bowie, in this context, offers an interesting answer.

BOWIE: I don't know. I really don't know actually. Wept . . . at least. But I can't even think of a hypothetical situation. I definitely would have reversed what I'd been doing some way or another. I had to for my own musical sanity. I had to do something where I felt more involved and less dispassionate. I had to get passionate again. I couldn't keep going the way I was going. It was shit or get off the pot.

Q: Your last two LPs – *Tonight* and *Never Let Me Down* – weren't terribly good, were they?

BOWIE: Mm. I thought it was great material that got simmered down to product level. I really should have not done it quite so 'studio-ly'. I think some of it was a waste of really good songs. You should hear the demos from those albums. It's night and day by comparison with the finished tracks. There's stuff on the two albums since *Let's Dance* that I could kick myself about. When I listen to those demos it's, how did it turn out like that? You should hear 'Loving the Alien' on demo. It's a wonderful demo. I promise you [laughs]. But on the album, it's . . . not as wonderful. What am I meant to say? [laughs]. (Deevoy 1989: 28–9)

As the interview progresses we listen to Bowie deal with further humiliation as other members of his band give their verdict on his more recent work. This is an interesting sequence in the interview. Bowie is partially able to admit his own disappointment with some of his recent recordings but he handles this embarrassment by revelling in a form of male bonding with other band members. It is as if his new tougher image has been invented to compensate for his excursions into pop and past disappointments. This time, Bowie suggests, unlike the candyfloss of the past two albums, it's 'for real'. Bowie's newly discovered heterosexist rock identity requires him to distance himself from the feminine (represented by Bowie's recent pop past) and homosexuality and bisexuality (again represented by his own past). In keeping with the normalization of his image throughout the eighties, Tin Machine enhances and deepens Bowie's projection of himself as a heterosexual male. Yet unlike most of the eighties, the set of identifications that are articulated by Tin Machine are excessive. Rather than simply normalizing his image, Bowie's heterosexual performance has a hypermasculine quality.

Tin Machine's first album contains two songs that are particularly striking in this respect. 'Pretty Thing', an obvious reference to the sexually ambiguous 'Pretty Things' recorded on

Hunky Dory, offers a celebration of straight phallic masculinity. The song opens with hard riffing guitars, banging drums and Bowie's voice shouting, 'something getting hard when you rock it up' ('Pretty Thing', 1989). The lyrics are more utilitarian than Bowie's usual efforts and rarely deviate from a banal heterosexual sexism. Their open misogyny and the driving music serve to dispel any sense of sexual ambiguity and impress upon the listener Bowie's 'straightness'. Perhaps even more revealing, however, is Bowie's treatment of John Lennon's song, 'Working Class Hero', which also appears on the first Tin Machine album. Bowie was particularly keen to record this song given that Lennon's son Sean had been around during the sessions. Yet the performance of the song is very different from Lennon's original 1969 recording. Whereas Lennon's vocals evoke vulnerability and pain, Bowie delivery is much louder and angrier. This arguably changes the meaning of the song. The chorus line, 'a working class hero is something to be' ('Working Class Hero', 1989), give Lennon's version a double-edged quality, recalling the hurt of his own childhood and the daily rituals of disrespect that are the markers of a class society. It is indeed the song's connection to Lennon's own biography that gives the music its resonance. These lines are delivered with a deadpan irony, making the listener aware they are not to be understood literally. Yet Bowie sings the same lines differently. Gone is any expression of vulnerability or troubled introspection. In fact Bowie's anger gives the song a strident quality, making it much more one-dimensional. The confident masculine delivery turns the song from one of private pain, connecting the personal and the political, into a clichéd protest song about social issues. The meaning of a song is surely determined by its performance. Indeed, Tin Machine's first album deals with a number of social issues from drugs ('Crack City') to the banality of visual culture and the decline of literacy ('I Can't Read'). These songs are interesting in respect of Bowie's earlier remarks about so-called political music but above all they lack the humour and poetic wisdom of punk and the personal authenticity of Lennon.

Many of these features are further in evidence in the second Tin Machine studio album, *Tin Machine II* (1991). Here even

Bowie's ability to deliver songs from the point of view of created characters (a hallmark of his performances in the sixties and seventies) comes into question. The symbolic effect of this material is not to create a different world view but simply mirror Tin Machine's dominant masculine ethos of desolate landscapes and unthinking sexism. Whereas Bowie in the early seventies tried to queer the pitch of rock music, by the late eighties he seems to have taken on its mantle, along with much of the 'rock' rhetoric and masculine posturing he originally sought to deconstruct. This was surely no way for David Bowie to rediscover his artistic vision and passion. The important cultural aspect of Tin Machine is that it reconstructs male heterosexual rock music *after* it has been deconstructed. In other words, the exaggerated masculinity evident in Tin Machine's cultural productions is there precisely because it recognizes its own instability.

Indeed many cultural critics have struggled to decide whether men can be said to have a gender in this respect. The radical post-feminist critic Judith Butler (1990) has argued that we do not 'have' gender, but 'do' gender. The argument here is that the masculine is not so much natural but has to be constantly performed as if it were 'natural' to give itself the 'appearance' of stability. In other words, gender identities are not fixed in stone and their very mutability means that our culture seeks to regulate their performance. At his most radical Bowie revealed gender and sexuality as cultural by performing it differently. However, in these terms Tin Machine is culturally conservative, the extent to which the performance of gender becomes 'naturalized'. Bowie attempted, through culture, to 'naturalize' his own gender and sexuality in ways that were always going to be difficult for the bisexual rock star of the seventies to pull off. This however did not appear to stop him trying.

Q: Have you made lyrics deliberately obscure in the past. Dressed ideas up?

BOWIE: Dressed them up? No. Watered them down. But certainly over the immediate period I simply haven't been allowed to. Reeves is quite correct and that's quite an insight for me. They didn't let me re-write. The lyrics were my first kind of feelings when the stuff was coming out. I just got it down as fast as I could. Do you know a guy came up to me the other day and said, 'Do you like pussy cats?' And I said, 'Yes I do but my name isn't cats!'

Q: Boom boom. (Deevoy 1989: 29–30)

It is as if Bowie is using the interviews and the music to insist on his own heterosexuality not only in order to repudiate both his own past but also to produce a stable and secure identity. In this masculine fantasy the only way to escape the entrapment of the music industry is to continually insist upon his rock 'authenticity'. Through the use of 'crude' jokes and sexist imagery Bowie aims to produce himself as heterosexual bloke in a band. This becomes the obsessional focus of Tin Machine. The instrumentality of the language, the avoidance of vulnerability, the harshness of the images and the 'cool' sexism all reconfirm the dominant aspects of mainstream rock music and heterosexual masculinity. This is actually less a new beginning for Bowie than the final move in an effort to normalize his music and image. Having banished any association with pop, sexual ambiguity, artistic experimentation or indeed literary pretension, Bowie has reached the final stage of his 'straight acting'. After Tin Machine, Bowie could either have become an increasingly boorish ageing rock star or have changed direction again. Thankfully, as we shall see, he chose the latter. Having rejected the initial sources of his creativity, it is not surprising he made some of the most genuinely depressing music of his career.

If David Bowie can be a 'straight' rock musician, then the set of styles and conventions he trades upon are surely less a matter of 'authenticity' than culturally learnt codes. At least during this period, we could argue, Bowie reminds us that gender is not a property of the 'personality' but a relationship between power and culture. This is however a generous interpretation and does not 'fit' with the overall sense to be gained from listening to the music of this period. If this was indeed what Bowie was up to with Tin Machine, the music would have been less excessive and desperate, and more obviously ironic in its construction. Indeed music critic Robert Walser (1993) defends the subversive quality of metal music on these grounds. Metal music in all its manifestations, argues Walser, both reproduces male dominance while simultaneously contradicting it. Metal music both allows female performers to utilize images of power and rebellion as well as giving men opportunities to engage in flamboyance and artifice. In more traditional gender codes, such features are usually 'off limits'. Metal music, by exaggerating gender, actually celebrates the mutability of gender. A similar argument could not be stretched to include Tin Machine whose 'normality' is straitjacketed into suits, the exclusion of women and the more predictable rituals of male-defined rock 'n' roll. While Tin Machine remains important for reminding Bowie that he could do something 'different', as a project its lasting legacy points to just how desperate Bowie's loss of artistic direction had become. At the end of the eighties, Bowie no longer signified a way of getting 'out of here' for his millions of fans but had become a further confirmation of popular music's ability to ape the mind-numbing conformity of the culture industry.

In sum, this chapter has mainly concentrated upon Bowie's artistic and cultural production during the eighties. This was the decade when Bowie risked becoming a blank commodity. His adoption of a normalized image meant (*Let's Dance* apart) that this was a period of accelerated creative decline. Many stars of Bowie's and indeed later generations never recovered from similar fates. Written off by a relentlessly market-driven music industry, their future careers were confined to greatest hits reissues and fan reunions. That Bowie still had a few more cards up his sleeve would seem to have surprised himself if no one else.

—— five ——

BOHEMIAN BOWIE

David Bowie was born David Robert Jones at his home in Brixton, London on 8 January 1947. His arrival meant he joined the lower-middle class home of his father John Jones and mother Margaret Burns. His older brother Terry, born in 1937 and the product of a previous relationship of his mother, was also part of the family. The Jones family left London's inner city for the suburbs of Bromley when Bowie was six years old. Living in the respectable suburbs just a short train ride away from the centre of London was crucial in forming the young David Jones's interest in popular music and stylist innovations. Much 'white' English popular music has its roots in dissatisfaction with the dominance of suburbia in contemporary society. Suburbia is often characterized by middle-class conformity, the desire to avoid conflict and the relative absence of strangers. Suburbia emphasizes defensiveness and an ordinariness which aims to curb the perceived excesses of the city (Silverstone 1994). In a great deal of popular culture, suburbia is represented as a trap for the young if a safe space for adults to bring up children. Generationally, suburbia is somewhere to both escape from and return to. The narrow confines of the suburb are the home of a particular gender and sexual politics where women have the principal responsibility for the raising of children and domestic labour. Suburbia increasingly involves privatized lifestyles where the home becomes the focus for respectable middle-class people.

Sociologist Simon Frith (1997) has argued that in British culture the Bromley of the young David Jones is probably the most significant suburb in pop history. By this Frith means that not only has Bromley produced a number of successful British popular music performers including Siouxsie from the Banshees and Billy Idol but that it has articulated a particular modern sensibility. If English suburbia is defined by safety and boredom then, particularly for the young, it fosters dreams of escape. These dreams, as we shall see with Bowie, help develop an intense interest in the city and the development of alternative lifestyles. The culture of rock 'n' roll offers a form of glamour and excitement not easily contained within the suburban sensibility. The teenage Bowie's deep interest in the American culture of rock 'n' roll, jazz and the beats allowed him the possibility of bringing the excitement of America into his own home. Music was a way of getting out of here. It was a way of removing himself from the humdrum of English small-mindedness and conservatism without having to travel geographically. Indeed, and this I think is key to Bowie's later appeal, if suburbia is what much popular music and culture is trying to get away from, then bohemia is where it leads. Part of the enduring fascination with David Bowie is that he is the prince of English bohemia.

The idea of bohemia is central to any understanding of David Bowie in our culture. Bohemia has a long historical lineage and is arguably as important to the shaping of modern society as suburbia. Indeed, it is probably true to argue that bohemia and suburbia have helped produce one another in an oppositional relationship. If suburbia is the outcome of a resolutely bourgeois domestic politics then bohemia is a subtle attempt to lessen its grip on the collective imagination. The original idea of the bohemian was someone who defended the status of art against the bourgeois philistine. The idea is that the artist is a special genius-like figure at odds with a predominantly utilitarian society. To quote Oscar Wilde, a key bohemian icon, the philistine was someone who 'knows the price of everything and the value of nothing'. Yet being a bohemian is more about the adoption of a particular pose or lifestyle than actually becoming an artist. It was the Romantics who first set the artist against the bourgeois philistine. Here the most reliable proof of an artist's 'authenticity' was to fail to fulfil the debased expectations of the public. In this way, the bohemian is both a serious follower and producer of art, and a fake. To be a bohemian is to assume a way of living that shocks respectable society while continuing the search for new sensations and pleasures (Wilson 2000). The bohemian life-style was to allow Bowie the ability to work within mass culture while assuming the status of outsider and artist. The myth of bohemia has functioned for Bowie as a way to fuse together mainstream entertainment and artistic ideas without losing his 'credibility'. The adoption of a bohemian lifestyle in the sixties and early seventies meant he could both promote himself as an artist while selling millions of records the world over. The existential angst of the beats, new rock 'n' roll cultures, and later the desire for sexual experimentation all mark out Bowie as the bohemian of mass culture.

Historically the key figure mapping out bohemian identi-ties was the nineteenth-century French poet, Baudelaire. For Baudelaire (1995: 5) the artist needed to become 'the painter of the passing moment and all the suggestions of eternity that it contains'. While the artist in the broadest sense should be of the world, he or she should also have little to do with conven-tional understandings of morality and politics. The artist is better served by taking a childlike interest in the new, the fleeting and ephemeral. An artist becomes a 'passionate spectator' of the life of the city, observing (while remaining hidden) the ever-changing pleasures of everyday life. By seeing ordinary events with the innocence of a child, the artist can recover the beautiful from within the banal. Here the artist is searching for expressions of modernity, those rapid metamorphoses that are the expres-sions of contemporary experience. For Baudelaire the key figure who captures these dimensions the best is the dandy. The dandy is a man of wealth and notoriety whose main occupation is the pursuit of pleasure and personal elegance. It is the calling of the dandy to cultivate beauty and live life to the full. The dandy revels in his difference from 'ordinary' people and cultivates a personal form of magic. Baudelaire writes:

> first and foremost the burning need to create for oneself a per-sonal originality, bounded only by the limits of the proprieties. It is a kind of a cult of the self which can nevertheless survive the

pursuit of happiness to be found in someone else – in woman, for example; which can survive all that goes by in the name of illusions. It is the joy of astonishing others, and the proud satisfaction of never oneself being astonished. (1995: 27–8)

The dandy and the bohemian attempt to turn the self into a work of art. Perhaps where they differ is that the artist develops an intense interest in the gutter and in low life generally. While both share the need to produce the self in different and often shocking ways, it is the artist who is called upon to explore the obscure and the forbidden. The figures of the dandy and the artist captured by Baudelaire were not only granted a dominant role within sixties' culture but are historical figures traded upon and reinvented by Bowie's image and music.

David Bowie is simultaneously an artist who works in mass culture and an outrageous poseur and fake who dresses up the three-minute pop song as the new avant-garde. The critic Walter Benjamin (1973: 162) wrote of Baudelaire that he viewed the artist like a fencer in that 'the blows he deals are designed to open a path through the crowd for him'. It is the idea of the popular and yet avant-garde artist who revels in the freedom of the outsider that Bowie was to take as his central metaphor. The cultural critic Elizabeth Wilson (2000) has argued that the idea of the bohemian has entered mass culture in an ambivalent way. On the one hand, the pose of the bohemian is more available to many 'ordinary' people than ever before, but on the other, whereas bohemianism once meant a fanatical dedication to art, today it tends to signify cultural success that is just outside the mainstream. Whereas once artists were judged on their ability to turn their back on the market, today the word describes glamorous celebrities who are that little bit different. The bohemians of mass culture like Mick Jagger, Freddie Mercury (singer of 'Bohemian Rhapsody') and of course David Bowie were able to strike the pose of the doomed genius while selling stacks of records. The legacy of bohemia is itself a source of ambivalence. It both encourages an idea of work as play, promiscuity and a love of sexual ambivalence and flirtation with a number of more dangerous ideologies (like occultism and fascism).

The return of David Bowie

The end of Tin Machine saw Bowie embark on yet another greatest hits tour. The Sound+Vision tour of 1990 saw Bowie play 108 shows in 27 different countries. Looking back on this period, Bowie admitted he had begun to think about retirement and the need to make as much money as possible for his own financial security. He comments: 'More than anything else, I thought I should make as much money as I could, and quit. I didn't think there was an alternative, I thought I was obviously an empty vessel and would end up like everyone else, doing those stupid fucking shows, singing 'Rebel Rebel' until I fall over and bleed' (Cavanagh 1997: 92). The reason that this did not happen was that Bowie eventually found the emotional stability he had been looking for with his Somalian-born wife, Iman Abdulmajid. During the Sound+Vision tour, Bowie had split with his then partner, Melissa Hurley, and soon began a period of courtship with Iman. The couple married in early 1992. Since the divorce from Angie and the battle for custody of their son, Joe, that began in 1977, Bowie had had many relationships and short affairs. The settlement announced in 1980 granted Angela alimony but also placed on her a gagging order that prevented her from speaking of their marriage for ten years. It is hard not to speculate that the mask of normalcy Bowie wore during the eighties was hiding a good deal of emotional trauma as well as his bisexual self. Bowie would later claim that he had: 'a lot of the negativity about myself. I was convinced I wasn't worth very much. I had enormous self-image problems and very low self-esteem, which I hid behind obsessive writing and performing' (quoted in Cavanagh 1997). With his marriage to Iman and evidence of periods of self-reflection and therapy, Bowie begun to look like a man who might turn his career around. The way he did this initially was to reflexively re-engage in his own past work as well as embark upon ambitious new projects. For example, Bowie's next new album *Black Tie White Noise* (otherwise known as the 'wedding album' composed in honour of his new bride) re-employed Nile Rodgers from the successful album *Let's Dance*.

Whilst commercially the album did not do as well as *Let's Dance* (indeed this would have been difficult without the financial backing of EMI), it reached no. 1 in the UK and a creditable no. 39 in the US charts.

Bowie also performed at the 1992 Freddie Mercury Tribute Concert for Aids Awareness. This was a turning point for Bowie. While the big stars of that particular night were George Michael and Elton John (two performers who had maintained and developed a gay identity during the eighties), the fact that Bowie was present was a significant step. Having tried to mask his bisexual identity during the eighties, his appearance at such a public event began the process of reconnecting Bowie with his own past. Wearing a lime-green suit, Bowie sang 'Under Pressure' with Annie Lennox (the song he had written with Freddie Mercury), 'All The Young Dudes' with Ian Hunter and, perhaps most movingly, played 'Heroes' with Mick Ronson who at the time was dying of cancer. It was left to George Michael to deliver the most politically inspired speech of the evening, countering much of the propaganda of the eighties and reminding the audience that AIDS was not a 'gay plague' but a sexually transmitted disease. David Bowie, on the other hand, dropped to his knees at the end of 'Heroes', and led a packed Wembley stadium in the Lord's prayer. This might seem surprising at first, and yet Bowie had long explored spiritual and religious themes in his work without becoming a member of any particular church. The re-engagement with Bowie's past was only allowed to go so far during this period. This is most evident in his failure to attend either Mick Ronson's funeral or special memorial concert held at the Apollo in Hammersmith London. David Bowie undoubtedly had his own reasons for not attending these events, although it left many of Ronson's friends and supporters with a good deal of bitterness towards the star. Attending these events, Bowie would undoubtedly have met many of the people he had originally encountered during the Ziggy era of his career and this was something he was not yet ready to face.

In artistic terms, the real turning point comes with the recording of the soundtrack to the BBC television series, *The Buddha of Suburbia*. Here Bowie, in his own terms, attempts to fuse past and present by engaging his current working methods with those that he had used previously in the seventies. By moving back and forth between past selves and older ways of working, Bowie hoped to be able to capture a new musical form for the coming century. A bold ambition for a performer who had supposedly been considering retirement a few years hence. Bowie comments on this ambition on *The Buddha of Suburbia* sleeve notes:

> My own personal ambition is to create a music form that captures a mixture of sadness and grandeur on the one hand, expectancy and the organisation of chaos on the other. A music that relinquishes its hold upon the twentieth century yet searches out that which was stimulating and productive as a basis from which to work in the twenty-first century. (*The Buddha of Suburbia*, 1993)

This vision would take a firmer hold on his next album, *1. Outside*. Bowie's preceding album, *The Buddha of Suburbia*, started life as a musical accompaniment to the British BBC2's four-part adaptation of Hanif Kureishi's (1990) novel of the same title. The themes of Kureishi's novel made Bowie the obvious choice as the musician most suitable to attempt the soundtrack. Set in the Bromley of Kureishi's childhood the narrative tells the tale of Karim's transition from the dull suburbs into the alluring world of bohemian identity confusion. This replays Bowie's own escape in the sixties from the world of lower-middle class conformity into the urbanity of sexual experimentation, drugs, popular music and art. This album is important not only for its experimental nature but because it enabled Bowie to re-explore his bohemian roots.

The video for the single *The Buddha of Suburbia* shows Bowie wistfully strolling through a London suburb. Bowie, wearing a long raincoat, kicks at the leaves before settling himself on a front lawn to strum his guitar. While the single only achieved modest chart success, its deeper significance lies with Bowie's own reflexive engagement with his multiple cultural pasts. Bowie is caught reconnecting with his own experience of escape from the conservative world of middle-class conformity. It is Bowie's artistic re-engagement with his own self and cultural productions that helps pave the way for the development of the more interesting musical projects of the future. Like much music written originally for film or television, the album has an instrumental emphasis, although perhaps most significantly of all many of the tracks evoke some of Bowie's best work with the producer Brian Eno. Indeed Bowie's debt to Eno is again evident from the sleeve notes. Bowie, commenting generously on his friend's genius, writes: 'I should make it clear that many of my working forms are taken in whole or in part from my collaborations with Brian Eno, who in my humble opinion occupies the position in the late twentieth century popular music that Clement Greenberg had in art in the '40s or Richard Hamilton in the '60s' (*The Buddha of Suburbia*, 1993). Indeed with Eno's help, Bowie was to help destroy the myth that artists of popular music can never recapture their creativity once it has been surrendered. Such views are the common stock of journalistic opinion and are often recycled in the music press. David Bowie in his next phase was to defy such logic.

Outside

If Bowie's art had gone through two main stages thus far, it was about to enter a third. During the seventies, Bowie was able to utilize a sequence of arresting images and soundscapes in order to represent his difference from mainstream society. These representations drew upon excluded subcultures, obscure artistic sources and newly formed political movements like gay liberation. Bowie's cultural strategy aimed to critique the homogenizing impulse of mainstream society. The dominant culture seemed to impose a range of simple assumptions about what could be achieved in popular music, how men differed from women and the stereotyping of gay male sexuality that Bowie sought to arrest and challenge. This is the period when Bowie's art was at its most engaged and critical. The cultural legacy here is that of the sixties' rebellion against social and cultural forms of conformity replayed through a commodity culture. Bowie, it will be remembered, followed Dylan's critique of the counter-culture, and yet extended it by bringing into popular music a more performative and theatrical ethos. The eighties ushered in a period of mainstream conformity and commodification. During this period, as we have seen, Bowie adopted a mask of normalcy in keeping with the ideological agendas of the New Right. The New Right's agenda of heterosexuality and consumerism would find itself reflected in Bowie's artwork. Not surprisingly, during this period Bowie produced little work of any great note, and seemed to be struggling with an intense period of creative decline. Despite his initial commercial and popular success at the beginning of the eighties, Bowie was beginning to matter less and less. My argument is that Bowie's art enters into a critical new period during the nineties. Leaving the conformist eighties behind, Bowie began to move in more arresting directions.

If during the sixties and seventies there were still zones of cultural experience that were marginal, these had all but disappeared by the nineties. There were still cultural battles to be fought but Western societies had by and large adopted a more 'liberal' set of attitudes and dispositions in respect of the rights of minorities. Indeed, what was notable in this respect was how quickly cultural movements like punk had been both commodified and incorporated by a televisual and consumer society. The absorption of high and low culture into the culture industry was all but complete. There was, if you like, no 'outside' to the system. Yet with enhanced economic globalization, the development of worldwide media, the rise of the internet and new forms of visual art and the increased pluralization of lifestyles available in Western societies, it was evident that the world was changing fast. For Bowie a new artistic sensibility was required to grasp this emergent new society. Bowie returned to some of the postmodern themes of the early seventies, but this time with a difference. There is no doubting Bowie's ability to grasp the significance of the unfolding new culture. From this point on, Bowie retreated from the bland commodification of the eighties but he did not simply return to the youthful provocation of the seventies. Instead his new work, with varying degrees of success, became a contemporary and postmodern comment on our new society.

It is worth quoting at length some of Bowie's own comments on this cultural shift. He approaches many of these questions when explaining the direction of his latest album:

> It's either art or murder, ha ha! The strength in my work is when there's as much room for multi-interpretation as possible. I've always had an orientation towards combining contradictory information. And just seeing what happens. Messing about with structures, taking them apart. Dismantling toys and putting the wrong bits back together. I would have been great in Japan making those Godzilla-type things that become tanks, I'm sure. I treat music in the same way; what happens if you put that note with that word, what effect do you get? Because of that, it has its own informational output, that's sometimes more, sometimes less, than the two components. That's one of the fascinations of writing for me.

Later, in the same interview, he reflects:

> I think we as a culture embrace confusion. We are happy to recombine information, we take event horizons incredibly fast. The generations – and I can use that plurally now – underneath me have an ability to scan information much quicker than my lot, and don't necessarily look for depth that maybe we would. They take what they need for their survival, and their means to adapt to this new society. It is the inheritance of the sixties, not only with the breakdown of the American dream and the conflicts of that period, and the emerging pluralistic attitude towards society, but also a spiritual loss. A realisation that absolutes weren't law, weren't the thing that one could abide by. There's no absolute religion, no absolute political system, no absolute art form, no absolute this and no absolute that. Things weren't black and white like we'd been told (especially during the great stiff fifties). There are so many contradictions and conflicts that when you accept them for what they are, when you accept that this is a manifestation of chaos theory that's put forward, that it really is a deconstructed society, then contradiction almost ceases to exist. Every piece of information is equally as unimportant as the next. (quoted in Roberts 1995: 73–4)

The album Bowie is discussing is the 1995 release *1. Outside*, recorded with Brian Eno. Bowie's art needed to be re-charged with new ideas and concepts. This had failed to happen in the eighties. This time Bowie was seeking to articulate his postmodernism in the context of changing art and information cultures. What is striking is the sense of mission evident in the recording of *1. Outside*. It seems that Bowie was seeking to capture the contours of an emergent, information-driven society quite unlike that of the early seventies. Notably from 1994 onwards, Bowie begins to take himself much more seriously as a painter. His exhibitions during this period include 1997 at London ICA, 1998 at London's Chisenhale Gallery and in 1999 a collaboration with Laurie Anderson at the Museum Ludwig, Cologne. However, most significantly, in our context is Bowie's collaboration with Damien Hirst in June 1995 at the Arnolfini Gallery in Bristol, UK. If Bowie takes a number of ideas from emergent debates about the development of the internet and a global information culture, they become connected to the concerns of a younger generation of British visual artists during the nineties. This supporting context helps make *1. Outside* both startling in its complexity and its capacity to push Bowie's and Eno's partnership in new directions. While this does not mean that Bowie's music and visual art of this period is without flaws, it has undoubtedly become interesting again.

Discussing the album *1. Outside*, both David Bowie and the album's producer Brian Eno reveal something of the music's philosophical context. The conversation begins to trace the interconnections between a newly emerged information culture and what was becoming known in the media as Brit Art.

DB: Also it has something to do with the fact that the complexity of modern systems is so intense that a lot of artists are going back literally into themselves in a physical way, and it has produced a dialogue between flesh and the mind.

BE: Yes, it's shocking suddenly to say, in the middle of cyberculture and informational networks, 'I am a piece of meat'.

QUESTIONER: And is shock also a necessary part of a definition of art?

BE: At some level I think it is, yes. It doesn't only have to be that kind of shock.

DB: The shock of recognition is actually more what it's about, you know. I think that's what it does for me, anyway. That, for me, Damien [Hirst], of whom I am a very loyal supporter, it's the shock of recognition with his work that really affects me, and I don't think even he really knows what it is he is doing. (Wells 1995: 101)

Later in the interview Bowie takes the opportunity to reaffirm his newly rediscovered bohemian identity.

DB: I'm an artist, a painter and a sculptor. Why should I be afraid? Seemingly the only other thing I'm supposed to be afraid of is whether people thought it was any good or not, but I've lived that life since I began, publicity, of whether I'm any 'good' or not, for nearly 30 years, so that comes with the territory. (Wells 1995: 101–2).

The influence of Damien Hirst and Brit Art are mostly evident on *1. Outside*'s first single release 'The Heart's Filthy Lesson'. The video of the single shows Bowie in a warehouse that is slowly being transformed into an art gallery. This is indicative of Brit Art, given many of the most prominent artists who are usually spoken of under this label initially presented their work in abandoned buildings. In the video, Bowie appears as an artist making life-size plaster casts of 'primitive' human beings. He and the other assembled artists are shown eating human flesh, holding human organs (notably a human heart) and wearing masks of dead animals. The central plaster cast is eventually supplied with an animal's head and at one point a mouse appears with a human head. The video is shot through a brown lens, giving the scene the appearance of either rotting flesh or of excrement. As the video progresses, Bowie can be heard moaning 'if only there was some kind of future'. Throughout, the song has a discordant and urgent feeling that is simultaneously compelling and uncomfortable. The overall effect, in terms of Bowie's work, revisits the dystopian landscapes of the *The Man Who Sold the World* and *Diamond Dogs*. Seen in this context, the deliberate blurring of boundaries between humans and animals has a kinship with some of Bowie's earlier transgressions. David Bowie, by re-engaging his more bohemian instincts as pop star-cum-artist, continues to deconstruct the ordinary categories of experience between men and women, different sexualities and animals and humans.

Critic Steve Baker (2000) argues that artists like Damien Hirst are concerned to ask philosophical questions about the boundaries between animals and humans. Damien Hirst is perhaps best known for the practice of bringing animal corpses into the gallery. By displaying carcasses of dead sheep or a shark frozen in a tank, Hirst is trying to provoke us into questioning the nature of mortality while deconstructing the boundary between animals and humans. As alluded to in the album's title, it is these questions that are currently 'outside' of ordinary, taken-for-granted assumptions which give art its shock effect. The Bowie video discussed above is evidently trading on similar issues. Lest we try to reconstruct Bowie (or indeed Hirst) as a 'serious' artist, we would do well to remember it is the posturing that interests Bowie. The problem with conceptualizing either Hirst's or Bowie's work in these terms is that it misses its evident humour. Bowie, perhaps like Hirst, is only ever half serious. If Bowie continues to be interested in such questions, he keeps them firmly in his back pocket, using diverse fragments and ideas in his own artwork rather than working out a fully realized philosophical position. Not surprisingly many have found this lack of earnestness to be a major flaw of Brit Art. Julien Stallabras (1999) has suggested that British artists like Damien Hirst have more in common with celebrities like Bowie than many think. Stallabras argues that what was distinctive about British art during the nineties was its emptiness and commodification. Like Bowie, Damien Hirst deliberately utilizes shocking images in order to attract the attention of the mass media and is better known as a celebrity than as an artist. Rather than asking disturbing questions about the human condition, Hirst's work is deliberately spectacular and attention grabbing. It is not surprising that Bowie and Damien Hirst ended up working together. Like Warhol and Pop Art, Brit Art stands accused by its radical critics as being populist, celebrity endorsing and consumerist in orientation. Alternatively for its supporters and backers like David Bowie, Brit Art seemed a form of provocation that sought to critique more established art's seriousness and elitism by attracting ordinary people into art galleries. Brit Art deliberately cultivated enthusiasm for the vulgar, money, mass culture and publicity rather than being explicitly concerned with pleasing more established art critics. Brit Art very quickly became canonized by the hugely popular 1997 *Sensation* exhibition held at the Royal Academy of Arts organized by the millionaire art collector, Charles Saatchi.

Other critics trade upon different objections to the so-called post-human environment embraced by Bowie. Turning rotting corpses, severed human heads and ripped-up body parts into either art or entertainment is morally problematic. Paul Virilio (2004) argues that Western societies have inherited a tendency to view art that breaks taboos as being progressive. The overall effect of this supposedly radical practice has not been the questioning of boundaries, but the desensitization of human subjects and cultures to suffering. If art is constantly pushing the limits of the morally acceptable, what prevents us from viewing torture as a form of mass entertainment? Like those issues posed above, these important questions can only be explored in passing. More important in this context is the idea that *1. Outside* is not principally concerned with taboo-breaking. More to the point, as we shall see, are the proliferating layers of human culture and experience that electronic cultures increasingly make commonly available. Indeed, indifference to suffering may form a central aspect of our modern visual culture. It is perhaps no longer shocking for us to see victims of torture, genocide or starvation on the evening news. The real point of modern media and information cultures is that they institute a form of 'presentism'. As Bowie sings on the album's title track, 'It's happening now, not tomorrow' (*1. Outside*, 1995). The new information culture requires us to be constantly 'up to the minute' or indeed 'up to speed' with our information. The rapidity of the turn of events very quickly converts the present into the past. In an age where everything is displayed on screen, Bowie seems to be asking whether we can still meaningfully talk of a cultural outside. The large galleries very quickly incorporated Brit Art and the album *1. Outside* was released by RCA records (owned by the media multinational Bertelsmann corporation). The title track of *1. Outside* could indeed be read literally as Bowie resurrecting the pose of the bohemian artist. This is right, but I think he is also asking what constitutes 'outside' in a culture that quickly incorporates and domesticates the radical and the shocking.

Modernity has delivered its consumers fast food, assembly line production and instantaneous communication; this, Bowie suggests, changes our sense of ourselves. It also begins to blur the boundaries between humans, technology and animals. The cultural theorist Donna Haraway (1991) has argued in these respects that modern culture has created the myth of the cyborg. As Haraway (1991: 154) puts it, 'a cyborg world is about lived social and bodily realities in which people are not permanently afraid of their joint kinship with animals and machines, not afraid of partial identities and contradictory standpoints.' It is perhaps not surprising that a celebrity who brought us electronic music, science fiction, the mutability of identity and gay politics would be interested in such a concept. Its cultural politics seems to offer 'queer' possibilities beyond complaints about commodification or the desensitization of the human subject for exploring the possibilities and considerable dangers of the new information culture. *1. Outside* does not ask us to embrace the cyborg world where relations between animals and machines are blurred, but to at least be open to the potential for exploring it.

In an interesting reversal, by bringing these ideas into popular music Bowie was actually positioning himself just 'outside' the mainstream. During the early and mid nineties, British popular music was dominated by the laddish Brit pop of bands like Oasis, Supergrass and Blur (Harris 2004). In this context, Bowie's philosophical ponderings on the Internet or concerns about a post-human future was given the brush-off by a younger genera-tion of critics. Brit pop, like Brit Art, was concerned with mass popularity. It was the kind of laddishness Bowie had exhibited in the early nineties with Tin Machine that was to become the focal point for popular music. The invention of the category 'new lad' meant a new lease of life for many of the masculine icons from the seventies. These included footballers like George Best, Rodney Marsh and actor Phil Daniels. Notable here is Bowie's comparative invisibility. The seventies, during this period, represented a male heterosexual utopia before the advent of 'political correctness' and what many of the new range of men's magazines identified as castrating forms of feminism. The 'new lad' exhibited nostalgia for a period when straight masculinity was supposedly less regulated by questions of sexual equality. Yet lad culture had its contradictions, given the 'softer' forms of masculinity evident in pictures of David Beckham and Damon Albarn although the emphasis was usually firmly placed on their laddish credentials. Further, Brit pop in terms of its sexual politics arguably contained more critical elements especially in the form of Suede's Brett Anderson and Pulp's Jarvis Cocker who both found inspiration in Bowie's music from the early seventies. Both Anderson and Cocker delivered high profile interviews with Bowie, claiming him as a major influence on their homoerotic stage performances. Again David Bowie became connected to popular music that was both commercially successful and bohemian.

If *1. Outside* is hardly laddish in its artistic pretension, it managed to re-engage Bowie's more sexually ambiguous past. It will be recalled that Bowie had previously fused together images of outer space and bisexual forms as metaphors for alienation. These features were revisited on the album track and re-recorded single, 'Hallo Spaceboy'. Similar cultural metaphors are also available in black popular music. The futuristic projections of black popular music in the seventies included Earth, Wind and Fire, George Clinton and Sun Ra. In this instance, technological and futuristic images are being drawn upon to imagine utopian futures free of race and racism. In these are evident parallels with the way Bowie fuses together a utopian imagination, gay politics and glam rock in the early seventies. In an updated version of such projections, Bowie sings, 'Do you like girls or boys?', later adding, 'This chaos is killing me' ('Hallo

Spaceboy', 1995). This frenetic song, with its screaming guitars and synthesizers backed by equally intense drumming, evokes a sense of informational confusion. This song, re-recorded for single release with the Pet Shop Boys, went on to be the most successful track released off the album, reaching no. 12 in the UK charts in 1996. This time, under the direction of Neil Tennant, the music's disco remix gives the song a more overtly camp sensibility. The accompanying video features a postmodern bricolage uniting the more pop personas of the Pet Shop Boys with the bohemian Bowie. Throughout the flow of the film it is punctured by the informational overload of seventies disco, budget science fiction movies from the fifties and crashing cars. This is the point where the uncertainty of the flows of information meets the ambivalence of modern sexuality. As the cultural critic Alberto Melucci (1996: 43) says, 'in the age of speed, we no longer possess a home'. In an information society, Melucci is arguing, our society becomes increasingly complex while our identities lose any sense of permanent anchoring. We are overwhelmed by new forms of information while becoming unsure as to the shape of our identity. In such a culture we cannot help but fashion ourselves in the light of new information. Which food we should eat (or indeed avoid), what clothes we decide to wear and which political positions we seek to adopt are all in a permanent state of flux. We participate in a culture which continually reminds us that we might have made different choices and fashioned different identities. The emergence of a simultaneously more information-based and uncertain culture means a life of both multiple possibility and the prospect of exclusion or addiction. It is this dimension of changing human experience that Bowie and Eno have grasped on their formidable album. In such a climate 'it's all deranged' and there is 'no control' ('No Control' 1995). Given the more confusing set of co-ordinates which now shape our lives, it is not surprising that many seek to retreat from the irreversibly cosmopolitan nature of contemporary culture, but such a strategy is unlikely to succeed. In 'The Motel' which follows 'Hello Spaceboy' on the album, Bowie is heard to mutter 'we're living in a safety zone', but then asserting to chilling effect, 'there is no hell like an old hell'. If we cannot keep the world the same, we are then forced to respond to new situations, refashion our sense of self and become different people. Bowie revisits the possibility of identity, but this time in the midst of an information age and culture. While 1995 was to hear many both inside and outside the academy proclaim the internet to be the saviour of a lost humanity, such optimistic projections are less evident on *1. Outside*. Here there is a pervasive sense of anxiety and uncertainty. However, the album's brilliant closing track ('Strangers When We Meet') reminds the listener that, despite troubling uncertainty, this is still a world where genuine intimacy is possible. While the mutiplication of information and complexity of culture may have unsettled the ground beneath our feet, we can still hold onto our humanity and connect with the other.

The almost seamless sequence of music (or as a friend of mine put it, its lack of punctuation) stretches over nineteen different tracks. Indeed *1. Outside*'s deliberately opaque sleeve notes (taken from the diary of an invented character called Nathan Adler) seems to have given many the impression that the album is a straightforward concept album. This adds yet another cultural layer to an already complex piece of music. Nathan Adler's occupation is to investigate art crime (this, it seems, is another reference to British art in the 1990s). These 'crimes' are works of art that are not really worthy of public support. Over the course of the album we also hear from Romna A. Stone (an artist), Baby Grace (a disembodied voice) and Mr Touchshriek (a broken man and exile from the information society). These voices add to the album's hypertextual quality which suggests different labyrinths and journeys available to its listeners. While the album has some dominant themes (in my view at least), it has been deliberately constructed to make any simplistic or unified meaning impossible. How many Bowie fans will have bought this album and been troubled by the meaning of these songs, images and pieces of text? In this respect, I think we should take Bowie at his word when he suggests wanting to leave the text open to a number of different interpretations. Overall the album is actually one part postmodern novel (the Nathan Adler Diary), one part critique of the information society and one part inspiration drawn from Brit Art.

Such large themes and brushstrokes, we would do well to remember, are unusual in popular music. At a time when Brit pop dominated the airwaves it will not surprise many readers that some of the journalistic reactions to the album were extremely critical. Such a recording would always be too pretentious for many, but could hardly be criticized for its lack of artistic ambition or originality. There are undoubtedly many potential themes in my own understanding of this ironic, serious, shambolic masterpiece that I will have passed over. It does, however, remain one of Bowie's most important pieces of music, signifying the third stage of his career. In this respect, the album should be welcomed for Bowie's (and indeed Eno's) ability to combine and move between a multitude of resources and perspectives taken from contemporary complex societies.

The Thin White Duke, race and the road to Berlin

That Bowie's artistic renaissance should come about during a period when he both reconnects with Brian Eno and certain bohemian ideas around art is of course rooted in Bowie's own biography. Central to our understanding of Bowie's bohemianism and his pose as the artist who only ended up in popular music 'by mistake' is the two years he spent in Berlin. This decision, as he repeatedly told journalists, was an attempt to get away from America and Los Angeles where he had been living since 1974. The relocation to Europe in 1976 found Bowie travelling between his home with his wife Angie in Vevey, Switzerland, the recording studios in Paris and Berlin, a sightseeing tour of the Eastern bloc and his apartment with Iggy Pop at Hauptstrasse 155 (also in Berlin).

The initial move from Britain to America and on to mainland Europe had an important effect upon Bowie's musical direction. His earlier move out of London to America, thereby breaking up the Spiders, had been an ambitious attempt to project his music onto a world and North American stage. Living in Los Angeles in 1975, Bowie was widely reported to be in a poor mental and physical state. Cocaine was his drug of choice, and he was reputedly living on a diet of peppers and milk. His increasing frailty was noted by many of his friends at the time. Bowie's features were drawn and many reported that he was beginning to resemble a ghost. Such was his physical appearance when he attended the Grammy awards that year that Aretha Franklin quipped, 'I'm so happy, I could even kiss David Bowie.' His exploration of American culture and his high profile status as a global star of popular music was, it seems, having an extraordinary impact on Bowie. During this period, he lived a mostly secluded life and became intensely interested in occultism, black magic and the Kabbalah. If this was not enough, Bowie had also developed a well-documented obsession with Nazism and his relationship with his wife Angie was close to its end. According to the rock critic Ian MacDonald (2003), Bowie's interest in Nazism was never conventionally political. MacDonald, one of rock 'n' roll's most astute observers, argues that Bowie's fascination with Nazism was an outgrowth of his earlier Nietzschean ideas. It was not that Bowie was a fully-fledged Nazi, but that he flirted with what seemed to be forbidden. Many punks, it may be remembered, wore Nazi armbands not because they were sympathetic with German National Socialism, but because they had a desire to shock. However, it seems that Bowie's fantasies went quite a bit further than he and many critics would be comfortable admitting. Bowie loved to entertain and startle the music press, always giving them good copy and ensuring a place on the front page or in the headlines. That British popular and official culture continually replays the culture of the Second World War meant that any mention of Nazi sympathies was likely to receive a media torrent of reaction. The cultural critic Paul Gilroy (2004) has pointed out that in British culture the symbolism of the Second World War is continually figured in football chants, state ceremonies, popular film and documentaries. This is done, argues Gilroy (2004: 96), so that 'Brits can know who we are as well as who we were and then become certain that we are still good while our uncivilised enemies are irredeemably evil.' The continual replaying of the fault line between a free and democratic Britain and a Nazi Germany acts as a way of displacing recognition of current problems. What Gilroy skilfully detects within the continual reference to an anti-Nazi war is Britain's inability to mourn the passing of its empire and to develop a more hospitable attitude towards a multicultural present. The current clinging of the British parliament to America's coat-tails and the so-called 'special relationship' is further evidence of this cultural condition.

Such is the allure of this period within British culture it is not surprising that someone like Bowie would find it worthy of exploration. Just as Bowie's gay posing in the early seventies was intended to provoke a reaction, the same could be said of some of Bowie's pronouncements during the mid seventies. Interviewed in a breathless style by the *New Musical Express*, Bowie revels in his ability to court attention. First, Bowie declares rock 'n' roll to be a 'toothless old woman'. He then goes on:

> There will be a political figure in the not too distant future who'll sweep this part of the world like early rock 'n' roll did. You've got to have an extreme right front come and sweep everything off its feet and tidy everything up. Then you can get a new form of liberalism. The best thing that can happen is for an extreme right government to come. It'll do something positive, at least, cause a commotion in people – and they'll either accept the dictatorship or get rid of it. It's like a kaleidoscope . . . No matter how many colours you put in, that kaleidoscope will make a pattern. That's what happens with TV – it does not matter who puts what in the TV, the TV puts over its own plan. (*NME* 1976/2004: 139)

While many will dismiss these projections as the ramblings of a drugged rock star, such a response seems too easy and forgiving. Bowie's views are in part a comic reflection of his own cultural power over his fans, but there are more disturbing elements being drawn upon here, although it is not clear what needs in Bowie's terms 'to be cleared up'. These comments are similar to others espoused by Bowie at this time. The most controversial of these interviews is the 1976 interview with *Playboy* magazine. In the early part of the interview Bowie is claiming 'nothing matters except whatever it is I'm doing at present. I can't keep track of everything I say. I don't give a shit.' He then moves on to give details about his flirtation with 'fast drugs' and claims, 'I really have nothing to say, no suggestions, no advice, nothing.' This paves the way for Bowie to pronounce his most often quoted views on fascism:

> PLAYBOY: You've often said that you believe strongly in fascism. You also claim you'll run for Prime Minister of England. More media manipulation?
>
> BOWIE: Christ, everything is a media manipulation. I'd love to enter politics. I will one day. I'd adore to be Prime Minister. And, yes, I believe very strongly in fascism. The only way we can speed up the sort of liberalism that's hanging foul in the air at the moment is to speed up the progress of the right wing, totally dictatorial tyranny and get it over as fast as possible. People have always responded with greater efficiency under a regimental leadership. A liberal wastes time saying, 'Well, now, what ideas have you got?' Show them what to do, for God's sake. If you don't nothing will get done. I can't stand people just hanging about. Television is the most successful fascist, needless to say. Rock stars are fascists, too. Adolf Hitler was one of the first rock stars. (*Playboy* 1976)

Again this is both a playful commentary upon Bowie's relationship with the media and further evidence of his postmodern confusion. Bowie, it seems, is drunk on celebrity, both fascinated by and contemptuous of the attention his every move seems to receive from the world's media.

Not surprisingly, many at the time were outraged by Bowie's views on National Socialism and Hitler. The impression of Bowie as a Nazi sympathizer was further strengthened on 2 May 1976 when Bowie arrived at London's Victoria Station and was photographed in an open-topped limo throwing a Nazi salute. Bowie later denied this and claimed to be only waving to the assembled crowd. Whatever the 'truth' of this event, that Bowie would seek to pull such a publicity stunt is certainly in keeping with the comments he had previously made. Indeed, the subtle ambiguities of Bowie's posturing were lost on many British neo-Nazi groups who became interested in him during this period, as well as the organization Rock Against Racism who campaigned against rock stars perceived to have racist sympathies. Bowie's defenders have pointed to the considerable amount of drugs he was taking at this time and to his quick apology for these and other remarks. His detractors, however, have rightly claimed that Bowie made too many statements of this kind for them to be dismissed. It seems that Bowie's desire to shock his audience had gone too far this time. Indeed, Bowie's antics are all the more disturbing when connected to his interest in the British politician Enoch Powell at the end of the sixties. Powellism in the British national context paved the way for Thatcherism during the eighties. Powell, a conservative MP, made a speech on race relations in 1968 that warned that Britain's streets would become 'rivers of blood'. While dismissing such talk as inflammatory, the popular press, police and government agencies during the seventies became increasingly anxious about black male muggers. 'Moral panic' led the police to claim new powers and to target young black men in the fight against street crime. Claims about the increase in black crime always lacked hard evidence and the deliberate persecution of an excluded minority was undoubtedly racist. In October 1975, the National Front organized a march through the East End of London, spurred by stories in the tabloid press about black muggers and scroungers on the dole. Behind this attack on young black Britons were white fears about the decline of Britain as an economic power and an increasingly authoritarian state seeking to intervene to reverse a perceived 'moral decline' (Hall et al. 1978). It is against this background that we have to locate Bowie's irresponsible and reactionary posing.

The argument that Bowie is undoubtedly drawing upon racially inspired imagery is strengthened if we consider the final character Bowie invented during the seventies, The Thin White Duke. Reminiscent of Halloween Jack (*Diamond Dogs*), what is conspicuous is this character's explicit whiteness and his tough, emotionless masculinity that builds upon the earlier image. The Thin White Duke is usually associated with the set of performances generated by Bowie's 1975 album *Station to Station*. Bowie, his complexion powder-white, hair slicked back, dressed smartly in black and white, has described this image as a 'very Aryan, fascist type – a would-be romantic with absolutely no emotion at all' (Dalton and Hughes 2001). The racial 'purity' and emphasis upon the 'whiteness' of Bowie's image is significant in retrospect. This particular album begins Bowie's turn away from America towards more 'European' influences, trading upon the German electronic music of Kraftwerk and Neu as well as the black-and-white imagery of German expressionism. This is combined with visual images of a white masculinity that seems to have been heavily influenced by the Nazi period. In terms of Bowie's own description of The Thin White Duke, what is noticeable is how he brings together 'whiteness', authoritarian masculinity and a lack of emotion. It is the theatricality of Nazism rather than the ideology that attracts Bowie. The work of cultural historian Klaus Theweleit (1989) can perhaps help us understand why Bowie might have been drawn to these images at this time. Theweleit's work has been important in developing our understanding of fascism not just as a form of politics but as a way of seeking to develop a specific culture. In the popular images of German manhood that accompanied Hitler's rise to power, Theweleit skilfully detects a masculine obsession with hardness, destruction and self-denial. Indeed many of the images and transcripts that were inspected by Theweleit during his analysis suggest a narcissistic attraction to leader figures who are able to repudiate more feminine needs for warmth and physical security. The body is imagined as a machine that is fearful of its own needs for nurturing and care. The masculine fantasy apparent here is that through self-discipline these 'figures of steel' will successfully eliminate the need for emotion and intimacy from the psyche. The authoritarian male in this cultural logic seeks to control emotion, irrationality and anxiety. Not only is The Thin White Duke not responsible in terms of Britain's racialized politics but also his creation potentially satisfied the needs of a rock star who was going through a period of intense emotional turmoil. As we saw earlier, in respect of Tin Machine (which was more 'blokeish'), this would not be the first or last time that Bowie turned to images of masculine hardness as a way of dealing with personal difficulties.

Again Bowie had to find a way of escaping a prison house of his own making. He was on the run not so much from America but from himself and the harsh, cruel and in parts fascistic self that he had helped create.

The Berlin albums: *Low* and *'Heroes'*

Berlin had long featured in Bowie's imagination as the bohemian capital of Europe. The Berlin of the 1920s and 1930s, before Hitler's rise to power, had been a world of shady nightclubs and cafés for poseurs and for sexual and artistic experimentation. Berlin in the 1920s, like Greenwich Village in New York and Montparnasse in Paris, became the focus for alternative bohemian artistic activity. During the seventies, Bowie had become fascinated by the romance of Berlin, stimulated by the novels of Christopher Isherwood (whom he continued to name-drop during this period) and the popular success of the 1972 film, *Cabaret*. However, an equally, and often neglected attraction, was Lou Reed's 1973 album, *Berlin*. Lou Reed's (former lead singer of the Andy Warhol-produced Velvet Underground) previous album, *Transformer*, had been produced by Bowie and Mick Ronson. This recording continues to be hugely influential today and includes songs such as 'Perfect Day', 'Vicious' and of course 'Walk on the Wild Side', which combined camp and glam in equal measure. The bohemian classic *Berlin* is less well known and is considered an artistic rather than a commercial success. The careers of Lou Reed and David Bowie were connected by friendship, sexuality and artistic involvement. It is noteworthy that the recording of *Berlin* was in fact prompted by the break-up of Reed's own marriage and offers a stark and uneven narrative of two drug addicts living together in the city (Bockris 1995). Despite the romantic gloss of the title track, *Berlin* is an unsettling story that includes a suicide attempt, male violence, resentment and class hatred, family break-up and eventually sadness and acceptance. *Berlin* is like a vessel for negative emotions and feelings that finally offers redemption. This, it seems, is what Bowie was looking for when he came to Berlin.

The Berlin discovered by Bowie and Iggy Pop was quite different from that of the bohemian myths generated by the 1920s. Berlin had become symbolic of the Cold War, a segmented city in a Europe divided between the capitalist West and the communist East. The Cold War was perpetuated by both stability and instability – a divided Europe as well as a divided city while sustaining the memory of the Second World War. The Cold War put the globe on an almost permanent war footing. The threat of nuclear holocaust and the destabilization of democratic regimes that did not fit with the ambitions of America and the USSR saw the world living in the shadow of its own destruction. These factors were particularly apparent in Berlin whose division was marked by the concrete symbol of the Cold War, the Berlin Wall. The Wall not only represented a city split between two different economic and political regimes but imposed a cultural divide across which families, citizens and relatives found it almost impossible to communicate. In this respect, Berlin stood for the tragedy of a divided Europe that had never fully recovered from the nationalist violence and genocide that marked the twentieth century. If Bowie wanted to go somewhere where the myths about National Socialism were likely to be dramatized and contradicted he could not have chosen a better place. Berlin, at that time, represented not only a divided continent, but one that had witnessed the near destruction of democracy and civilized values by totalitarianism. Berlin was a place of hope, given that it had demonstrated that freedom could survive in the face of adversity, but also of deep sadness, given the social and political repression that the Wall had come to symbolize.

Both performers kept a lower profile than would have been possible in either London or Los Angeles. While their accommodation was comfortable, it was far from glamorous and they spent their time visiting punk clubs and gay bars, walking the streets and frequenting the various galleries and museums that Berlin had to offer. Bowie and Iggy lived near the poor Turkish quarter of the city and witnessed first-hand the poverty and ill treatment of its residents. Years later Bowie commented: 'Suddenly I was in a situation where young people of my own age whose fathers had actually been SS men. That was a good way to be woken up out of that particular dilemma, and start to re-function in a more orderly fashion . . . I came crashing down to earth when I got back to Europe' (Dalton and Hughes 2001: 45). It was time for Bowie to begin to let go of some of the dangerous and disturbing fantasies that had begun to penetrate his music and his psyche. The masks that Bowie had hidden behind were beginning to crack. The extremist delusions of The Thin White Duke had no place in Berlin. Talking of his experiences a few years later Bowie comments:

> For years I daren't walk down the street alone. I was paranoid about it, terrified. It still takes me courage to walk from A to B and not think, 'This person walking down the street is David Bowie and everybody's looking at him.' Now I look at other people. I even go into the shops and, if somebody talks to me, I chat back. Three years ago I could have no more done that than fly – literally. They couldn't drag me onto an aeroplane screaming, at one time. Now, every day, I get up more nerve to try to be more normal and less insulated against real people. (quoted in Rook 1979/1996: 163)

Pointedly, the metaphor of the wall works in a number of ways here. The walled separation of Berlin and the brittle masculinity of The Thin White Duke are both barriers in need of deconstruction. Bowie had constructed an internal wall based upon playing the media and taking on the attributes of characters he had invented in his music and on stage. Now that Bowie was beginning to realize a new freedom in a city where he was able to form a more reciprocal relationship with his own self and others, he had to abandon the rigidity of his earlier creations. It was also a time to escape from the pressures of stardom and a failing marriage and to begin again to concentrate on his music. The popular fascination with Bowie's partial disappearance in Berlin is inflated by the fact this proves to be one of the most creative periods of his life. The recordings of *The Idiot* and *Lust for Life* (with Iggy Pop) and *Low* and *'Heroes'* (released under Bowie's name) would prove to be genuinely groundbreaking albums, creating popular music that influenced generations of musicians and fans for years to come. Here Bowie's bohemianism exhibited a more creative context. If bohemianism can lead to a flirtation with extremist political ideologies, it also traditionally engages with lifestyle experimentation, forming more reciprocal relations with excluded racial and sexual minorities, and developing a more playful disposition in respect of work. That Bowie was able to tap into these dimensions not only temporarily saved him but also formed the creative background for his next two albums.

The recording of *Low* under the stewardship of Brian Eno began in September 1976 at Chateau d'Herouville near Paris. While Bowie had previously recorded *PinUps* at the same location, this proved to be a very different kind of album. In particular, Brian Eno, whose previous career had included Roxy Music and a string of successful solo albums including *Another Green World* (1975), was widely regarded as an intellectual who, like Bowie, borrowed ideas from both high and popular art. Eno not only drew upon his own inventions in ambient music, but also sought to connect his music to some of the more experimental features of the avant-garde, drawing inspiration from composers like John Cage. In particular, the recording of *Low* is remembered by many of the musicians who worked on the album for Eno's *Oblique Strategies* cards. The idea was quite simple, if challenging for musicians who were not used to working in this way. During the recording of *Low* and *'Heroes'*, Eno would hand out cards which had imprinted on them a series of aphorisms or instructions. The randomness of this process recalls Bowie's use of William Burroughs's cut-up technique. Some of the cards were quite baffling, containing messages like 'use an unacceptable colour': others, such as 'emphasize the flaws' had more readily understood meanings. The aim was to disrupt the recording process productively, introducing spaces for the unexpected, accidents and mistakes. Similar to cut-up, such processes ensured that the music evident on *Low* and *'Heroes'* went beyond the usual repertoires of popular music. Not surprisingly, these two pieces of music initially confounded many critics, although they attracted attention from the classical world with Philip Glass recording his own versions of these two albums. For many, listening to these albums today is an arresting experience as they break many of the expectations that listeners usually have about popular music. Although they could both be put in the broad category of art rock, along with artists like Pink Floyd and Radiohead, they were not what Bowie fans had come to expect, even from someone as unpredictable as David Jones. Never, it seems, had Bowie's music been so simultaneously autobiographical or so abstract. Initially issued on vinyl, the first side of the long-player contains some glorious pop moments intertwined with a good deal of experimentation. Here Bowie's singing is kept to a minimum and can be heard recounting the pain of the past few years. The songs evoke a world of personal isolation, fragmentation and the search for intimacy. The sound of the album appears to emphasize Bowie's separation from the world. The lyrics have a seamless quality which expresses feelings of personal dislocation, an effect enhanced by the electronic unpredictability of the music. Further, there is an intimation of dread in respect of an uncertain and unpredictable future.

The overall feel of the album, however, is melancholic rather than depressed; if anything, it hybridizes the blues and 'electronic music'. If the 'blues' were originally invented by black Americans to give voice to their troubles and heartaches, Bowie had seemingly done the same for a more individualized world of listeners. During my interviews with fans, I was struck by how many people mentioned listening to *Low* as a way of helping them through depressive periods. The mournful music of *Low* gave voice to Bowie's own inner turmoil and also helped many of his listeners deal with their own. This mood is continued and to some extent deepened on the second side of *Low* where the vocals almost completely disappear and are replaced predominately by the undulating sound of synthesizers. If anything, the second side is not so much a switch in mood but in focus from Bowie's own self to the external climate of Berlin and Europe. The mood is intensified in instrumental pieces such as 'Warszawa' (perhaps indicating the Soviet-controlled Polish city of Warsaw) or the more obviously referenced 'Weeping Wall'. Bowie evokes a different idea of Europe. Europe is neither celebrated as the birthplace of democracy, but nor is it dismissed as the place of angry nationalist violence or of war. Bowie's Europe is a Europe of sorrow and suffering in terms of its own past and possible futures. What Bowie captures here is an idea of European decline. Where once Europe could conceive of itself as the cradle of civilization, the Europe of the Cold War tells a story of occupation, continued repression and the fading splendour of its capital cities. The album in this sense provides the European antidote to The Thin White Duke, evoking the passing of its own omnipotence and splendour. Here the personal and the political are fused together. Just as Bowie gives up his own illusions about his ability to master and order himself, the same could be said of the European continent. Rather than the official state-sanctioned talk of European success or failure, the album articulates a loss of harmful delusions and postulates the possibility of reconstructing the self and our world views. This points to an understanding of Europe that might move beyond competition between jealous nationalisms or a single dominant civilization while opening the possibility of something different.

In many respects *'Heroes'*, recorded soon after the release of *Low,* is a companion piece. The 'something different' that might be achieved becomes apparent as the album makes space for 'other' cultures, European art and diverse subjectivities and sexualities. To the bemusement of many critics at the time, Bowie described the album *'Heroes'* as 'compassionate'. As with Bowie's previous offering *Low*, *'Heroes'* articulates feelings of personal distress, but this time with the occasional slice of hope. If anything, *'Heroes'* gives voice to a Bowie who exhibits personal and social wakefulness. If the racist clichés and far-right posturing, aided by a drug-fuelled lifestyle, induced a zombie-like existence, living in Berlin had helped shatter a few myths and evoke a sense of worldliness within Bowie's art. Echoing *Low,* much of the album's second side (again on the original vinyl album) is instrumental, Bowie's vocals only reappearing on the album's sublime final track, 'The Secret Life of Arabia'. Before we reach that moment, 'Sense of Doubt' communicates a feeling of doom, while 'Moss Garden' adds a Japanese flavour with Bowie playing koto, and finally 'Neuköln' (which Bowie later revealed was written about the Turkish quarter of Berlin) mixes synthesizer and saxophone, communicating a dark atmosphere of repression. Despite the sense of pessimism, Bowie's 'compassion' is also on offer. In Bowie's video performance of 'Heroes', he appears silhouetted in a black leather jacket, in a pose designed to emphasize his bisexuality and sense of otherness. If *Low* is mainly mournful, then the 'compassion' of *'Heroes'* is located in the space it provides for difference and otherness. While reference is made to other cultures and art worlds ('Joe the Lion' refers to the performance artist, Chris Burden), it is really Bowie's own personal difference that is again being celebrated. Perhaps Bowie's most requested and best-loved song, 'Heroes,' revisits the filmic quality of his earlier writing evident in songs like 'Five Years'. This time it is the possibility of making intimate contact despite social and cultural division that is proposed. The image of two lovers connecting with each other seemed heroic to Bowie in a city blighted by the Wall.

That Bowie is trying (if only in part) to deal with questions of cultural domination is again evident on his next record, *Lodger*. Bowie often referred to this as the third Berlin album, despite its being recorded in Switzerland. There is however a continuity in its themes and musicians (Brian Eno amongst them). In terms of Bowie's career, the album also began to pave the way for the more 'mainstream' successes of *Scary Monsters (and Super Creeps)* and *Let's Dance*. This time the music had a more obviously commercial appeal but the themes it attempted to tackle are no less complex. David Bowie's Berlin period is crucial in the history of popular music. It perhaps equates with Bob Dylan's artistic achievement in the recordings *Highway 61 Revisited* and *Blonde on Blonde* in the mid-sixties. By this I mean that Bowie's cultural invention offered a break from the past and unintentionally influenced generations of musicians. Yet Bowie's art had reached a turning point where his whiteness and his masculinity would either become increasingly extreme or would be reformulated in the search for different artistic dimensions. That he chose the latter is now a matter of popular history. Bowie's interest in cultural difference remains at the heart of the album with tracks like 'African Night Flight' and 'Yassassin (Turkish for: Long Live)'. If Bowie had not yet gone far enough to banish media interest in his Nazism, he was now expressing liberal sentiments more openly: 'They wipe out an entire race and I've got to write it down' ('Fantastic Voyage' 1979).

In the two years after the recording of *Low* and *'Heroes'*, Bowie embarked upon a world tour (eventually resulting in the live album *Stage* in 1978) and finally reached a divorce settlement with his wife, Angie. What was beginning to happen was that Bowie was becoming less the politically volatile bohemian and more the liberal bohemian. We saw earlier how *Let's Dance* (mostly unsuccessfully) articulated a concern for cultural imperialism. In the aftermath of his fascist posturing, Bowie no longer needed to claim to be apolitical but was giving voice to a more responsible and tolerant liberalism. Such pronouncements became bland in his later music but here they still dealt explicitly with questions of cultural domination. For example, on *Lodger*, Bowie penned both one of his best and most politically committed songs. The powerful narrative and music of 'Repetition' articulates a sense of frustration and emotional repression. The song is sung largely without emotion to evoke the everyday nature of the situation being described. The 'repetition' of the domestic violence being articulated is captured by the hypnotic and jagged sound of guitar and synthesizer. This song was later covered by the radical feminist group the Au Pairs on their album *Playing With a Different Sex* (1981). Without trying to sound worthy, it seems that Bowie was beginning to explore many of the dynamics of traditional masculinity. Again it is important to view 'Repetition' and 'Boys Keep Swinging' as an attempt to provide an antidote to the excesses of The Thin White Duke. As Bowie's career progresses, however, the more critical aspects of his liberalism are sidelined. This is partly a result of the stadium-star status Bowie acquired in the eighties but it is also linked to the shifting terrain of his career. However, as we shall see, Bowie is a star whose liberal concerns, after his flirtations with fascism, were (no matter how diluted) never far from the surface.

Millennium Bohemian and the liberal self

The 'liberalism' of Bowie is evident in his more 'mainstream' music of the eighties, prompting appearances at charitable events and support for noble causes. Many saw the marriage with Iman and *Black Tie White Noise* (1993), produced by Nile Rodgers, as ending any suspicion of a racialized Bowie. The record is important in that it allowed Bowie to break away from the depressing music of Tin Machine. The album offered a celebration of liberal multiculturalism in the face of the 1991 Los Angeles race riots. This is suggested through the jazzy and dance-oriented rhythms of the music (including as it does Lester Bowie on trumpet) and Bowie's image as a streetwise hipster. Bowie's image seemingly moves between being an angst-ridden yuppie and a jazzman in a trilby hat. The music self-consciously searches for a 'harmony' between different cultural styles, while the music video which accompanies the release of the album features Bowie backed by black and white singers dressed in black-and-white suits. In an interview that accompanies the album, Bowie expands on these themes:

> We are all heading towards equality, but integration will take longer. We are now at the point where black and Hispanic communities are no longer oppressed. To cap that we can and should be positive. I think we will head towards equality but integration will take longer because there are so many forces working against it and the only way to overcome that is to be aware of it and there is no desire on the greater part of Western society for integration. If we can accept that and start appreciating the differences and not look for sameness, white sameness within everybody then we have a much better chance of creating a real and meaningful integration. I wanted to get some of that in the song [laughs]. ('Black Tie White Noise', music video 1993)

Admittedly this is not territory many 'white' artists would have felt confident enough to enter. The song Bowie is referring to is the album's title track, 'Black Tie White Noise'. A duet with black singer Dave Richards, the song sought to articulate the feelings of mistrust that black and white Americans felt towards each other. It is perhaps important not to be over-critical of such an enjoyable album. Bowie after all had made a successful commercial recording which actually dealt with questions of race. The problem would seem to lie with both the music and Bowie's own need to be 'positive'. The liberal multiculturalism apparent on the album has little passion or conviction. Not surprisingly this is multiculturalism for the 'comfortably off'. The more discordant search for identity that was so prominent in many of Bowie's earlier offerings had been replaced by a slick commercial sound. There is little sense of burning anger and outrage at the way that racism privileges whites and humiliates black people. Like *Let's Dance* (also recorded with Nile Rodgers), *Black Tie White Noise* is an album of stylish production and easy appeal. Bowie's old postmodern radicalism and use of arresting images, at this point at least, had been replaced by a 'responsible' rock star persona who tries to distance himself from the excesses of his own past. This does not mean the record is not enjoyable to listen to (this again draws parallels with *Let's Dance*) but rather that the album's self-confessed political concerns are weakly realized.

Today David Bowie is no longer the postmodern radical of old. In a recent interview, music journalist Paul Du Noyer (2003: 87) says of Bowie that 'his conversation nowadays – hesitantly high-brow, earnestly left-liberal – suggests a Manhattan academic.' The interview effortlessly moves between discussions of September 11th, the literature of Peter Ackroyd and Tom Wolfe and postmodernism. Bowie, it seems, is still concerned with intellectual and postmodern issues, commenting: 'If you can make the spiritual connection with some kind of clarity then everything else would fall into place. A morality would seem to be offered, a plan would be offered, some sense would be there. But this evades me' (Du Noyer 2003: 89). The discussion then turns to Bowie's recording *Reality* (2003). Earlier in his career, such a title might have signified a postmodern attempt to reveal the 'natural' as 'cultural', challenging conventions of representation. This is perhaps still present, given Bowie's cartoon image on the front of the album. More in evidence is the philosophical postmodern question of what to believe, in a fragile and dangerous world. Bowie works different metaphors of spiritual dislocation into his lyrics and songwriting. Bowie is no longer the perverter of art and literature but adopts the position of the decent liberal trapped in a culture colonized by fear and fundamentalism. Questions of sexual and gender ambiguity have long been abandoned with the adoption of a *Hello!* magazine image of a happily married celebrity. Similarly to his previous album *Heathen (2002)*, *Reality* resonates with connections between September 11th and broader spiritual questions. This is most evident on 'Looking for Water', where Bowie sings, 'I don't know about you but my heart's not in it' ('Looking for Water', 2003). The song is a complex mediation on notions of commitment and belief in a city (New York) which has been shattered by a global terrorist attack. The overlapping metaphors evoke sceptism in respect of President Bush and Prime Minister Blair's war on terror and the painful search for truth. The search for 'water' within the song evokes something not easily found. We are left to muse that this could be either the infamous weapons of mass destruction or more spiritual forms of sustenance. The frantic nature of the music builds, until Bowie spits 'Baby dumb is forever'. We are left without any final point of arrival, but with a warning not to turn away from difficult personal and political questions. Despite this heavily coded discomfort with the 'war on terror', Bowie's political commitments stopped short of many American artists like Bruce Springsteen, REM and others who sought to galvanize support for more liberal alternatives. Bowie remains a liberal bohemian but one who is shy of joining causes. This is not surprising, given some of the irresponsible posturing of Bowie's past. Yet after a life journey from Brixton to New York, Bowie remains one of the few global celebrities who persists in connecting his art with broader philosophical themes that go beyond ordinary understandings of politics.

Bowie's liberalism, one could also argue, contains a tough centre as found in his warnings against fundamental solutions offered by either terrorists or the Christian Right. Bowie courageously, at a time when many are seeking simpler explanations, rejects the allure of moral certitude. What is missing, however, is the extra dimension that made Bowie so fascinating to begin with. If in the Berlin period Bowie took his music apart from the inside in order to propose alternatives to cultural domination, he currently offers enjoyable mainstream rock for the middle-aged consumer. If Bowie has traded bohemian disaffection for a business suit, then his art has inevitably suffered in the process. However, that he may yet again confound his critics cannot be ruled out, given Bowie's enduring mutability.

six

BOWIE FANS

When I was just sixteen in 1977, David Bowie seemed like the biggest star currently making new music. Yet while he was evidently popular and still selling records, he did not appear to be 'mainstream'. This was a time when punk had come along and was claiming to sweep away everything that was middle-aged, predictable and conformist about the record industry. Yet Bowie – already an established star – not only survived, but his light began to shine even more powerfully. Despite being a star from a different era Bowie seemed to be oddly at home in punk. Bowie was also a secret who had been passed down through the generations. His mystery in this respect was that while being the subject of mass consumption his interest in the art of image manipulation seemed to signify a 'depth' lacking in his rivals. His singles may have got him on the popular television chart show Top of the Pops, *but his back catalogue required a more specialist, 'insider' knowledge.*

I can still remember the first time I encountered Bowie's image and music. I was spending the evening round at a male friend's house listening to music. We did this a lot as we were too young to go to a pub, and we were both avid record-collectors and wanted to share our passion for music. At one point during the evening, my friend's elder brother came in and suggested we listen to Bowie's album Diamond Dogs. *I remember looking at the cover art and listening to the music, thinking this was far more radical than anything to which I was currently listening. This was my first glimpse at the prince of bohemian pop. My second was at home with my Mum, Dad and sister on a Thursday night watching* Top of the Pops. *The video for 'Boys Keep Swinging' came on the television and I could not believe my eyes. I was fascinated, but at the time I did not know what with. I knew that David Bowie was a man and yet he dressed like a woman. This was all at once confusing, alarming and appealing.*

From this point on I was hooked. I bought Bowie's most recent albums 'Lodger' and 'Scary Monsters' in quick succession. I also noticed the passion with which I had defended Bowie against the scepticism of my then girlfriend's father. Bowie mattered to me because he embodied something beyond the small Midlands town where I lived. Bowie's interviews in the music press were different from those of other musicians and performers. He seemingly took himself very seriously whilst talking about his music in the language of projects, works and above all else as art. He stressed the importance of not confining himself to music but of wanting to appear in films, to act in theatre and to paint. Bowie represented a different masculinity to the laddish aggression of some punk groups like Sham 69 and the Sex Pistols and the head-banging clubbishness of the then still popular heavy metal acts like AC/DC and Saxon. Seemingly he had more in common with the art rock and sexual ambivalence of contemporary music like the Buzzcocks, Magazine, Penetration, X-Ray Specs and Siouxsie and the Banshees. His masculinity seemed at ease with sexual difference and cultural experimentation, allowing himself to stand out from those around him.

Bowie's exoticism and aesthetic strangeness were also signalled through his interest in literature. He seemed to have a foothold in a European art world that he represented not only through his music and connections with Berlin but also in the novels he spoke about. His interest in the literature of Burroughs, Isherwood and Mishima was well known. These writers for me represented a canon of creative writing which was not the English literature of Hardy, Austen and Dickens that I associated with middle-class culture. It was not that I was particularly turned off these writers by school, but more that they were part of 'official culture'. I was searching for something 'different'. Indeed it was not even that I went away and read these particular writers; it was more Bowie's persona as an artist who was working within popular culture that struck a chord with me.

For a white working-class male who had just left school with few career prospects, Bowie represented a form of middle-class 'cool'. I loved his affinity with the world of travel, art, books and no doubt glamour. It all seemed a long way from the parochial and small-town world in which I lived. He represented the possibility that upward mobility could mean more than simply passing exams and getting a slightly better job. Indeed, it was in identifying with Bowie that I began to push away my working-class self, and started taking an interest in anything that was European rather than British. This included reading European fiction, listening to electronic music and watching avant-garde films.

148

Above all, Bowie was a way of getting out. In identifying with Bowie, I began a career in what I felt at the time to be self-improvement, passing exams and refashioning my identity. Bowie represented the possibility of becoming different. He did not create these elements within me, but entered into my world on these terms.

I wrote the words printed above. I wrote them at the start of this project before I had really begun to analyse the music or think very deeply about Bowie's career. The words you see are obviously written from the point of view of the present. I am not sure I would quite so readily have used terms like 'masculinity' or 'avant-garde' back then. Yet they do capture the beginnings of my own interest in David Bowie. Two aspects are immediately noticeable as I re-read the extract reprinted from a notebook I have been keeping during this project. First, that for me the drama of David Bowie was mainly about class and masculinity, and my hoped-for 'escape' from what I evidently felt to be the 'confines' of my then location. Valerie Walkerdine (1990: 92) makes a similar point about girls' comics when she argues that they 'provide solutions and escapes, ways out, in fantasy and in practice, by the proffering of what and who one might be'. She continues that girls' comics in this respect embody a form of realism in that they inform the fantasy life of the reader. Commercial culture is always more than a matter of media bias or lack of realism, but should instead be understood as the creation of meaning through diverse patterns of identification. In this section of the book, I am less concerned with how we might unravel Bowie's images and music than I am with the different ways he has come to have significance in the lives of his fans. Secondly, already in re-reading my own experience, I can identify aspects of other fans' accounts. I have spent the best part of the past two years listening to lifelong Bowie fans like myself. Undoubtedly they all had their own individual reasons for becoming Bowie fans, but as I listened I began to notice similarities and differences between their stories and my own.

Before moving on to examine my meetings with Bowie fans in more depth, I just want to deal with the question of why I think this is relevant. Some readers might be wondering, having got this far in the book, why a discussion of fans matters. Surely this is meant to be a book about David Bowie, not the people who happen to listen to his music? Here I want to make a number of related arguments. What I have offered the reader thus far is my interpretation of the music, images, interviews and above all what I take to be the relevance of David Bowie to our culture. Arguably another author (and indeed on Bowie there are many others) would have made quite different interpretations of his art and life to those presented in this volume. This is of course inescapable. What has interested me is how my own understanding of David Bowie has changed over the course of writing this book. At first I was enthusiastic, then I became quite negative (Tin Machine indeed has a lot to answer for) but by the closing stages I was able to offer what I hope is a more nuanced view beyond either blind devotion or cynical criticism. This, then, is no 'objective' account of Bowie's cultural production but is unavoidably my assessment of his cultural significance. There will be both more and indeed less sympathetic books written in the future as there have been in the past. This is perhaps just another way of saying that had I not been a fan of David Bowie since 1977 then I would have written a very different book. Yet, as I hope the opening reflections of this chapter make clear, 'something' is missing from the argument so far. Up to this point I have mainly been concerned to trace the different commercial strategies, representations and forms of cultural commentary that have become associated with Bowie. The picture I have presented thus far is necessarily partial as I have not yet begun to consider seriously why he might have attracted such devoted fans. We can easily imagine a hypothetic celebrity who produced a very similar output yet simply failed to attract such a wide audience. As is well known, popular music is littered with stories of one-hit wonders, spectacular failures and many more moderate forms of success than that represented by David Bowie. Another way of expressing this is that if David Bowie's celebrity can be understood through the complex interplay of image, provocation and the music industry, how he has come to have significance for his fans is important. Arguably these questions cannot really be answered by examining his music, but requires that we actually talk to people who describe themselves as Bowie fans. So this is what I have done. Before moving on to address these questions in more detail, I want briefly to review some of the cultural studies literature on fan culture. This is important in positioning my interpretations in a wider critical framework.

Fans: social and cultural perspectives

Cultural and media studies, in my view, have something distinctive to offer the study of the relationship between fans and celebrity. In particular, cultural and media studies attempt to understand the various cultural processes that are involved in being a fan. To be a fan is a fairly ordinary phenomenon. We all know people (if not ourselves) who are fans of football, soap operas, cult television shows or stars of cinema and popular music. Being a fan might mean that we follow the careers of particular celebrities with an intensity that is less evident in other cultural arenas. Usually being a fan means it matters to us if our favourite team wins or loses, whether our favourite band has entered the charts at no. 1, or that the television schedulers have just deleted a favourite show.

Most of the work that has been done in this area has sought to avoid turning people who identify with celebrities into an 'other'. The claim this work is seeking to subvert is that only abnormal or psychologically disturbed people form intense one-sided relationships with celebrities. It is easy to see where this idea comes from. Much of the official media's reporting of fans represents them as dangerous and out of control. Fans are perceived as stalkers creeping into the bedrooms of their favourite stars, or as lonely obsessives who spend a lifetime hunting down trivial artefacts connected in some way with their hero or heroine. Much of the cultural and media studies literature has sought to argue that this creates not only a misleading picture, but one that makes it difficult to admit our own fandom to others. Fans may want to keep their enthusiasms to themselves (unless they know it is safe to do otherwise) for fear of being labelled mad, bad or dangerous.

These projections are perhaps understandable, given that there is indeed something about the behaviour of some fans that goes beyond narrow definitions of rationality. In the cold light of day it may be hard to understand the emotionality and intense waves of feeling and affect that can become associated with fan experience. These outbursts of emotion unsettle a dominant culture based upon rationality, self-control and the ability to keep our feelings in check. This is not to say that all fan activity is of this kind. The celebrations of football fans or the enthusiasm evident at a popular music concert usually evokes a high degree of emotionality not so evident in other areas of social and cultural life. However, we need to be careful here in suggesting that all fan activity and involvement is of this type. Much of the fan literature emphasizes the relatively banal nature of being a fan – collecting sporting programmes, searching for obscure CDs or chatting to other fans on websites. None of these activities are likely to induce intense emotional states, although this cannot of course be ruled out.

For these reasons, media and cultural studies have sought to understand fans through less overtly judgemental frameworks. If the dominant view of fans tends to suggest a combination of obsessive behaviour and irrationality, the cultural and media studies literature uses a different tactic. If being a fan of a celebrity or group of celebrities is a much more ordinary experience than our society usually likes to admit, how might we build a different model of interpretation that both steers clear of making sweeping assumptions (accounting for the difference among fans) and makes sense of a wide range of fan activity? Similarly, it is not usually considered 'the done thing' in educated circles to pay too much attention to the culture of celebrity. Being caught reading a copy of a celebrity magazine (as I know to my cost) can lead to a questioning of your status by fellow academics. This is because 'official' forms of culture like to look down upon more supposedly 'ephemeral' cultures like celebrity. Instead of adopting this approach I have sought to take 'seriously' what

the many people I interviewed have said to me and to appreciate the importance that David Bowie has in the context of their
everyday lives.

Interviewing Bowie fans

These features guided much of my research into Bowie fans. I
also came to question many of the assumptions made by some
of the media and by cultural studies literature. First, I found it
comparatively easy to get people to talk about their fandom.
Important within this was presenting myself as a David Bowie
fan. This helped build up a rapport between myself and the
person being interviewed. Whereas most of the cultural studies
literature currently emphasizes the cultural productivity of the
fans (their active engagement in fan culture), I was more struck
by the emotional connection that many of the fans had with
Bowie and the reverential language they employed to describe
his evident star quality. This was often indicated by religious
metaphors. These were occasionally used ironically, but more
often usage expressed their intense admiration for David Bowie.
Many of the fans I interviewed claimed to have been artistically
inspired by Bowie (more of this later) but more evident was
their devotion or deeply felt connection to a star whose image
had been constructed by the mass media. Overwhelmingly I was
left with a sense of the power of the media to provide the symbolic resources through which ordinary people live their lives.
Interestingly, some of the cultural studies literature is silent on
these points lest it imply that ordinary people are the passive
dupes of mediated culture. My argument is that many of the
fans I interviewed actively identified with Bowie (more of this
later) and this has helped perpetuate the cultural power of some
images and representations rather than others. Some writers have
emphasized the power of the emotional connection of many fans
to icons while others have been too quick to write this out of
their accounts. The other problem I have with some of the existing literature is that it tends to suggest that fans are most often
people who are low in social and cultural status. This assumption

was not borne out by my research where many conventionally successful people strongly identified with David Bowie. Many of the people I interviewed had secure, middle-class forms of employment and were university educated. The reasons why the current literature makes this error is too complex to go into here, but I think we need to dispense with the argument that only the socially and culturally marginalized can be fans. Being a fan is an everyday and ordinary experience in a mass celebrity culture. If university professors, the unemployed and clerical workers can be fans, then so can we all.

The people I interviewed are listed below:

Sheffield: male musician
Sheffield: female lecturer
Derby: female clerical worker
Derby: unemployed male
Nottingham: female fashion and beauty consultant
Nottingham: male artist
Sheffield: male professor
Manchester: male clerical worker
Sheffield: unemployed male
Stoke: male information technology worker
Sheffield: information technology couple (man and woman)
London: female graphic artist
London: male journalist
Manchester: male television scriptwriter
Nottingham: male warehouse supervisor
Derby: IT worker

As can be seen, most of the people I interviewed were white, male and middle class. However, three of my respondents were from working-class backgrounds and two were currently out of work. Further, about a quarter of my sample were women, all of whom were 'white'. All small-scale sample groups are largely determined by the methods used to get into contact with potential interviewees. There is no scientific or neutral way of doing this. I mainly relied upon contacting people through Bowienet (David Bowie's official website) or through friends, family or students who knew someone who was a fan. This usually meant meeting a comparative 'stranger' in their home or in a public place that was not too noisy. The conversations lasted between one hour and one hour and a half and were all tape-recorded. Most of the people I interviewed were lifelong Bowie fans and were aged between approximately thirty and fifty years old. This is again not surprising (I am in this age range) as most people 'discovered' Bowie at the height of his fame during the seventies and early eighties. This meant that for most people following Bowie, taking an interest in his career, was something that had occupied them for a relatively large part of their lives.

This obviously marks a difference from the usual way that celebrity culture is understood. For many, celebrity culture – to borrow a phrase from the literary critic George Steiner (1974: 174) – is about 'maximum impact and instant obsolescence'. Most of the people I interviewed had a relationship with Bowie that developed over time. Here we have to proceed with caution as there was undoubtedly a masculine bias towards keeping in touch with Bowie over the decades. Like the men, the women I interviewed had mainly come across Bowie during their teenage years but this interest seemed to take a back seat as they got older. There were however exceptions. This is not to argue that the men I have interviewed maintained a sustained level of inter-est in Bowie over the years. More often periods of intense inter-est alternated with relative disinterest. Many spoke about how they had rediscovered Bowie in later life. The level of their focus on David Bowie was determined both by the rhythm of their own lives and by their favourite star's new releases and tours. This picture is further complicated by the fact that many of the women who claimed currently to have little interest in Bowie's recent career still described themselves as fans, while some of the men claimed that their interest had actually peaked during their late teens or early twenties. We cannot neatly package male and female fans in this respect although as we shall see there was a marked difference between them. Gender was still the main point of differentiation amongst fans, although as we shall see other differences like class and ethnicity were also appar-ent. Hopefully then this research will suggest a different picture from 'celebrity-obsessed women' and 'rational and indifferent men' which is currently such a staple of masculine discourse. Overall it was men rather than women who seemed to maintain a lifelong connection with Bowie, although the reasons for this are quite complicated.

In what follows I present what I call a series of discursive repertoires. These are ways of talking about Bowie, evident in conversation with fans, that I took to be significant. It is through the creation and interpretation of these discursive repertoires that fans make sense of Bowie as an icon and incorporate him into the fabric of their everyday lives. There has been a considerable amount of argument in social and cultural studies about the status of discourses. Some writers more closely allied to a structuralist tradition argue that discourses are linguistic codes that restrict and regulate the production of culture. Without going into too much detail, this approach has been rightly criticized for giving language and culture a fixed and objective character. Instead, following Volosinov (1973) and Williams (1977), I also wish to emphasize the idea that speech and talk are actually dependent upon human creativity and praxis. The discursive repertories are both produced and reproduced out of a dialectic of constraint and creativity. In other words, what I represent below is not simply what the culture of celebrity makes of its consumers, but what we make of it. As we shall see, in listening to the talk of fans we need to search for patterns of commonality, difference and creativity. Discourses are not only drawn upon to make sense of celebrity, they are also actively created in different social settings.

Before I move on to looking at the discursive repertoires produced by the Bowie fans I want to stress the ways in which many fans utilized their long-distance relationship with Bowie in order to help them construct their own individual biographies. The media's ability to be able to move texts and images through time and space opens the possibility of what J. B. Thompson (1995) has described as 'intimacy at a distance'. The audience's relation to celebrity is different from that with persons who are co-present. A non-reciprocal relationship of intimacy depends upon the scrutiny of the celebrity by the audience and not the other way round. Viewed positively, such relationships may help fans or audiences construct their own biographies, yet in other instances such relations can become moulded by addiction and compulsion. In an increasingly individualized society, the culture of celebrity can offer people reflexive resources as they attempt to sustain a coherent identity. As we shall see, in certain instances, given that the culture of celebrity is promoted by a consumerist society, there are evident dangers for the self in this process. Our mediated world is a world that is literally full of stories, some of which change every day and others which are built over time. These routinely include news stories, soap operas, tales of celebrities and of course sporting heroism. Unlike any other age, perhaps, our daily lives are constantly interrupted by the cultural production of stories. This is perhaps a more significant feature of our lives than we might currently be aware if we consider that to have an identity is to have the ability to be able to tell a story about yourself. The philosopher Paul Ricoeur (1991) has famously argued that our identities are like stories in that they are constantly being retold and revised in the light of new circumstances. If we take some of these features together we might begin to understand why a person like Bowie has been so important for many people. Bowie, as I have sought to argue in the first four chapters of this book, offers a compelling story that fuses together a narrative of fame, success, bohemian posing, gender uncertainty, bisexuality, loss of creativity and of course tragedy and redemption. Not surprisingly, in an age where the production of the self is increasingly an individual responsibility, many people look to celebrities to offer a 'guide' in the project of building an identity. In the next section, I highlight these features in terms of some of the interview material.

The cultural production of the self in postmodernity

As indicated above, many (although not all) of the men I interviewed had an interest in Bowie that helped them construct a sense of themselves across time. This feature was not so evident amongst the women, although there were exceptions to this general picture. In particular, many of the men suggested that they turned to Bowie in times of trouble and personal uncertainty.

> GUY: People tend to go back to it when they're having problems, they deal with it by secluding themselves through Bowie and turning to him for, like a guide, inspiration, whatever like, or just to cope with it, I mean so many people have said that.

Seemingly during periods of stress and emotional turmoil, many male fans suggested that Bowie's music helped.

> NS: How has he inspired you?
> LEE: Certain points of my life when I have been down or happy. He can be quite uplifting when I have been down. It can encourage you at certain low points. 'Low' (the album) doesn't depress me at all. It helps.

During the course of the interviews, both these men made it clear they were referring to particularly intense periods of economic insecurity and to the break-up of intimate relationships. What was evident was that being a Bowie fan meant that, while you might listen to other music, Bowie would be returned to over and over again. It was as much a case of growing old with Bowie as it was of growing up with him. Later in the same interview, we returned to the question of what this fan got from being so intensely interested in Bowie.

> NS: So you'll stick with him?
> LEE: Yes; if he stopped it would be sad. It will be a sad day when he stops. It's sad, people look at his age and say he's past it. That's just ageism. It's too simple to say that. Sometimes you can see in his work he's looking at himself, you know and he's fifty, but that's not a bad thing. It's interesting to watch how he's grown. You know he had his second child. You can tell he is happy, but not always. You can watch him through different periods. I mean I have supported the same team (football) all my life but it has not affected me in the same way. I can't remember that football match ten years ago, but I can remember that track on that album.

NS: So not like football?

LEE: There is an emotional attachment in an appreciation of art.

NS: Can't football be emotional?

LEE: It can be but it's instantaneous. It isn't like you listen to it constantly. It stays with you. I mean not just David Bowie, but music all the time. This I can play back, you know, keep listening, keep replaying.

Bowie's image and music provide an emotional resource for fans that can be drawn upon in good times and bad. What is distinctive here is the intimacy of the relationship when compared with that of supporting a football team. The intense scrutiny of Bowie's career and image by his fans helps foster a sense of relationship with an individual rather than with a group of people who make up a football team. Indeed, the comparison between following a football team and being a fan of a celebrity like Bowie was made more than once. Another fan makes a similar point:

ZAK: Whereas football, it's almost the same every time you go. I know that it is a different game but you are still seeing the same fifteen guys kicking a ball around for however long ... you go to see Bowie you see different sets, different levels, different audiences ... taking home with you the CD or listen to it at home, and you think I know there are some other Bowie fans out there doing the same.

While we shall return to this point later, it can be seen here that a sense of intimacy with an image and an individual is intensified when it is shared with a like-minded community. The intense scrutiny of Bowie's image and music seemingly provides fans with a reflexive resource they can call upon in different periods of their lives. Most of the people I interviewed were fans of a variety of popular music, although for many of them Bowie held a special place in the collections that they had built up over a number of years.

JAMES: I'll forget about it and then rediscover it. Now I have all the albums on CD; it's a periodic thing.

Fans have converted Bowie into a cultural resource that can be reinterpreted in the context of their changing life situations. Here Bowie acts as a kind of hypertext with fans reading interviews, listening to music, looking at images and searching out new information and inspiration. This information is then reinterpreted and understood in the context of their own changing lives. What is noticeable is Bowie's position as a cultural authority. Bowie is valued as a 'teacher', as a 'good mentor', as someone whose work and music can act as a continual inspiration over the years. During many of the interviews, I was struck by how a connection to Bowie has acted as a relatively permanent anchor in many people's lives. In a society where the traditional coordinates of family, class and church are weakening, people search for new sources and meanings in order to make sense of their lives and ongoing experience.

At this point we encounter something of a paradox; if Bowie has given shape to these fans' lives by providing a semi-permanent presence, then he has done so by encapsulating change. In other words, Bowie has encoded the possibility of reinventing oneself and handling change over a long career. The fans see Bowie as representative of change and the passing of time. That you never know what he is going to produce or become next was commented on by everyone I interviewed. As one fan put it 'you never know what's round the corner'. Indeed, this comment could equally apply to the life as well as the career of David Bowie. If he has dealt publicly with both personal and artistic change, he has done so in a way that has inspired many of his fans. Those I interviewed remained loyal and continued to buy his music over the years because the next album was always likely to be different. A fairly typical response in this respect was the following:

> GUY: When the next album comes out I'll buy it, I'll buy it because he has always been there and I know there is always a chance it is going to be a corker.

While Bowie's experiments and changes were not always successful, he was seen to be a man who had endured a great deal of personal suffering and tragedy but had pulled through. Bowie was a survivor in a double sense: in terms of his musical career and of having come through periods of intense drug use, creative inertia, loss of friends and family and divorce. Further, he was managing to grow old gracefully in an industry seemingly dominated by young people and fading rock stars.

> MIKE: You see Jagger today doing the same routine he did years ago, Bowie doesn't. He does not pretend he is a twenty-year-old, he's not a sixty-year-old bouncing around.

Bowie is valued precisely because he can both respond to change, but does so in a way that is appropriate for a man at his stage of life. He offers a model of how to grow old with dignity, but rather than becoming old and stale he is capable of responding to new ideas and influences. Bowie is valued as someone who can help you respond to change in your own life, and some of the people I interviewed suggested to me that they were potentially overwhelmed by change. The sheer pace of technological and social change was threatening their sense of self. As we know, a life of constant change can be both exhilarating as well as threatening and dislocating. Bowie's capacity for self-reinvention was something that was admired by nearly everyone who followed his career. In the context of their own lives, the need to reinvent the self seemingly put many of the fans under intense amounts of pressure. This, it seems to me, is apparent in the following interchange on the future of the music industry:

> NS: So where do you think music is going?
>
> SIDNEY: I'm not sure. But the pace has changed, particularly in the environment that I work in. If I take the sort of work that I do in IT, the pace of change in IT is frightening. I'm sometimes envious of people who maybe chose plumbing or bricklaying as a career, yeah they're hard skills to learn and you spend five or six years at college learning them but once you have got them they are yours for life. Plumbing ain't going to change, laying bricks ain't going to change, but IT is a nightmare . . . you don't know how it's going to pan out. Will there ever be an artist like Bowie again or whether every artist will be flavour of the

month, Justin Timberlake is this year's and Britney Spears the year before and someone else the year before that I don't see any big stayers anymore . . . I mean Elvis fans are still Elvis fans even though he's been dead for thirty years. People will always love the Beatles, if they loved the Beatles, they will love the Stones, if they love the Stones; they will never go off it. It's like my old man, my dad, he's a Bob Dylan nut and has been a fan since 1962. I think he still buys the albums; my dad is pensionable age in seven years' time, he's still buying Dylan records. . . .

NS: Can you see yourself being like that?

SIDNEY: Yeah, quite probably. I think it could be with me until I'm dead, hopefully in a nice way, and that Bowie will die before me, unless there is something up with me I don't know about, but I imagine I will still be a Bowie fan after he's dead.

There are a number of important features here. Most obviously there is the idea of lifelong fandom and someone to stick with over the life course. Forming an intense connection to Bowie as a 'survivor' of cultural change offered hope in the capacity of the self to be able to adapt to a fast changing society. To be modern means embracing a culture of transformation and growth, and yet at the same time such a culture constantly threatens to destroy everything that we are (Berman 1982). The accelerating pace of change offers new possibilities as well as the destruction of our ways of life, hopes for the future and our current identities. The future may destroy our current skills, ways of life and communities but we can remain consistent in our tastes. This is particularly evident in the reference to this man's father who had maintained a lifelong interest in Bob Dylan. This situation is seemingly threatened by current transformations in the nature of celebrity. The cult of big stars is currently under threat from social and cultural change and the age of instantaneous celebrity.

Many older male fans expressed a concern that popular music was currently under threat because of the capitalist orientation of the music industry and technological change. In this respect, artists like Bowie were probably the last of a long line of mega-stars. In some fans this concern evoked lingering feelings of nostalgia for the more innocent world of the early seventies and in others it illustrated the decline of British national identity. There remains a specifically racial politics connected with these concerns that I want to return to later. For now, I note that there was a concern that music was increasingly driven by commercial imperatives and would not foster the necessary talent required to develop great artists. The anxiety is what will happen in the future to what we currently value? Fears of atomization, disintegration and above all meaninglessness are apparent in these and similar reflections. The anxiety is not just about what will happen to Bowie but also about what will happen to ordinary people in a fast-changing society. In an age where personal relationships are experienced as increasingly fragile, there are no more jobs for life and individuals are having to rely upon their own resources, figures like Bowie seemingly provide some comfort from the maelstrom. The hope is that investment in stars like Bowie will grant the self the resources it needs to carve out a more reflexive biography, although as I have been arguing this hope masks a considerable amount of anxiety. Just as the culture of celebrity has shortened the time between impact and obsolescence, so the pace of technological change means many now have to retrain and update their skills over the life-course. The culture of celebrity, far from being superficial, can be understood as the dramatization of permanently insecure individuals who can count on very little in a fast changing and insecure world. Indeed, as shown in the previous interview, this was not the first time that anxieties about human mortality were evident.

A fan comments on Bowie's recently reported heart murmur:

LEE: Then came the news the other day. The flash about the heart scare. I thought – shit – what if there is no more work. It's really selfish I know but I can't imagine there being no new work, as well as being concerned for the man himself, I can't imagine a world without him in it.

If Bowie offers his fans a resource for dealing with change, or at the very least cultural resources for handling difficult life events, then his own destruction is also feared. The fan being interviewed notably did not want to appear 'selfish'. His 'real' concern is if Bowie disappears then his personal 'guide' that allows him to navigate this difficult, risky and uncertain world will also be lost. If you like, if modern life is built upon constant change, then he will lose his way and his grip on what he might become.

Here I want to draw attention to the numerous religious metaphors that are apparent in many of the quotes above. This will not have escaped the attention of careful readers. To refer to Bowie as a 'teacher' or a 'guide' is more than just a reference to his cultural status and perhaps indicates something deeper. Other commentators have remarked upon the intimate connection between stars of popular music and the existential themes usually associated with religion. In particular, dead stars like Elvis Presley or John Lennon have long been treated like 'living' gods by many of their followers and fans. John Frow (1998) has argued that while cultural studies has long recognized the effect of star texts, it has had little to say on why mediated texts become appropriated in terms of the sacred. Basically, Frow argues that by identifying with a star, we attempt to defeat death. By connecting with a more-than-human being, we seek to move beyond human temporality into the mythic and the sacred. By identifying with an image that outlasts the death of any individual (including the real body of the star), we attempt to displace our anxieties in respect of our limited lifespans. Such a view undoubtedly has something going for it. We have already seen that Bowie is valued for his longevity and witnessed the anxiety that seems to be connected with his passing. In many of my interviews, Bowie was indeed identified as having a religious significance for his fans. This was evident in many of the metaphors drawn upon by fans to describe Bowie's cultural power. Particularly striking in one interview was a fan who had encountered many personal, family and social problems and who gave me the strong impression that if it were not for Bowie he would have had little reason to go on. He said little during the interview and was very reserved for most of our conversation. Eventually, he seemed to grow tired of my questions and gave me one of the most evidently passionate responses that I heard during my time interviewing fans:

MARTIN: You see, Nick, I live only for David.

In many of the fan accounts I have collected there is a discernible search for a figure of deeper meaning beyond the superficial cycles of commercial culture. As I said earlier, if modern life and commercial culture is increasingly signified by change, then identifying with a figure that has seemingly survived the accelerated fluctuations of musical fashion offers something more permanent. In the past it has been the job of the church to give meaning to life, birth and death; the search for symbols of ultimate value is still with us today. In these post-traditional times, however, such symbols may well have a multitude of sources. For example, David Lyon (2000) has argued that in a consumer culture individuals are increasingly prone to adopt a pick-and-mix approach to religion rather than simply conforming to a specific sect or tradition. Religious belief and sentiment is not so much in decline (as many have argued) but is increasingly individually negotiated. In our own terms we can extend these ideas. Bowie fans are not a religious sect (this would indeed be an overstatement) but use the language of the sacred to describe their different connections to David Bowie. For many of the men and women who participated in my study, Bowie has come to have an almost spiritual significance. That David Bowie could occupy such a role within many people's lives might seem surprising at first. Yet he was consistently referred to as 'the Pope of Pop' or as a 'god', someone who is 'up there' – 'he was like an icon, he was the ultimate, he was you know, God'. These religious metaphors are occasionally used ironically but more often they reveal a sense of devotion to Bowie as a cultural authority.

What of Frow's argument that this is an existential attempt to defeat death? While I don't think we can rule this out, I favour a different interpretation. Instead I think the religious metaphors of deep meaning and the anxiety in respect of death are more concerned with questions of individualization. In a fast-moving world, who can afford to stand still? The decline of class loyalties and bonds (along with growing income inequalities) means that individuals are increasingly thrown back on their own biographies, with human relations increasingly becoming susceptible to individual choice. For sociologist Ulrich Beck (1992), the classic plea of industrial society, 'I am hungry', is replaced with 'I am afraid'. Individualization means the disembedding of the ways of industrial society and the reinvention of new communal ties and biographies. As more areas of social life are less defined by tradition, our biographies involve choice and planning. We are therefore living in the age of DIY biographies. For Beck, 'people are invited to constitute themselves as individuals: to plan, understand, design themselves as individuals and, should they fail, to blame themselves' (Beck 1999). Individuals are condemned to become authors of their own lives. We are increasingly what we make of ourselves. Such a situation, I have been trying to suggest, is both liberating and threatening. We may not have to live by the 'old' rules, but who should we become and how should we live in these increasingly uncertain times? Indeed if Bowie has, as I suggested in chapter 3, been addressing such questions in his art then so, it seems, have his fans in their own lives. Fans are not, as popular stereotype would have it, sad, pathological or disturbed personalities. They are instead nomads, making sense of an increasingly fragmented social and cultural world with the cultural resources that they have to hand.

If Bowie can offer a sense of security by helping his fans handle change, there are evident perils in this distanced relationship. If we are increasingly a post-traditional culture then we are also increasingly a commodified culture. In this respect, Bowie's star image is a deep source of ambivalence. This was particularly striking in one case where a fan (like me) had followed Bowie since he had visited a friend's house when he was sixteen. His relationship with Bowie had been a source of confidence for him but in other respects had threatened the production of his own identity. Here I think I captured a more nuanced picture of the engagement of Bowie fans than is usually evident in more optimistic readings of fan accounts. For example, Jackie Stacey (1994), in her study of cinema audiences, found that, despite the 'other worldly' nature of stars, spectators regularly sought to take on aspects of their identity. That is, an intense relationship with a particular star or stars offered fantasies of personal transformation. By bringing the star or stars into the self, many reported that they were able to take on their attributes and characteristics. Women reported that they were able to fashion more rebellious forms of femininity or to gain personal confidence. Missing from this account is the pain of those who are unable to realize such dreams. Many undoubtedly feel themselves to be too poor or overweight to achieve media-defined standards of bodily perfection (Bird 2003). There may be many fans who feel that a relationship built over time with a star has mainly had positive consequences but who are blind to some of the more negative implications. Such features seemed particularly evident with one fan:

NS: Do you think he has influenced you?

MICKY: The image of Bowie is important. He has the sort of image that says come on, stand up for yourself. Be yourself. He gave me confidence. He was brave in 1972, to do what he did and has always been one step ahead. I think [patting his stomach] if I was a smaller person I would have done. The style changes, the haircut. You have to be able to engage with that. I didn't feel I had it in me. I couldn't do it . . . [falls silent].

This was a lifelong male fan who evidently felt he had been given 'confidence' by Bowie and yet had found it very difficult to maintain his appearance and body image in the same way as Bowie. In this respect, Bowie is literally 'up there', someone to be admired and be inspired by, but few people could realistically hope to be able to control their body shape in the way that Bowie has done. Indeed, as is well known, consumer societies are obsessed with thinness and the ability to be able to control your body. According to anthropologist Susan Bordo (1995), we currently live in the age of the 'plastic' body, viewed as a machine to be subjected to our will. In this respect, consumer societies regularly bombard the consumer with images of lean, controlled bodies as well as fat, unacceptable or out-of-control bodies. The image of Bowie may well have been inspirational. But it has also delivered an image many in more ordinary contexts find difficult to live up to.

With another fan, I explored at some length why it was better to be a follower of Bowie than to have a religion. This particular fan was unusual in that he recognized the link between the two. He had been describing how it was better to follow someone who actually existed rather than a being whose existence we could not be sure about.

NS: So you follow someone you can know about?

GUY: Well, you can see Bowie, you can listen to him, and it talks . . . you feel connected . . . one of the things in there [book made by the fan from fan websites] said, 'you feel you're connected to him, like your soul's connected to him, you have the same fundamental beliefs as he has.' And he's said so many things over the years that I just think, that's exactly what I feel like. That's exactly what I do. The image changes because you get fed up with it. People think, I can't do this and I can't do that, so I've always done that. I've always been the same as him. If you get fed up with something, change it. It's not for me . . .

NS: But do you think it's easier for him to change things?

GUY: Well, yeah, I know what you mean. It's obviously . . . it's going to be easier for him because he's his own boss, kind of thing . . . he genuinely believes that, that if you are bored and fed up with something then for God's sake change and if you want to do something else, do it . . . .

The ambivalence I tried to describe earlier between what can be gained from a star relationship is in evidence here. In a positive sense Guy – an unemployed working-class man in his fifties – argues that Bowie's image and music has had a profound effect upon his life. A great deal of the interview was spent describing to me how Bowie had helped him carve out an 'individual' identity and had sustained in him a sense of personal difference from his host culture. Guy's desire to become a writer and musician had meant he had to embark on a long, hard struggle. He had left art school after only a few months due to his lack of resources. Indeed much of his story, about doing it his own way, was also about the barriers he had encountered. When I asked him the question about whether change was easier for Bowie, I could tell that this was not something he had consciously thought about. Lacking the resources, security and cultural capital of a major star, 'doing you own thing' was evidently a lot tougher for Guy. Later in the interview, Guy (an experienced football fanzine writer) told me that he was currently trying to save £150 so that he could publish 300 copies of a planned Bowie fanzine. This was proving to be difficult. For Guy, the fact that his ideals were also Bowie's was the most important thing. Again what is most striking here is both Bowie's creativity and the power of his image. Indeed when I asked, as I did of many fans, whether they ever felt exploited by the Bowie industry, I consistently received the same response.

NS: Do you ever feel exploited by Bowie?
GUY: No. I think he gives them what they want. If you want to pay the prices you will pay them.

While Guy's individualism and intense connection with Bowie was a recurring theme of the interview, I could not help but think that sometimes this tended to obscure the fact that, for the music industry, fans of big stars are obviously an enormous market that they ruthlessly exploit. Most of the Bowie fans that I interviewed argued that it was important to be 'realistic', that they could not afford to buy everything Bowie-related that was readily available. Yet the argument that we are all sovereign individuals, deciding what to buy in the market place, does not really fit with either the intense affective connection many felt towards the star or a powerful music industry relentlessly reinventing Bowie's back catalogue for new waves of consumption.

So is it the case that Bowie's female followers do not build up such intense biographical connections? This is difficult to judge, given the inevitably limited number of people that I interviewed. What was noticeable was that it seemed common for some men to rediscover Bowie during times of crisis. This could be due to the often commented upon difficulty that men have in forming intimate relationships. Despite the shifting dynamics of masculinity, it seems that the giving and receiving of emotional support is still more often the common fare of women's relationships. Many heterosexual men often fear the emotional forms of vulnerability required of intimate relationships in case they be thought effeminate or homosexual. Further, men in our society continue to be taught that to be a man is to be able to be self-reliant. To have emotional needs is often understood as a sign of weakness. The idea that 'real' men do not need other people and are better served by putting their feelings to one side remains a central feature of modern culture. Indeed, as sociologist Victor Seidler (1997) comments, the dominant images and representations of masculinity often suggest the necessity of rejecting the past and disconnecting from personal relationships as a way of maintaining control over your biography. That a 'real man' stands alone continues to be a feature of much popular culture from Clint Eastwood to the more recent inventions of Eminem. As far as fans are concerned many men find it easier perhaps to receive emotional support from a relationship based on distance than they do from relationships based upon proximity. It is noticeable, as I indicated above, that Bowie is rediscovered at times of intense insecurity or emotional vulnerability. However, women too form intense relations with Bowie during times of emotional difficulty, the difference being that this tended to happen during adolescence.

One female fan told of her feelings of 'abandonment' at being sent to boarding school and another of identifying with Bowie as a way of dealing with the conflicts of her Jewish identity. Unlike most of the male interviewees, both these female fans were aware of and able to express the sexual dimension of this identification. The relationship formed with Bowie's star image was more significant at the time than the usual tales about being a fantasy boyfriend.

PATRICIA: I loved watching him. I mean I was obsessed with him physically, that androgynous thing of that time when you are still growing, almost non-gender, almost, that was for me what I really liked about him you know.

KATIE: I think it was about his ambiguous sexuality and the fact that he had different coloured eyes . . .

Both these women obviously enjoyed Bowie's ambivalent sexuality. Despite the taboos in this respect, some of the men I interviewed were aware of the homoerotic element of the relationship with Bowie, although their embarrassment was also evident.

LEE: It was moving and connecting. It meant something to me. It was like I was meant to find him. I was sixteen and still at school. I am heterosexual but I found him very attractive. You know, like you see lots of actors on films. Like James Dean. I just could not take my eyes off him.

MICKY: There is nothing more embarrassing than a forty-year-old bloke fawning over him. But at a concert, during 'My Death', you know the Jacques Brel song, they played that you know-when they shout 'me, me, me'. Well I was the first person on the front row to shout that. Got me some strange looks from Dorothy [girlfriend]. Side of me she didn't know. Best not say any more. [We both collapse with laughter.]

This aspect was mostly avoided by the other men that I interviewed. Again the reasons for this are complex, although admitting sexual feelings for another man is still difficult in a culture where men are encouraged to be ashamed or embarrassed about such feelings. Such feelings are more evidently policed in some social settings than others. The visual pleasure of men viewing other men is a feature of popular music and other aspects of visual culture that is perhaps not encountered in other areas of social life. This is not to argue that the men I interviewed are 'repressed' homosexuals, more that sexual pleasures are more ambivalent than much of mainstream society would like to believe. Throughout I was struck by how Bowie offered both men and women a different sense of what they could become by representing the partial unfixing of the scripts of dominant masculinity and the exploration of other, ambivalent possibilities.

> SIMON: I was just totally drawn in after seeing them do the *Top of the Pops* thing [Bowie singing 'Starman' with his arm around Mick Ronson]. I mean, loads of people around then at school were into, like, the heavy rock stuff. The people into the music became like the heavies and then there'd be a small pocket of people who were more into glam stuff and, like, I had Roxy Music's first album. You took it to school and it was, like, gorgeous women but it was like you were considered effeminate for liking a band like Roxy Music or Bowie.

For both the men and women I interviewed, it was evident that following Bowie offered (if mostly in their imaginations) the possibility of subverting the expectations of a parental world that sought to order, regulate and control the younger generation. Despite some of the differences between the men and women I interviewed, this issue was consistently returned to as a shared theme and concern. Listening to Bowie was a way of exploring imaginative alternatives to a world of rules, regulations and cultural norms that perhaps also represented a world beginning to crumble. Many of the people I spoke to told me how they did not 'fit the mould' and that Bowie gave them a relatively safe way of exploring difference. While I want to return to these themes later, what was evident for many of the people I met was that Bowie not only represented continuity within change but also that he was able to represent a society whose rules in respect of identity were beginning to loosen.

Fandom as a postmodern community?

So far I have concentrated upon the way that many Bowie fans, by forging a relationship with a distant other, were able to draw upon symbolic resources in their construction of self. Many recent commentators have been drawn to fans' cultures because they represent alternative forms of community. Seemingly much of the research on fandom is actually interested in how these new or postmodern forms of community might differ from or compare with communities based upon a shared sense of place. For example, Henry Jenkins (2003) has observed that many fans come together as virtual communities on the internet. Fans are increasingly able, due to the impact of the internet, to share their experiences, interact with other fans and make a new form of community based more on affinity than locality. Many of the fans interviewed were contacted through Bowie's official website, Bowienet, and I was keen to find out how significant this or other sites were to their fandom.

Part of the argument this debate is seeking to address is that the breakdown of old-style communities has left people isolated and fragmented, living increasingly lonely lives. People retreat to the internet when existing public spaces are privatized and wither away. This pessimistic view sees a society of strangers who have little contact with their actual neighbourhoods and only interact with people online. The withdrawal into the home as the centre of entertainment has meant that the ideal of community is under threat and in an increasingly fragmented world exists only, in this view, in the distant past. Virtual communities become sticking plasters for an increasingly isolated society. However, the French sociologist Michel Maffesoli (1996) rejects the idea of the isolated individual alienated by the operation of mass culture and points to what he calls the 'tribalization' of the social. The new tribes are based upon shared sentiments, whether they are regular visitors to an internet site, football supporters or even regular readers of a newspaper. These new emotional communities are constructed upon fleeting acts of identification and periodic warmth rather than on the stability of traditional ties. The argument here does not so much bemoan the ways in which capitalism has destroyed traditional forms of association as investigate the creative ways in which social solidarity might be reimagined in the postmodern age. This is the age of 'elective sociality' where we choose our own community (Maffesoli 1996: 86). This condition presupposes a society based upon a plurality of lifestyles and ethical investments where solidarity can be experienced through the practices of consumption, mediated images and computer networks. These new communities are easy to join, require little in the way of obligation and ensure that exit remains a permanent possibility. What they offer is intense experience of communal belonging; but this time the individual can withdraw if the experience proves to be unsatisfactory. On this view, the community or communities we belong to are always the result of individual choice.

Can we accurately describe Bowie fans as constituting a postmodern tribe? My argument would be that they fit the kind of community described above but with a number of important qualifications. One fan told me that he liked Bowienet as it offered him an experience of diversity in that Bowie fans were from a range of backgrounds. He had actually made some friends through the site and it transpired that most of these friends were men of a similar age and social status. He described in some detail how he was now part of a regular group that would meet up and go to Bowie concerts. This group had originally formed by chatting on the net about their shared interest. When I pushed him further to describe what this community meant to him, he commented:

> ZAK: Why I like Bowienet on the internet is 'cos you can get together with like-minded people; you're not ploughing a lonely little furrow somewhere.

Later in the same interview he expanded on this theme:

> ZAK: To me it's like a lot of lonely islands dotted around the place that all come together, becoming a big land mass. You don't feel alone anymore . . . part of something.

This feeling of being 'part of something' was significant, given that other parts of the interview concentrated upon the loss of his original community and background. Furthermore, meeting up with other fans can also take the edge off the suspicion that there is something peculiar about your own fandom.

174

ZAK: It's maybe a bit of reassurance that you are normal, you're earning a living, you know, and there are other people who feel the same way.

For another fan, chatting on the net about Bowie had led to the formation of a long-term relationship.

GUY: We first started communicating by e-mail, and, er, I said, 'Do you fancy a chat about Bowie?' and she said, 'is the Pope a Catholic?', like, and that were it, we were off, and it's just we found we had so much in common because of Bowie ... it's just like gone on and I am two weeks away from moving to be close to her.

Another couple I interviewed had not met on the internet but it played a key part in a new relationship. They both described to me how an interest in Bowie had been key to bringing them together, and they had recently visited Japan to see Bowie on the 2004 Reality tour. Yet what was more important for these fans was how the internet created a more intimate relationship with Bowie himself.

RICKY: He reads a lot of the fan mail on his website, doesn't he – you can see. And he does rehearsals on the net; he did one the other week and he said 'this is a new song, but not for those fans on the internet who've already got it' [laughs]. So you get this really fast feedback between him and his fans now, which isn't unique to him – a lot of bands, like REM, do that.

NANCY: Yeah and in that way the internet has helped that, hasn't it? It has just made it possible to do that stuff where the band answers questions and he [Bowie] puts his diary up there and engages with people and responds to questions and comments.

RICKY: .... I had a chat with four members of the band and I sat there at three o'clock in the morning, it could have been anyone but I thought that it was the band [laughs].

For many fans, the sense of being connected to other Bowie fans is important, and it seems that some relationships struck up on the net can be anything but fleeting. However, many other fans seemed less interested in joining a postmodern community and much more interested in gaining a closer relationship with Bowie. The invention of interactive websites seems to convert Bowie from being a remote star into a persona with whom you could forge an intimate relationship, albeit at a distance. The need for intimacy with Bowie has meant many of his fans have actually met him in person. This decision is a risky one as meeting your hero could prove to be a disappointment. Most of the fans I met talked about the risks that may be involved, should they try to meet Bowie in the future. This is a different image of a fan from that of the stalker we often read about in the tabloids. All the fans I met simply wanted to thank Bowie for giving their lives a meaning it might not otherwise have had. One describes a fairly typical encounter with Bowie:

> ZAK: The HMV signing he came to in Oxford Street to sign stuff, I managed to get in there and shook the guy's hand; that was the big Holy Grail, to shake his hand and say thank you for thirty years of my life and that was just fantastic. Again it was like a dream; it was over in a flash – I shuffled in, saw him in a flash and shuffled back out again, with the album signed.

None of the fans who had met Bowie had found it an anti-climax and most wanted to keep their distance and simply give their thanks to someone who had meant a great deal to them personally. In all of these instances there is a sense of community, or intense 'we' feelings, created by the Bowie fans. For some, this comes through keeping up with the latest Bowie news, while for others chatting and meeting up with fellow fans was an important experience which gave them a sense of belonging in a shifting world.

When speaking about fan communities, many interviewees made a distinction between real and fake fans. This, it turned out, was mostly a masculine obsession with record and CD collections but it points to the idea that there are actually communities within communities that identify different rules of belonging. To be a 'real' fan was not about being on the internet but having a collection which included Bowie's back catalogue, rarities and 'major' recordings. Particularly for male fans, this was indicative of status within the Bowie community.

> BENNY: You judge a fan by the record collection. If they only have the greatest hits, you are quite disdainful of someone like that. They don't understand the music, they haven't understood it like the real fans. They are just a casual listener.
> NS: What makes a fan?
> BENNY: The record collection is a sign.

Another fan summed up this attitude:

> MICKY: If you look through my record collection you'd know I was a David Bowie fan.

For many, the desire to mark themselves out as 'real' fans went well beyond collecting music, although this was always considered central. Another fan (who informed me he literally had 'thousands of pounds worth of stuff') revealed there was always someone who had a better or more developed collection. The anxiety was that as a fan you could never be 'real' enough. Clearly this fan felt that some fans were more authentic in their fandom.

> RICKY: There is this guy in Stoke. I mean he had like one hundred versions of 'Space Oddity' from every single country in the world it was released. I mean I have probably got ten 'Space Oddity' ones and he has got hundreds of them, thousands of them, just 'cos he wanted every single copy of every single version. I mean these people have got like 2,000.

Partly such statements are made to avoid the stigma of being obsessed. Many of the fans I interviewed were concerned about this particular label. Yet another part of the story relates to a fandom of one-upmanship, where buying a greatest-hits album and enjoying the music can be dismissed as 'casual listening'. Being a real fan is an identity you can only claim relative to other people. While you may dismiss some fans as not being serious, there is always the risk you will encounter someone else who will be equally dismissive about your collection. Here 'the collection' acts as a metaphor for masculine identity more generally. In this respect, the collections of real fans can never be full enough. It is like a hypermasculine form of identity that can never be achieved and is always insecure. As the feminist sociologist Lynne Segal (1995) has argued, masculinity (like the record collection) is always incomplete; men must possess the power to assert control over women, other men and themselves. The contradiction that real fandom and traditional masculinity have to deal with is that each time they assert themselves, they also call themselves into question. Just as powerful masculinity is dependent upon the relative weakness of the other, so with real fans their sense of authenticity is dependent upon the inadequacy of other people's collections. While many of the women fans recognized the obsession with record collections as 'blokeish', some male fans withdrew from the competitive nature of possession. One fan described to me how he was not a 'completist', that he did not really understand the need of many fans 'to try and have everything' and that 'some people say to be a completist you've got to have more money than sense or be obsessional.' This fan explained to me how bringing up a family on a tight budget meant that he did not have the income to be too obsessional. If some fans were able to fly to concerts across the world, others had only seen Bowie a few times, mostly at local venues. This was demonstrated to me in a moving story from a currently unemployed man who had waited over thirty years to see Bowie:

GUY: I got into him in '72 and it was 2002 before I ever saw him live. First I wasn't old enough, then he went to America, then he came back and I was unemployed at art college, so I couldn't see him on the Station-to-Station tour. I wasn't that bothered about seeing him live on the Let's Dance tour . . . I thought I was never going to see him live, and finally in 2002 he played Old Trafford. It was going to be thirty quid. I couldn't afford it. Like anyway, me two daughters and me brother came round to the house the night before I moved out, 'cos like me marriage split was amicable so I was living in there until I moved in here, they came round one night and me eldest daughter said to me put your favourite David Bowie track on dad and I went 'why?' and she went 'just put it on, just put it on', and I thought strange, but honestly I had no idea whatsoever, so *Heathen* had just come out so I put 'Slow Burn' on. She went right, 'this is from us' and gave me a ticket, I literally just froze. I couldn't believe it.

The divisions of class make the achievement of 'real' fandom a more difficult achievement for some people than others. Whatever their class position, the authenticity of fandom was an ongoing concern for many of the men.

NS: What makes a proper fan?

MICKY: You would have to look at the record collection. You see I'm a bit of a Bowie fascist. You have to look at their record collection to see what they've got; they have to be able to name your three tracks off *Buddha of Suburbia*. You have to look through their record collection to see what they've got. They have to have Outside, Black Tie.

NS: Right.

MICKY: I suppose I am overboard.

Here we can see how talk of a Bowie community partially masks its own internal hierarchical nature where some fans are presumed to be more 'authentic' than others. Such was the power of this discourse I often found myself doubting whether I was actually a Bowie fan myself, having previously bought greatest hits' collections and admittedly only buying all the albums because I happened to be writing this book. Despite many postmodern writers claiming that fans build alternative communities and networks, what was apparent was the overtly masculine nature of this community where a sense of inclusion was largely governed by the size of your record collection. In conversation male participants would stress that they were mostly interested in 'the music' before moving on to discuss Bowie's image. Again, being overly concerned with 'the look' or with Bowie's image was supposedly indicative of a more feminine set of concerns.

BENNY: It's essentially a music thing.

Despite many men's prioritizing of 'the music', it was apparent that their interest in the singer was also tied to Bowie's image.

> BENNY: I've been to '70s fancy dress parties. If I go, I go as Ziggy Stardust. With my thirtieth birthday coming up, I thought I am not going to do that. I have done that before. Actually in [Midlands town] about four or five years ago I did go to a '70s night with work. Most people go in big Afros, I went as David Bowie.
>
> NS: How did you feel?
>
> BENNY: A bit ridiculous.

In another part of the interview, this fan said he had been aware of wanting to be David Bowie, and then had pushed this idea away, as he told me he was happy as himself. As we saw earlier, identifying with a star rarely signifies the desire to change places but rather the need to take on an aspect of their personality. It was obvious from my interviews that for many men this was often experienced as internally troubling. The reason for this I think can be found again in the dominant ideas of masculine self-sufficiency. If a real man stands alone, then his identity should be his own authentic self-creation. In this respect, it is easy to see why so many men are attracted to Bowie. Not only does he periodically reinvent himself but he does so in an uncompromising way. The irony is that despite Bowie's flirtation with gay and bisexual politics, it is his ability to be able to control his identity and self-image that is so highly valued. According to psychoanalyst Jessica Benjamin (1990), the idea of the self-sufficient individual is not only masculine in origin but remains the hegemonic cultural ideal. Such a view suggests individuals should simply stand on their own two feet without relying upon other people or the community for support. This ideal is masculine as it attempts to banish more 'feminine' considerations such as nurture, responsiveness and the need for more physical forms of comfort. These latter features are usually associated with the kind of relationships mothers have with dependent children. The emotional logic of this situation roughly translates as: if he is able to transform himself, then the same should apply to me. We have already seen how similar processes can be detected in some of Bowie's invented characters like Halloween Jack and The Thin White Duke. As I also argued earlier, many fans evidently found it difficult to live up to the example set by their 'guide'. In order to cope with divorce, one fan decided to change his hair colour to try and maintain a youthful image. Rather than enjoying his capacity to transform himself, more complex feelings were not far from the surface.

NS: What was the reaction at the time?

MICKY: Shock. Not my partner as she helped me do it. She is quite open to ideas. She helped me. It came as a surprise. I'm not the sort that does this.

NS: How did you feel?

MICKY: At first I enjoyed the fact I could do something to shock people. That validated it; I wasn't just a middle-aged bloke. I could get a reaction. It was validation.

NS: Is 25 middle aged?

MICKY: It felt like it at the time. My marriage was breaking up. I was suddenly married and then divorced. It was kicking against this bloke who'd been married and divorced. It still crosses my mind [laughs]. But that was the end of the hair-dying phase [said sadly].

Many fans appear gripped by Bowie's capacity to both control and transform his identity. Seduced by the possibility of becoming something different, they find changing one's hairstyle will not necessarily deflect more troublesome feelings.

If class and gender divide the Bowie community, the same can also be said of race. At times the pleasure gained from Bowie's music was expressed by the fans as a kind of defensive 'white' Englishness.

SID: I don't know, and certainly please don't take this the wrong way or anything racial, but black music I just don't, I don't like black music. I suppose I don't like music where dance or rhythm is emphasised above lyrical context perhaps. I get quite hooked on songs with meaningful lyrics as well as a hook or two and a rhythm.

Elsewhere in the interview, this fan claimed that, whereas Bowie's music was 'intelligent', black music on the contrary was more about the body and rhythm. The explicitly racial overtones of these remarks were rare but they do link into ideas about national decline evident in the interview material. Indeed I often wondered whether the belief that rock music was in decline depended less on the impact of capitalism (as indicated earlier) than on the way that an essentially 'white' category had been displaced by other genres such as rap, reggae and dance music that were less securely located in a specific ethnic identity. Such belief seems to be borne out in the following exchange.

NS: It's often said the English like eccentrics.
MICKY: Yes but there is not many of them left. They are few and far between these days. It's the old island mentality, we are used to being set apart from everything. But today everything's just a big corporation. In the music business now it's just music by committee.

It may not be pressing the point too far to suggest that the regret expressed in respect of the decline of the 'big' rock star is a coded way of mourning national decline. For some, fandom is expressive of the decline of a white 'island race' into the shifting and less certain world of the multicultural present. The cultural critic Paul Gilroy (2004) has argued that, in the British context, national melancholia is often linked to the perceived erosion of a white Englishness. While Britishness remains a contested term, the nation continues to refuse to face its own imperial and colonial past, which would mean reconstructing itself as a multicultural nation. Indeed, just as many fans appear to take refuge in the ebbing privileges of masculinity, so do they in 'whiteness'. Yet as with masculinity, we need to tread carefully since for many fans Bowie offers an escape from Englishness into a more European identity:

PETER: It takes me right back to the time, it was all very exciting . . . straight out of boarding school and in London doing art,
which is doing what I wanted to do. That was a good time. It
evokes the time, but also that kind of European thing as well. I
think that is one of the things that drew me to Bowie's work.

This is less dismay at Britain's relative decline than the exploration of other possibilities beyond exclusively defined national
communities. Such is the complexity of the fans' identification
it is clear that the Bowie community is not a homogeneous one,
but equally it is not always a community that celebrates difference. In particular the structuring capacity of class and the
overtly masculinized and racialized rhetorics evident should be
enough to complicate any simplistic talk of an easily accessible
and shared tribalism or escape from loneliness into the warmth
of shared enthusiasm.

The consuming self: outsiders, rebels and everyday magic

In this final section, I want to outline some of the discourses and
repertoires that became apparent as the fans sought to understand what an interest in Bowie had given them. So far I have
been mainly concerned with how fan identities seek to anchor
a narrative of self and sustain a sense of community with or
exclusion from others. Here I am less concerned with differences than with a set of common narratives and discourses that
were drawn upon by most of the people that I interviewed. Lest
anyone doubt the significance that Bowie had for many of the
people I interviewed, I want to borrow a phrase from Annette
Kuhn (2002) and argue that David Bowie for many people
represents a form of 'everyday magic'. By this is meant that the
connection many fans felt with Bowie was articulated in terms
that went beyond the category of rationality and became more
associated with a sense of wonder and mystery. These special
moments took different forms and often involved ideas of fate
or significant turning points in people's lives. This points to

a connection between stars, fans and religion. Many fans find within Bowie a sense of the sacred. Indeed, as I have already indicated, other research into fandom has identified similar patterns. Daniel Cavicchi (1998) discovered many American Bruce Springsteen fans talked of being 'converted', going on 'pilgrimages' and of 'bringing him into their lives'. Yet the 'magic' I am seeking to describe both goes beyond the 'ordinary' but has no necessary connection to the sacred. To offer two examples from the many I listened to:

NS: And you have seen him live quite a few times?

ZAK: Yeah, quite a few times.

NS: Can you remember the first time?

ZAK: I can tell you what should have been the first time, that is quite interesting, what should have been the first time was 1973, erm, Glasgow at Greens Playhouse. I was on my way to school, this is why I know that I was meant to be a David Bowie fan (. . .) I was interested in him anyway and I can't remember if I had [missed words] how big a fan I was at the time but I was on my way to school and came across this waste ground and I looked down at the ground and I saw a purse, a girl's purse and I picked it up and had a look inside and it was full of ticket stubs and there was all sorts of ticket stubs in there, everything that came to Glasgow, but amongst that there was one full ticket, one full ticket for David Bowie in Glasgow. There was no name, no address, nothing in the purse, nothing of value except for this one ticket and I struggled with my conscience: what do I do with this ticket, do I go to the concert? At that time I'd never been to a concert before and I said, I thought what if I go to the concert and she has got a friend in the next seat and she knows that I've got her ticket and she might think that I have stolen this purse. So in the end I didn't go, but I kept the ticket. I don't have it any more, it's gone.

NS: That's a really nice story.

ZAK: But that's when I knew that there was something about this guy – something was there, someone up there wanted me to go and see him, but my conscience wouldn't let me go.

A female fan told me that, after seeing Bowie on *Top of the Pops* in 1972, 'my life turned around':

WENDY: When I first passed me driving test and had a brand new red Escort and and I went out in it, I felt fantastic, windows open, music blaring out [Bowie], it was really good.

Both of these experiences can also be attributed to the ability of the consumer society to offer relatively pleasurable forms of escape and the dream-like promise of a world of abundance rather than of austerity. These hedonistic moments are part of the considerable allure that consumer societies wield over their citizens. The temporary escape from the mundane into a realm of short-lived fantasy is the stuff of popular desires, enjoyed (however guiltily) by many people in today's society. In terms of celebrity, it seems some of the magic of star personality temporarily rubs off on the fans. By associating ourselves with the stars, we too can live (if only for a moment) with a sense of enchantment. As we saw above, this can entail a connection with a star that was 'meant to be' or simply signify a momentary transition.

Despite Bowie's everyday magic, there were two discourses or repertoires articulated by almost everyone I interviewed when I asked them to ponder their own personal connection to Bowie. I now want to discuss these before bringing this chapter to a close.

'The outsider'

Many fans recognized Bowie's image as that of the 'outsider'. Bowie was the man who did not quite fit in, who was not mainstream, who operated at the margins. Further many fans then linked this – with little prompting from myself – to periods of their own life when they felt themselves to be outsiders. This was usually, although not exclusively, during their teenage years.

MICKY: I was an outsider. If like a lot of teenagers you did not belong to the gang or get that feeling of the outsider, that was the main thing. Bowie made a lot of sense. He still does to a degree but not as much as he used to. He still has that outsider. I think that was the main thing. I can only assume going back to the seventies. Watching Starman on *Top of the Pops*. As a lot of teenagers, if you don't belong to a group or set then Bowie makes a lot of sense. Because he does not fit in – well he does now to a degree; there was always the feeling of the outsider there. I didn't feel part of the crowd.

The mistake here I think would be to suggest that Bowie fans are isolated individuals, when actually the sense of not being part of the 'in-crowd' is an experience most people can identify with at some period in their lives. Bowie's popularity and the intense loyalty he inspires in his many fans is built upon feelings of isolation to which so many can relate.

> NS: Why does he resonate with you?
> MARTIN: Definitely felt like the outsider. You know you are not as involved in things as you should be . . . he likes that, he likes outsiders. There is that aspect. In that sense, you feel like he is singing to you, and I know people say that. I'm not a loner, but I've never been the life and soul of the party, but I've been on the edge watching other people and I think, yeah, that does come into it.

Some of the ways that people identified with Bowie 'the outsider', hence reaffirming their own identity as outsider, were very creative. For example, one woman I interviewed explained how for much of her teenage years she had felt both depressed and excluded by her schools and her parents' own personal problems. Her interest in Bowie as an outsider came through a book she had read about Christina X. The book tells a story of a young Berlin woman's life as a prostitute and drug addict. Yet this fan was clear she did not want to be Christina X, but she identified with the story as being about abandonment. As Bowie provided the soundtrack to the film this led to an interest in him and she soon purchased the Berlin albums, '*Heroes*' and *Low*.

> MAXINE: I loved to be like Christina X so I had jeans and a jean jacket. I hennaed my hair, looked sallow [laughs] I was kind of morose, I cultivated a heroin chic without the heroin and before it became chic, and I didn't listen to anyone else. I pooh-poohed

everything else. I actively . . . [pauses] what's the word I am looking for, dismissed it.

While the primary identification was with Christina X, the image seemingly maps onto the sense of alienation also associated with Bowie. What was noticeable was that while still a fan, this woman rarely listened to Bowie anymore. The more she talked, the more she began to realize why. The memory of the isolated young woman she used to be was evidently still painful.

> MAXINE: I don't listen to Bowie now because you don't have to that much. Also because I got into a lot of trouble at school . . . I was very disruptive at school and it carried on really and I was disruptive at home and it really carried on to my 'A'levels and till just before I went off to college. So, yeah, I guess that although I clearly really loved the music maybe listening to the music now makes me think about that teenager, and actually that is really quite painful and we weren't a family that were able to deal with me depressed.

Not surprisingly given these associations, she had not continued to follow Bowie's career. Other fans claimed the outsider as a more positive identity, although as we shall see it is a source of considerable ambivalence.

> GUY: You see I've always had to do this kind of thing. You see, it's not like . . . I've tried it a few times, I used to try and conform to what society, I suppose, would like me to be. I can't do it, I've tried, I just can't do it.

This fan went on to describe how, after a number of relationship breakdowns and attempts to adopt a male breadwinner role, he had reconciled himself to living quite differently. He had written football fanzines, a book (as yet unpublished) about Bowie and played for a number of years in a Bowie tribute band. Specifically, his identification with Bowie as an outsider had helped him sustain a positive identity despite the evident difficulties he had also had to negotiate.

'Respectable rebels'

The image of the outsider also resonated with a sense that many people had of themselves as rebels. Yet what I noticed here was that they were all concerned about going too far; they were 'respectable' rebels. This does not mean that being a 'rebel' could be dismissed as trivial. For many this had proved to be an enduring aspect of their identity. There was an ongoing sense of 'break the rules, be yourself, but don't go too far'.

> GUY: I'm like a pleasant anarchist, if you like, you know what I mean?
> NS: That's a nice phrase.
> GUY: Well, I try to live by me own rules, I try to do what I wanna do, when I wanna do it, like, I'll eat when I wanna do it, like, I'll eat what I eat, sleep when I wanna sleep, sing when I wanna sing, stuff like that, but I won't allow myself to upset other people.
> NS: What does it take to be a rebel?
> MICKY: Doing your own thing with talent. You know, kind of like an eccentric.

Another fan described to me how, having grown up on a Greek island, her parents were somewhat relieved that she had discovered David Bowie rather than joining the anarchists who were engaged in a particularly violent conflict with the authorities. There was a sense of rebellion, but of always knowing there was a line you should not cross. The displacement from their surrounding community that many fans had found in Bowie was part of an ongoing concern that had significantly shaped their teenage and adult lives. This was particularly evident in the account of a Jewish woman whose lifelong quest was to adopt a different identity to that expected of her by her family and the wider community.

> KATIE: I think I'd already had a tendency towards that sort of weirdness in dressing and stuff like that; and then I got into the music as well, at that time. And then I think I just happened

to gravitate towards them because they were into that more unconventional, not particularly Jewish thing. Because as you can imagine there's sort of various people into religious stuff, then there's people sort of into Zionist, socialist groups and I did that a bit, but these people were just a bit more, a bit more fun I suppose.

As we have already seen, identifying with Bowie can mean joining an 'alternative' community, but in this instance it was a group of young Jewish men and women who liked to dress up, listen to music and go out with each other to local clubs. While 'rebelling' in terms of dress, when Katie began going out with non-Jewish men, she kept it secret from her parents. Such 'rebellion' always stopped short of renouncing her Jewishness despite her need to articulate her personal difference while continuing to belong.

KATIE: I did not want to be Jewish.
NS: You did not want to be Jewish?
KATIE: No, no, oh God no, I was totally in denial. For me it stood for everything I did not want to be, I didn't want to do. It was all about you can't do, you can't eat that, you can't do this, you can't go out on Saturday night, you can't go out on Friday night.

Throughout the interview, the need to belong yet still carve out a sense of personal difference was clear.

NS: You were visually different then.
KATE: Well, I am a bit visibly different now, as well, because I don't – people comment on what I wear, or jewellery I've got something like that, because I can kind of pick out things that are a bit different. But I don't fit the mould. A lot of them don't work – the women that is – they have a stereotypical life-style, sort of pampered blah blah blah. And I'm like this manic woman who works full-time and runs around like a lunatic – they just don't get me.

Evidently these remarks could be understood in terms of individualization, the need to choose your own identity in different situations. But I think this takes us only so far. I noticed that almost everyone I interviewed connected a discovery of Bowie with a search for personal distinctiveness. Such was the power of his image that fans felt the need to keep consuming it over and over again. This meant that despite talk of the sovereign consumer ('if you don't want it, don't buy it'), I was more struck by the huge personal and financial investment many fans had in Bowie. A female fan captured this:

> NANCY: I mean, he has become this kind of icon, this idol, this amazing man who seems to have the capacity to keep reinventing himself, reinventing new stuff.

Through the discourses of the 'outsider' and the 'respectable rebel', Bowie is able to find a link with fans across the globe. It is quite possible that his ability to transmit these features into popular music best accounts for his commercial and artistic success amongst his many followers.

We are all Bowie fans

Viewed romantically, Bowie fans are a community of outsiders. I think the term 'respectable rebels' is complex in that what they actually represent is a society where no one actually wants to 'fit the mould'. Bowie's emergence as a celebrity and star of popular music during the seventies and eighties came at a time when most people of the post-sixties' generations did not want to be perceived as part of the traditional order. Ours is a society where tradition is increasingly questioned but people still have a strong need to belong while also wanting to be themselves. Again for many fans, Bowie is attractive because through his music, image and style he is able to dramatize this ambiguity. My claim is not that Bowie fans are interesting because they represent a relatively marginalized subculture. On the contrary, as I argued earlier, anyone can be a Bowie fan. Instead, what Bowie fans highlight is the search to reconcile personal difference and a sense of belonging. Bowie fans embody not so much a world of potential stalkers but the need to create significance that gives the self a sense of continuity in a shifting and uncertain world. What Bowie fans do is help to highlight a culture where many people feel deeply uncertain about who they should become. In this respect, people are looking to stars and celebrities to offer inspiration as to how they might realize the self. These features are identified in much of Bowie's music which deals with these and similar questions. As we have seen, despite the ideology of instant transformation so beloved by the consumer age, some are in better positions than others to utilize this particular message. Further, we also saw how so-called alternative communities continue to be distinguished by features such as class, race and above all gender. While many fans look to the pleasures of popular culture as a way of escaping the mundane, they inevitably remain trapped by a number of powerful features that continue to structure modern society. These fragments, then, I hope demonstrate more about the ambivalence of individual freedom than they do about the supposed pathology of the Bowie fans that I had the pleasure of meeting.

seven

CONCLUSION: DAVID BOWIE TODAY

This book has told the story of a celebrity who became a star. It is true that Bowie's star no longer shines as brightly as it once did, but his story tells us a great deal about the times in which we have lived. David Bowie now lives in New York with his wife Iman and his young daughter. Part of his image these days is that of the happily married man who has put behind him the radical bohemianism of youth to become a liberal bohemian. As many of his fans will testify, Bowie no longer tries to act like a twenty-year-old and is proof positive that it is possible to grow old gracefully in popular music. However, as many of his recent television appearances indicate, part of the continued fascination with Bowie is his masculinity and his body. Most of his recent interviews are less concerned with his new art but if anything offer narratives of survival. Bowie, nicknamed 'the Dame', has come through the unpredictable twists and turns of a theatrical life full of incident. That he is still with us and making music despite the drugs, alcohol and rock 'n' roll lifestyle is a source of constant intrigue for many. Outside of his devoted fans, people are perhaps more interested today in Bowie's fitness regime, diet and home life than they are in his music. How could Bowie defy the ordinary logic of bodily decline and mortality that has been so cruel to many of his generation? That Bowie has made the transition to being a heterosexual family man still invites comment and conjecture. Bowie, in his art and his life, makes no secret of his past inventions and resists the idea that they can simply be dismissed as youthful fancy.

For those of us still interested in his music, questions of mortality have come into sharp focus on some of his most recent recordings. The most important of these has been the 2002 Mercury Music prize nomination, *Heathen*. The album beautifully articulates a sense of an unwritten future while pondering some of the risks and fears of the present era. Undoubtedly the events of September 11th have had a profound effect upon Bowie. Gone it seems is the period of optimism which followed the end of the Cold War. The new global era is dominated by the threat of terrorism, potential ecological collapse and the uncertain flows of money. What *Heathen* depicts is the sheer impossibility of protecting yourself from the risks and dangers of our shared world. If someone as rich and powerful as David Bowie is anxious, then we should all be looking over our shoulders. It was reported that during the attack on the twin towers in New York, Iman witnessed the events not live on television but from the couple's apartment window. Bowie at this time talked about leaving the city that he loves, possibly to return home to London. That he has not done so says more about his reluctance to give up life in New York where the sighting of stars is an everyday if not banal occurrence.

Part of *Heathen*'s success was to convey a sense of the fragility of all our lives. We all live in a potentially dangerous world where the future offers few guarantees for our children or ourselves. The title *Heathen* refers to the fact that we have to face such a future without any certainty of what will happen to us now or indeed in the afterlife. This, as I have argued at some length, is a recurrent theme in Bowie's artistic output stretching back at least as far as *Hunky Dory* and *The Man Who Sold the World*. What are we to become in a godless universe where we are confronted by many possibilities and dangers? Bowie has struggled with these questions long and hard while making some of the most affecting music ever to grace the canons of popular song.

Such are the anxieties surrounding the decline of Bowie's body that there was a furore over his recent heart scare. Britain's bestselling newspaper ran with the headline, 'Bowie had Heart Attack' (*Sun*, Saturday, 10 July 2004). Inside, the paper speculated, 'Did Golden Years Catch Up With Ziggy Stardust'? Bowie it seems was finally paying the price of his past excesses. This indeed is a form of populist revenge that repeatedly informs us that popular music has helped deliver a society of irresponsible hedonism. But such a punitive logic goes against the grain of this book. That Bowie has at times been less than responsible is undeniable. However there is more to his story than the premature illness of a star who went too far. Bowie's is a story about the ambivalence of modern identity. Since the early seventies Bowie has done more than most to bring this question into the centre of our lives. Bowie has encapsulated a society that continues to struggle with questions of normality and difference. When most of the old certainties come into question, what to be is a central issue of our time. More than technological change or even globalization, such issues are probably troubling more people more profoundly than any other. Bowie has lived through a period which has seen the capacity of society to order identity go into decline or at least be redefined. This is the age of becoming. He has undoubtedly (sometimes not for the better) contributed to our understanding of these aspects of modern identity. His central message is the awareness that each of us must choose and fashion ourselves. Who would have thought that the old gender-bender of glam rock would become a happily married father? Who indeed would have predicted that his career would come to mean so much to so many, and that he would still be with us in the new millennium, asking us to think again? Part of the fascination with Bowie has been the way he has multiplied our shared sense of the possible. If I have not always been convinced that we all have the same opportunities to reconstitute ourselves in the way Bowie suggests, he has at least cracked many conservative ideas that we simply have to make do with who we currently are. Change is an ever-present if ambivalent possibility. Bowie has delivered this message over the years to popular audiences all over the world which is reason enough to continue to take him seriously. Whatever happens to David Jones, David Bowie will be with us for some years to come.

These points make it is hard to deny that Bowie resembles a blank commodity that keeps reproducing itself. If Bowie is a bohemian, he is also an astute entrepreneur. The figure of the cool businessman who first made his way into Bowie's repertoire in the early eighties has never been far away. The millennium saw Bowie develop an innovative website (www.bowie.net) and his own online bank (www.bowiebanc.com). Despite Bowie's creative re-birth in the nineties, it seems that the further along the path of commodification Bowie travelled, the more he has gone into artistic decline. Bowie's cultural difference now appears as the frills on top of a mainstream rock act, making interesting if not arresting music for a middle-aged audience. David Bowie's story is also about how Pop Art's attack on 'seriousness' ends with art simply becoming another commodity to be bought and sold in the market place. The tension that continued to exist during the seventies between artistic invention and the strategies of the music industry has finally collapsed amidst an endlessly repackaged back catalogue. Today it is Bowie's body and middle-aged vigour that invites media interest, his music being (sometimes unfairly) relegated to a secondary role. Bowie in this sense is the perfect expression of the depthless postmodern lifestyle experienced by the winners of late capitalism. If Bowie exemplifies change and adaptation, so does a restless postmodern capitalism that continually urges its products and subjects to search for competitive advantage. If Bowie is going to surprise us again, it is less likely to be with his music than with a new financial strategy as he seeks to keep ahead of the game in a cut-throat market.

Yet Bowie continues to inspire musicians and people who feel themselves to be 'outsiders' all over the world. The British-based *New Musical Express* magazine recently voted David Bowie the most influential artist of all time, ahead of the Beatles in third place (*NME*/30.11.2000). Since the millennium, Bowie has continued to work with a number of new musicians such as the Polyphonic Spree, Avril Lavigne and Arcade Fire, all hoping to be inspired by collaboration with a man who has changed popular music beyond all recognition. While his creative edge may never again be what it once was, his cultural and musical legacy is a story full of contradictions likely to be mined for some time to come.

DAVID BOWIE DISCOGRAPHY
(SELECTED)

David Bowie, Deram DML 1007 (June 1967)

David Bowie, Phillips SBL 7912 (November 1969)

The Man Who Sold the World, Mercury 6338041 (US November 1970, UK April 1971).

Hunky Dory, RCA SF8244 (December 1971)

The Rise and Fall of Ziggy Stardust and The Spiders From Mars, RCA SF8287 (June 1972)

Aladdin Sane, RCA RS1001 (April 1973)

PinUps, RCA RS1003 (October 1973)

Diamond Dogs, RCA APL1 (April 1974)

David Live, RCA APL20771 (October 1974)

Young Americans, RCA RS106 (March 1975)

Station to Station, RCA APL-1327 (January 1976)

ChangesoneBowie, RCA RS1055 (May 1976)

Low, RCA PL12030 (January 1977)

'Heroes', RCA PL 12522 (October 1977)

Stage, RCA PL02913 (September 1978)

Lodger, RCA BOWLP1 (May 1979)

Scary Monsters (and Super Creeps), RCA BOWLP2 (September 1980)

Christiane F. Wir Kinder Vom Bahnhof Zoo, RCA 4239 (soundtrack) (April 1981)

ChangesTwoBowie, RCA BOWLP3 (November 1981)

Let's Dance, EMI America AML 3029 (April 1983)

Ziggy Stardust – The Motion Picture, RCA PL84862 (October 1983)

Tonight, EMI America DB1 (September 1984)

Never Let Me Down, EMI America AMLS 3117 (April 1987)

Tin Machine, EMI-USA MTLS1044 (May 1989)

Tin Machine II, 8282721 (May 1989)

Discography

Sound+Vision (4 CD Boxed set) Rykodisc, RCD90120/21/22 (November 1989)

ChangesBowie, EMI DBTV1 (March 1990)

Tin Machine Live – Oy Vey Baby, Victory 828328 (August 1992)

Black Tie White Noise, Arista 7432113697 (April 1993)

The Buddha of Suburbia, Arista (November 1993)

1. Outside, RCA 74321310662 (September 1995)

Earthling, RCA 7432144944 (February 1997)

hours, Virgin CDV2900 (October 1999)

Heathen, Columbia 5082229 (2002)

Reality, Columbia 5125553 (2003)

BIBLIOGRAPHY

Adorno, T. (1991) *The Culture Industry*, London: Routledge.

Almond, M. (1999) *Tainted Life*, London: Macmillan.

Arendt, H. (1969) *On Violence*, New York: Harvester.

Baker, S. (2000) *The Postmodern Animal*, London: Reaktion Books.

Bakhtin, M. (1968) *Rabelais and his World*, Bloomington: Indiana Press.

Barthes, R. (1974) *S/Z*, London: Jonathan Cape.

Baudelaire, C. (1995) *The Painter of Modern Life and Other Essays*, trans. and ed. by Jonathan Mayne, London: Phaidon.

Bauman, Z. (2004) *Identity*, Cambridge: Polity.

Beck, U. (1992) *Risk Society*, London: Sage.

Beck, U. (1999) *World Risk Society*, Cambridge: Polity.

Benjamin, J. (1990) *The Bonds of Love: Psychoanalysis, Feminism and the Problem of Domination*, London: Virago.

Benjamin, W. (1973) *Illuminations*, London: Fontana Press.

Berman, M. (1982) *All That Is Solid Melts Into Air: The Experience of Modernity*, New York: Simon & Schuster.

Bird, S. E. (2003) *The Audience in Everyday Life*, London: Routledge.

Bockris, V. (1995) *Lou Reed: The Biography*, London: Vintage.

Bordo, S. (1995) *Unbearable Weight: Feminism, Western Culture and the Body*, California: University of California Press.

Bowie, A. (with Patrick Carr) (1993) *Backstage Passes*, London: Orion.

Bowie, D. (1980) *In His Own Words*, London: Omnibus Press.

Bradley, D. (1992) *Understanding Rock 'n' Roll: Popular Music in Britain 1955–1964*, Buckingham: Open University Press.

Bromell, N. (2000) *Tomorrow Never Knows: Rock and Psychedelics in the 1960s*, Chicago and London: University of Chicago Press.

Buckley, D. (1999) *Strange Fascination: David Bowie the Definitive Story*, London: Virgin Books.

Burroughs, W. S. (1969) *The Wild Boys: A Book of The Dead*, New York: Grove Press.

Butler, J. (1990) *Gender Trouble*, London: Routledge.

Cavanagh, D. (1997) 'ChangesfiftyBowie', *Q Magazine*, February 1997, <www.bowiewonderworld.com/press/press90.htm>

Cavicchi, D. (1998) *Tramps Like Us: Music and Meaning among Springsteen Fans*, Oxford: Oxford University Press.

Chambers, I. (1985) *Urban Rhythms: Pop Music and Popular Culture*, Basingstoke: Macmillan.

Cole, S. (1999) 'Invisible men: gay men's dress in Britain, 1950–1970' in A. de la Haye and E. Wilson (eds), *Defining Dress: Dress as Object, Meaning and Identity*, Manchester: Manchester University Press.

Coleman, R. (1972) 'A star is born', *Melody Maker*, 15 July 1972.

Copetas, C. (1974) 'Beat Godfather meets Glitter Mainman', in E. Gutman and D. Thompson (eds), *The Bowie Companion*, New York: Da Capo Press.

Dalton, S. and Hughes, R. (2001) 'Trans-Europe Excess', *Uncut*, 47, April 2001.

Denski, S. and Sholle, D. (1992) 'Metal men and glamour boys: Gender performance in heavy metal', in S. Craig (ed.), *Men, Masculinity and the Media*, London: Sage.

Deevoy, A. (1989) 'Boys keep swinging', *Q Magazine*, June 1989, <www.bowiewonderworld.com/press/press80.htm>

Dollimore, J. (1991) *Sexual Dissidence: Augustine to Wilde, Freud to Foucault*, Oxford: Clarendon Press.

Doyle, T. (1998) *The Glamour Chase: The Maverick Life of Billy Mackenzie*, London: Bloomsury.

Dyer, R. (1979) *Stars*, London: BFI Publishing.

Dyer, R. (1992) *Only Entertainment*, London: Routledge.

Dyer, R. (2002) *the culture of queers*, London: Routledge.

Ehrenreich, B., Hess, E. and Jacobs, G. (1991) 'Beatlemania: girls just want to have fun', in L. A. Lewis (ed.), *The Adoring Audience: Fan Culture and Popular Media*, London: Routledge.

Foucault, M. (1997) *Ethics, Subjectivity and Truth* (edited by P. Rabinow), vol. 1, London: Penguin.

Frith, S. (1988) *Music for Pleasure*, London: Routledge.

Frith, S. (1989) 'Only dancing: David Bowie flirts with the issues', in A. McRobbie (ed.), *Zoot Suits and Second Hand Dresses: An Anthology of Fashion and Music*, London, Basingstoke: Macmillan Educational.

Frith, S. (1996) *Performing Rites: On the Value of Popular Music*, Oxford: Oxford University Press.

Frith, S. (1997) 'The suburban sensibility in British rock and pop', in R. Siverstone (ed.), *Visions of Suburbia*, London: Routledge.

Frith, S. (2001) 'The popular music industry', in S. Frith, W. Straw and J. Street (eds), *The Cambridge Companion to Pop and Rock*, Cambridge: Cambridge University Press.

Frith, S. and Horne, H. (1987) *Art into Pop*, London: Methuen.

Frith, S. and McRobbie, A. (1990) 'Rock and sexuality', in S. Frith and A. Goodwin, *On Record: Rock, Pop and the Written Word*, London: Routledge.

Frow, J. (1998) 'Is Elvis a god? Cult, culture, questions of method', *International Journal of Cultural Studies*, vol. 1 (2), pp. 197–210.

Gamson, J. (1998) *Freaks Talk Back: Tabloid Talk Shows and Sexual Nonconformity*, Chicago: Chicago Press.

George, B. (with Spencer Bright) (1995) *Take it Like a Man: The Autobiography of Boy George*, London: Pan Books.

Gilbert, J. (1999) 'White light/white heat: jouissance beyond gender in the Velvet Underground' in A. Blake (ed.), *Living Through Pop*, London: Routledge.

Gillman, P. and L. (1986) *Alias David Bowie*, London: Guild Publishing.

Gilroy, P. (1993) *The Black Atlantic: Modernity and Double Consciousness*, London: Verso.

Gilroy, P. (2000) *Between Camps: Nations, Cultures and the Allure of Race*, London: Penguin Press.

Gilroy, P. (2004) *After Empire: Melancholia or Convivial Culture?* London: Routledge.

Goodwin, A. (1995) 'Popular music and postmodern theory', in N. Wheale (ed.), *Postmodern Arts*, London: Routledge.

Green, J. (1999) *All Dressed Up: The Sixties and the Counterculture*, London: Pimlico.

Hall, S., Critcher, C., Jefferson, T., Clarke, J. and Robert, B. (1978) *Policing the Crisis: Mugging, the State, and Law and Order*, London: Palgrave Macmillan.

Halperin, D. M. (1995) *Saint Foucault: Towards a Gay Hagiography*, Oxford: Oxford University Press.

Haraway, D. (1991) *Simians, Cyborgs and Women: The Reinvention of Nature*, London: Routledge.

Harris, J. (2004) *The Last Party: Britpop, Blair and the Demise of English Rock*, London: Harper Perennial.

Hebdige, D. (1979) *Subculture: The Meaning of Style*, London: Methuen.

Holmes, P. (1972) 'Gay rock', *Gay News*, 5 July 1972.

Hoskyns, B. (1998) *Glam! Bowie, Bolan and the Glitter Rock Revolution*, London: Faber and Faber.

Hunt, L. (1998) *British Low Culture*, London: Routledge.

Huyssen, A. (1973) *After the Great Divide; Modernism, Mass Culture, Postmodernism*, London: Macmillan.

Jenkins, H. (2003) 'Interactive Audiences?' in V. Nightingale and K. Ross (eds), *Critical Readings: Media and Audiences*, Maidenhead: Open University Press.

Jones, A. (1977) 'Goodbye to Ziggy and all that', *Melody Maker*, 29 October 1977.

Jones, T. (1987) 'Is this lad too sane for his own good?' *I.D.*, <www.bowiewonderworld.com/press/press80.htm#id1987>

Keightly, K. (2001) 'Reconsidering rock', in S. Frith, W. Straw and J. Street (eds), *The Cambridge Companion to Pop and Rock*, Cambridge: Cambridge University Press.

Koestenbaum, W. (2001) *Andy Warhol*, London: Weidenfeld.

Kuhn, A. (2002) *An Everyday Magic: Cinema and Cultural Memory*, London: I. B. Tauris.

Kureshi, H. (1990) *The Buddha of Suburbia*, London: Faber and Faber.

Laing, D. (1969) *The Sound of Our Time*, London and Sydney: Sheed and Ward.

London Gay Liberation Front (1971) 'London Gay Liberation Front Manifesto', in L. Richmond and G. Nogvera (eds), *The Gay Liberation Front*, California: Ramparts Press.

Lyon, D. (2000) *Jesus in Disneyland: Religion in Postmodern Times*, Cambridge: Polity.

MacDonald, I. (1995) *Revolution in the Head: The Beatles' Records and the Sixties*, London: Random House.

MacDonald, I. (2003) *The People's Music*, London: Pimlico.

MacInnes, C. (1980) *Absolute Beginners*, London: Allison and Busby.

Maffesoli, M. (1996) *The Time of Tribes: The Decline of Individualism in Mass Society*, London: Sage.

Marcus, G. (1997) *Invisible Republic; Bob Dylan's Basement Tapes*, London: Picador.

Marcuse, H. (1968) *Negations*, Boston: Beacon Press.

Marcuse, H. (1969) *Eros and Civilisation: A Philosophical Enquiry into Freud*, London: Sphere Books.

Marshall, P. D. (1997) *Celebrity and Power: Fame in Contemporary Culture*, Minneapolis: University of Minnesota Press.

Melly, G. (1970) *Revolt into Style: The Pop Arts in Britain*, London: Allen Lane; Penguin Press.

Melucci, A. (1996) *The Playing Self: Persons and Meaning in the Planetary Society*, Cambridge: Cambridge University Press.

Mendelssohn, J. (1971) 'David Bowie? Pantomime rock?' *Rolling Stone*, 1 April. Accessed at <www.bowiewonderworld.com/press>

Murray, C. S. (1984) 'Sermon from the Savoy', *New Musical Express*, 29 September 1984. <www.bowiewonderworld.com/press/press80. htm>

Murray, C. S. (1991) 'David Bowie: Who was that (un)masked man?' *Shots from the Hip*, London: Penguin.

NME Originals (2004) *Glam: Bowie, T-Rex, Queen and the Glory Years*, Volume 1, Issue 15.

du Noyer, P. (2003) 'Do you remember your first time?' *Word*, Issue 9, November 2003.

Orwell, G. (1990) *Coming Up for Air*, London: Penguin.

Pegg, N. (2000) *The Complete David Bowie*, London: Reynolds and Hearn.

Pichaske, D. (1989) *A Generation in Motion: Popular Music and Culture in the Sixties*, Minnesota: Ellis Press.

Pitt, K. (1983) *David Bowie: The Pitt Report*, London: Design Music.

Playboy (1976) 'A candid conversation with the actor, rock singer and sexual switch-hitter', September 1976.

Reynolds, S. and Press, J. (1995) *The Sex Revolts: Gender, Rebellion, and Rock 'n' Roll*, Cambridge, MA: Harvard University Press.

Ricoeur, P. (1991) 'Life: A Story in Search of a Narrative', in M. J. Valdes (ed.), *A Ricoeur Reader: Reflection and Imagination*, Hemel Hempstead: Harvester Wheatsheaf.

Roberts, C. (1995) 'Action painting', *Ikon*, October 1995, <www.bowie-wonderworld.com/press/press80.htm>

Rock, M. (2000) *Blood and Glitter*, London: Omnibus Press.

Rook, J. (1979/1996) 'Bowie reborn', in E. Thomson and D. Gutman (eds), *The Bowie Companion*, London: Macmillan.

Ross, A. (1989) *No Respect: Intellectuals and Popular Culture*, London: Routledge.

Rowe, D. (1995) *Popular Cultures: Rock Music, Sport and the Politics of Pleasure*, London: Sage.

Russell, J. (2001) *Queer Burroughs*, London: Palgrave.

Said, E. (1993) *Culture and Imperialism*, London: Chatto and Windus.

Sandford, C. (1996) *Bowie: Loving the Alien*, London: Warner Books.

Savage, J. (1990) 'Tainted love: the influence of male homosexuality and sexual divergence in pop music and culture since the war', in A. Tomlinson (ed.), *Consumption, Identity and Style*, London: Routledge.

Savage, J. (1997) *Time Travel*, London: Vintage.

Segal, L. (1995) *Slow Motion: Changing masculinities changing men*, London: Virago.

Seidler, V. (1997) *Man Enough: Embodying Masculinities*, London: Sage.

Seidman, S. (1997) *Difference Troubles: Queering Social Theory and Sexual Politics*, Cambridge: Cambridge University Press.

Silverstone, R. (1994) *Television and Everyday Life*, London: Routledge.

Simpson, K. (1969) Interview, *Music Now!* 1969.

Simpson, M. (1994) *Male Impersonators*, London: Cassell.

Sontag, S. (1994) 'Notes on "Camp"', *Against Interpretation*, London: Vintage.

Stacey, J. (1994) *Star Gazing: Hollywood Cinema and Female Spectatorship*, London: Routledge.

Stallabras, J. (1999) *High Art Lite*, London: Verso.

Steiner, G. (1974) *Extraterritorial*, Harmondsworth: Penguin.

Taylor, I. and Wall, D. (1976) 'Beyond the skinheads: comments on the emergence and significance of the Glam Rock Cult', In G. Mungham and G. Pearson (eds), *Working Class Youth Culture*, London: Routledge.

Theweleit, K. (1989) *Male Fantasies, Volume 2*, Cambridge: Polity.

Thompson, J. B. (1995) *The Media and Modernity: A Social Theory of the Media*, Cambridge: Polity.

Tevis, W. (1963/1999) *The Man Who Fell to Earth*, London: Bloomsbury.

Tremlett, G. (1996) *David Bowie: Living on the Brink*, Carroll and Graff: New York.

Vermorel, F. and Vermorel, J. (1985) *Starlust: The Secret Life of Fans*, Guildford: Comet Books.

Virilio, P. (1994) *The Vision Machine*, Bloomington and Indianapolis: Indiana University Press.

Virilio, P. (2004) *Art and Fear*, London: Continuum.

Volosinov, V. N. (1973) *Marxism and the Philosophy of Language*, Cambridge, MA: Harvard University Press.

Walkerdine, V. (1997) *Daddy's Girl: Young Girls and Popular Culture*, London: Palgrave Macmillan.

Walser, R. (1993) *Running with the Devil: Power, Gender and Madness in Heavy Metal Music*, London: Wesleyan University Press.

Watts, M. (1972) 'Oh You Pretty Thing', *Melody Maker*, 22 January 1972.

Weeks, J. (1981) *Against Nature: Essays on History, Sexuality and Identity*, London: Rivers Oram Press.

Welch, C. (1999) *Changes: The Stories Behind Every David Bowie Song 1970–1980*, London: Carlton.

Wells, D. (1995) 'David Bowie and Brian Eno', <www.bowiewonderworld.com/press/press80htm>

Werner, C. (2000) *A Change Is Gonna Come: Music, Race and the Soul of America*, London: Playback Press.

Whiteley, S. (1997) 'Little Red Rooster v. The Honky Tonk Woman: Mick Jagger, sexuality, style and image' in S. Whiteley (ed.), *Sexing the Groove: Popular Music and Gender*, London: Routledge.

Williams, R. (1977) *Marxism and Literature*, Oxford: Oxford University Press.

Williams, R. (1989) *The Politics of Modernism*, London: Verso.

Williams, R. H. (1982) *Dream Worlds: Mass Consumption in Late Nineteenth Century France*, California: University of California Press.

Wilson, E. (2000) *Bohemians: The Glamorous Outcasts*, London: I. B. Tauris.

Wollen, P. (1993) *Raiding the Icebox: Reflections on Twentieth Century Culture*, London: Verso.

INDEX

Abdulmajid, Iman 115, 143, 192, 193
Absolute Beginners (Colin MacInnes) 12
Absolute Beginners (film) 13, 98, 102
Absolute Beginners (video) 103
Ackroyd, Peter 144
Adorno, Theodor 48, 84, 92
Adventures of Batman and Robin, The (television serial) 53
affect *see* emotions
AIDS crisis 100–1, 105
Aladdin Sane 2, 52
Aladdin Sane 64–6, 69, 75, 85
Albarn, Damon 126
alien messiah 62
alienation 35, 87, 126, 187
'All the Young Dudes' 116
Almond, Marc 63
Alomar, Carlos 72, 77, 91
ambiguity and ambivalence 12, 13, 29, 66, 74, 75, 114, 192; *see also* sexual ambiguity and ambivalence; uncertainty
American influence 26, 60, 64, 66, 71, 112, 129–30, 192
Amis, Kingsley 9
Anderson, Brett 126

Anderson, Laurie 121
androgyny 19, 48, 53
angry young men 9–10
animals, boundaries between humans and 122–3, 125
Arcade Fire 195
Arendt, Hannah 41
art rock 77, 139, 148; *see also* progressive rock
Asher, Tony 101
'Ashes to Ashes' 77
Au Pairs, the 142
authenticity 28, 30, 42, 45, 50, 54, 58, 61, 109, 112; of fans 176–9
authority, challenges to, in sixties 9
avant-garde 37, 72, 73, 85, 87, 148

Baez, Joan 31
Baker, Steve 123
Bakhtin, Mikhail 59
Barbarella (film) 53
Barnett, Angela (Angie) 33, 43, 63, 71, 99, 115, 129, 130, 142
Barrett, Syd 41
Basquiat (film) 50
Baudelaire, Charles 113
Bauman, Zygmunt 46

BBC 17, 35, 41, 97, 116; *see also*
   radio; television
Beatles, the 9, 15, 16, 18–19, 20,
   28, 35, 47, 84, 89, 91, 162, 195
beats, the 9, 18, 113
Beck, Ulrich 166
Beckenham 43
Beckenham Arts Lab 26
Beckenham Free Festival 34
Beckett, Samuel 67
Beckham, David 126
Belew, Adrien 88
Bell, Edward 77
Benjamin, Jessica 70, 180
Benjamin, Walter 48, 114
Berlin 5, 72–4, 75, 88, 129, 135–42
Berlin (Lou Reed) 135
Berlin Wall 73, 136, 137, 141
Best, George 63, 126
Billboard magazine 77
Birmingham 92
Birmingham Evening Post 92
bisexuality 11, 25, 35, 66, 100–1,
   106, 116, 126, 141
black culture 9
black magic 130
black music 34–5, 71–2, 126,
   181–2
Black Sabbath 45
Black Tie White Noise 115–16,
   143–4
'Black Tie White Noise' 143, 179
Blue Jean (video) 105
Blur 21, 125
body, the 93, 167–8, 192–4, 195
bohemianism 9, 17, 18, 26–7, 43,
   44, 55, 111–46, 192, 195
Bolan, Marc 16, 41, 49
Bolder, Trevor 62
Bon Jovi, Jon 104
Bond, James 53

Bordo, Susan 167
Bowie, David: childhood 111;
   comments on his life and
   music 64–5, 71, 72–3, 75, 77,
   102–3, 115, 117, 118, 120, 137;
   comments on politics 36–7,
   131, 132; emergence 5, 8, 15,
   17–18, 19; first album 20–4,
   27; interviews 36–7, 41, 45, 72,
   95–6, 101–2, 105–6, 108–9, 120,
   121–2, 126, 131–2, 143, 144, 148,
   192; legacy 195; marriage to
   Angie Barnett 33, 63, 71, 75,
   99, 129, 130, 137, 142; marriage
   to Iman Abdulmajid 115, 142–
   3, 192; personal difficulties 32,
   71, 75, 78, 99, 115, 130,
   134–5, 139, 140, 161; present
   status 80–1, 144–6, 192–5
Bowie, Lester 143
Bowienet 154, 173, 174, 195
Boy George 63, 101
'Boys Keep Swinging' 76, 142,
   147
Bristol, Arnolfini Gallery 121
Brit Art 121–5, 129
Brit pop 125–6, 129
Brixton Neighbourhood
   Community Association 96
Bromley 111–12, 117
Buckley, David 4, 24
Buddha of Suburbia, The
   (album) 116–18, 179
Buddha of Suburbia, The
   (television series) 116
Buddhism 26
Burden, Chris 141
Burns, Margaret 111
Burroughs, William 9, 49, 66–70,
   82, 138, 148
Butler, Judith 76, 108

Cabaret (film) 135
Cage, John 138
Cale, John 55
Cambridge, John 43
camp 27, 51, 52–4, 61, 63, 79, 127, 135
capitalism 13, 14, 15, 27, 29, 48, 51, 52, 83, 85, 87, 88, 92–3; fans and 162, 173, 182, 195
carnivalesque 59–60, 69
'Cat People' 93
Cavicchi, Daniel 184
CBS 90
celebrity and celebrity culture 1–4, 72, 74, 103, 114, 123, 132; fans and 58–9, 150, 152, 154, 155, 156, 162, 163, 185, 190, 191, 192
Chambers, Ian 56
change 2–3, 7, 9, 24, 32, 86, 194, 195; fans and handling of 160–72
Changes 80
'Changes' 52
ChangesBowie (1990) 98
ChangesTwoBowie (1981) 98
'character' songs 21
Chic 91
Christian themes 62–3
civil rights movement 19, 31–2
class 39, 49, 84, 107; fans 149, 154, 155, 166, 179, 181, 183, 191; teenagers 12–13; *see also* middle class
Clockwork Orange (film) 56
clown figure 77
Cocker, Jarvis 126
Cold War 136, 140, 193
Coleman, Ray 57
Collins, Phil 91
Cologne, Museum Ludwig 121

Coming Up For Air (George Orwell) 23–4
commercial culture and commercialism 9, 29, 30, 46, 47, 50, 61, 83, 87, 149, 163, 165; *see also* commodification; consumer culture
commodification 7, 13, 15, 49, 51, 52, 166; of Bowie 71, 82–110, 118, 119, 194–5; *see also* commercial culture and commercialism; consumer culture
communalism 78
community 84; fans 159, 166, 172–83, 189, 190, 191
conservatism 40
consumer culture 7, 8, 11, 12–13, 14, 17, 49, 85, 88, 89, 119; and cultural imperialism 93–7; fans 157, 167–8, 174, 185; *see also* commercial culture and commercialism; commodification
contestation 7, 8; *see also* rebellion
context, and image 65
contradiction, cultural 3, 29, 36, 71, 85–6, 195
Costello, Elvis 21
counter-culture 7, 8, 16, 22, 24–30, 39, 55, 89; decline 30–7, 40, 41, 42, 45, 46, 49, 118–19
'Cracked Actor' 86
Crawford, Joan 53
creativity 28, 34, 51, 85, 137–42; decline 5, 79, 82, 98–9, 101–2, 104, 110, 119, 161, 195; fans and 156, 169; rediscovery 5, 116–29
Cribbins, Bernard 20

Crosby, Bing 99
cross-dressing 21
cultural cynicism 32
cultural domination and
    imperialism 58, 93–7, 141, 142,
    145
cultural nationalism 23, 58
cultural politics 18, 23, 83, 125
cultural power 1
cultural studies 48, 151–3, 156,
    164
culture 4, 7; fifties and sixties 5,
    7–37; *see also* high/low culture;
    popular culture
culture industry 4, 45, 48, 79, 82,
    83, 86, 110; *see also* commercial
    culture and commercialism;
    commodification; consumer
    culture
Cure, the 45
cut-up technique 49, 67–8, 138
cyborg 125
'Cygnet Committee' 33
Czechoslovakia, invasion
    (1968) 19

Dancing in the Street 102
dandy 113–14
Daniels, Phil 126
David Bowie (Deram album)
    20–4, 27
*David Bowie: Man of Words, Man
    of Music* 29–36
David Live 90
Davis, Bette 53
Dean, James 11–12, 54
death *see* mortality
Decca 13–14
DeFries, Tony 90
Deram album 20–4, 27
Diamond Dogs 67–70, 123, 147

Dietrich, Marlene 53
difference 58, 118, 141, 172, 190,
    194
discourses 156
Doherty, Pete 4
Dollimore, Jonathan 71
'Dreamers, The' 80
dreaming 79–81
drugs 9, 35, 107; Bowie's
    problems with 71, 75, 90, 99,
    130, 132, 133, 161
Du Noyer, Paul 144
Dudgeon, Gus 36
Dyer, Richard 22, 44, 53
Dylan, Bob 4, 28, 31–2, 36, 50,
    118, 141, 162
dystopianism 22, 41, 67, 68, 123

Eastwood, Clint 170
ecological collapse 21, 42, 193
Edwards, Bernard 91
elective sociality 173–4
electronic blues 139
electronic music 72, 148
Elephant Man, The, Bowie's stage
    appearance 98, 99
EMI 13, 90, 91, 99, 100, 102,
    116
Eminem 58, 170
emotions: fans 6, 58–60, 152,
    153, 159, 170; masculinity and
    independence 70, 133–4, 170,
    180–1
Englishness 20–4, 182
Eno, Brian 50, 72, 76, 88, 118,
    121, 127, 129, 138, 141
ethical issues 12, 80
ethnicity *see* race and ethnicity
Europe 134, 139–40; fans 148,
    182–3; *see also* Berlin; fascism

everyday life: aestheticization of 51; commodification of 13
everyday magic 4, 73, 183–5

'Fame' 72
fame 56–66, 72, 74, 82; *see also* celebrity and celebrity culture; stars and stardom
fans 5–6, 73, 75, 81, 92, 147–91; construction of self 57, 139, 156–72; interviewing process 153–7; nature of 190–1; personal experience of author 147–9; as postmodern community 172–83; social and cultural perspectives 151–3; and Ziggy Stardust and Aladdin Sane 57, 58–9, 65
'Fantastic Voyage' 75–6
fascism 5, 21, 94, 114, 130–5, 140, 141
'Fashion' 77
fashion 7
femininity 10, 41, 69, 70, 106, 167
feminism 10, 60, 142
Ferry, Bryan 50
'Fill Your Heart' 55
film stars *see* stars and stardom
films, Bowie and 50, 62, 98, 102, 148
'Five Years' 56
folk music 26, 28, 31–2, 48
folk rock 26, 32, 33
Foucault, Michel 78
Franklin, Aretha 35, 130
freak shows 68–9
Freddie Mercury Tribute Concert for Aids Awareness (1992) 116
freedom 7, 19, 28, 191
Fripp, Robert 77
Frith, Simon 89, 111

Frow, John 164, 165
fundamentalism 145

Gabrels, Reeves 103, 104
Gabriel, Peter 94
Garbo, Greta 53
Garland, Judy 14, 53
Garson, Mike 64, 69
gay culture 87
Gay News 63
gay politics 28, 35, 36, 37, 52–3, 60–1, 118, 126
gayness 18, 25, 63–4, 67, 100–1, 106, 118; *see also* camp
gender 2, 30, 39, 44, 53, 62, 82, 89, 108, 109, 110; change 5, 21; fans 154, 155–6, 157, 169–72, 178, 181, 191
gender-bending 12, 63; *see also* bisexuality; sexual ambiguity and ambivalence
gender identity 11, 84, 108
gender politics 8, 66, 80, 111
Genet, Jean 49, 67
German expressionism 134
Gilroy, Paul 130–1, 182
Ginsberg, Allen 9
girls' comics 149
glam rock 47–56, 61, 63, 89, 126, 135
Glamour calendar 77
Glass, Philip 138
Glass Spider tour (1987) 98, 103
Glitter, Gary 49
global brand, Bowie as 5, 82, 91, 94
Growth newsletter 26
Guns N' Roses 104

Haddon Hall, Beckenham 43–4
Haley, Bill, and the Comets 16

Halloween Jack 69, 133, 181
Halpern, David 53
Haraway, Donna 125
Harris, Bob 41
'Heart's Filthy Lesson,
    The' 122–3
Heathen 145, 179, 193
heavy metal *see* metal music
Hebdige, Dick 49
hedonism 194
Hell, Richard 67
Hello! magazine 145
'Hello Spaceboy' 126–7
Hell's Angels 31
Hendrix, Jimi 9, 56
Henson, Jim 102
'Heroes' 72, 73, 74, 77, 78, 98,
    137–42, 186
'Heroes' 73, 116, 141
heterosexual masculinity 10, 12,
    16, 17, 18, 61, 63, 76, 93, 126,
    142, 192; Tin Machine
    103–10
high/low culture 13, 25, 26, 30,
    48, 82, 119
hippy culture 49, 61
Hirst, Damian 121, 122, 123–4
Hitler, Adolf 132, 134
Hong Kong 92
Hoskyns, Barney 48
hours 79–81
'Hunger City' 69
Hunky Dory 50, 53–5, 62, 90, 98,
    107, 193
Hunter, Ian 116
Hurley, Melissa 115
hypermasculinity 70, 106, 178
hypertextuality 128, 160

icons 62, 86; Bowie as 76, 153,
    190

identity: ambivalence of 194;
    and change 2–3, 9, 60–1, 75;
    fans 149, 157, 172, 180–1, 187,
    188–90; in fifties and sixties 9,
    11, 12–13, 17, 27, 38; in
    information culture 127, 128;
    Pop Art and 51; postmodern
    Bowie 5, 39–40, 45–7, 60–1,
    71–81, 82, 84–5; *see also* self,
    selves
ideology 7–9
identity politics 4, 7, 38–9, 87
Idiot, The 137
Idol, Billy 112
Iggy Pop 41, 49, 56, 90, 98, 99,
    101, 104, 129, 136, 137
image(s) 2, 7–8, 86, 87;
    contemporary 145, 192;
    fans 147, 150, 167, 168,
    169, 179–80; normalized, of
    commodified Bowie 93, 96,
    98–110, 115, 119; postmodern
    Bowie 45, 48, 52, 54–5, 65–6,
    68, 75
imagination 80
individual and
    individualization 3, 14, 70,
    166, 180, 189
individualism 7, 28, 41, 46, 49,
    70, 82, 84–5, 169
information culture 119–29, 174
interactive websites 176
internet 121, 128, 173, 175, 176;
    Bowienet 154, 173, 174, 195
Isherwood, Christopher 135,
    148

Jackson, Michael 87, 91
Jagger, Mick 16, 19, 102, 114
Japanese kabuki theatre 56
Jay, Dave *see* Bowie, David

jazz 9, 14, 64
Jenkins, Henry 173
John, Elton 41, 116
'Join the Gang' 22
Jones, David *see* Bowie, David
Jones, John 25, 32, 111
Joplin, Janice 9
Juke Box Jury (television
    programme) 14

Kabbalah 130
Kemp, Lindsay 26–7
Kerouac, Jack 9, 10
King, Jason 63
King Bees 15
Kinks 21
Konrads 15
'Kooks' 55
Kraftwerk 134
Kubrick, Stanley 35
Kuhn, Annette 183
Kureishi, Hanif 117

Labyrinth (film) 102
laddishness 125–6
Laing, D. 15
Lancaster, Phil 18
Lavigne, Avril 195
Lee, Hermione 32
Leiber, Jerry 101
Lennon, John 16, 19, 41, 42, 72,
    99, 107, 164
Lennox, Annie 116
Let's Dance 88–97, 98, 110, 115,
    116, 141, 142, 144
'Let's Dance' 94–5
Let's Dance tour 98, 178
'Letter to Hermione' 33
liberal bohemianism 141, 142–6,
    192
liberalism 5, 119

lifestyle experimentation 8, 11,
    19, 24–5, 28, 39, 43, 112, 113,
    135
literature: Bowie's interest in 25,
    148; influence of William
    Burroughs 66–70
'Little Bombardier' 23
Little Richard 10–11
Live Aid concert 96, 97
Lodger 72, 74–6, 78, 87–8, 141,
    142, 148
London 5, 8, 16, 91, 92; Bowie's
    art exhibitions 121
'London Boys' 22
'Looking for Water' 145
'Loving the Alien' 106
Low 72, 73, 74, 78, 98, 137–42,
    158, 186
Lower Third 15, 16, 18
Lust for Life 137
Lydon, John 4
Lyon, David 165

MacDonald, Ian 28, 130
MacInnes, Colin 12
MacKenzie, Billy 63
Madonna 87, 96
Maffesoli, Michel 173
MainMan 90–1
Man Who Fell to Earth, The
    (film) 62
Man Who Sold the World, The
    41–7, 54, 55, 85, 123, 193
Mandela, Nelson 96, 97
Mannish Boys 15
Marcuse, Herbert 27, 29
Marley, Bob 89
Marquee club 16
Marsh, Rodney 63, 126
masculinity: ambiguous, of
    James Dean 11–12; Brit

pop 125–6; commodified Bowie 85; contemporary 192; fans and 148, 149, 170, 178, 179, 180–1, 183; in fifties and sixties 10, 15–16, 17–19, 27; postmodern Bowie 44, 61–2, 63, 68–9, 70, 71, 79, 133–4, 137; *see also* heterosexual masculinity

mass communications 8, 14

mass media *see* media

meaning, created nature of 46–7

media 1, 6, 14, 101, 123, 124, 130, 132, 151, 153, 156, 174, 195

media studies 151–3

Melly, George 16

Melody Maker 63

Melucci, Alberto 77, 127

'Memory of a Free Festival' 33–4

Mercury, Freddie 99, 100, 114, 116

Merry Christmas Mr Lawrence (film) 98

metal music 104, 110, 148

Michael, George 116

Michelmore, Cliff 17

middle class, conformity and rebellion 9, 111–12, 117, 148

mime 26–7, 56

miners' strike (1984–5) 96

Minogue, Kylie 84

Mishima, Yukio 148

misogyny 107

mod movement 16–17, 18, 61

'Modern Love' 93

modernity 3, 125

Monroe, Marilyn 54

moral panic 100, 133

morality, challenges to, in the sixties 9

More, Thomas 22

Morris, William 22

Morrissey 4

mortality 123, 162, 163–6, 192–4

'Moss Garden' 140

'Move On' 87

multiculturalism 131, 143–4, 182

Munich 91

Murray, Charles Shaar 72

music hall tradition 21, 24

music industry 4, 13–14, 15, 29, 71, 74, 83–4, 89–91, 110, 150, 161–2, 169, 195

Music Now! 36–7

music videos 76, 93, 94–5, 103, 117, 122–3, 141

National Front 133

national identity, decline 21–4, 163, 182–3

naturalism 58, 108; *see also* authenticity

Nazism *see* fascism

'Nelson Mandela' (Special AKA single) 97

neo-liberalism 7

Neu 134

'Neuköln' 140

Never Let Me Down 102–3, 104, 106

New Musical Express 20, 92, 131, 195

New Right 83, 96, 100–1, 119

New Romantics 76, 80, 88–9

new social movements 27, 35, 118

Newley, Anthony 20

Nietzsche, Friedrich 41, 42–3, 46, 47, 85, 130

1984 (George Orwell) 67

non-conformity *see* rebellion

normality 17, 53, 93, 96, 97,
  98–103, 115, 119, 194; Tin
  Machine 103–10
nuclear threat 42, 96, 136

Oasis 125
occult 41, 71, 114, 130
O'Jays, the 72
Old Grey Whistle Test (television
  programme) 41
Outside (album) 179
1.Outside 117, 120–9
Ono, Yoko 99
Orwell, George 23–4, 67
Osborne, John 9, 10
otherness 63, 66, 77, 80, 141, 151
outsider image 9, 18, 21, 43, 56,
  93, 113, 195; fans and
  185–7, 190; marginality and
  information society 118–29

Pang, May 99
Paris 91
patriarchy 70
*Peace on Earth/Little Drummer
  Boy* 99
performativity 2, 26–7, 45, 61–2,
  76, 93, 119
permissive society 7, 19, 100
personal/political fusion 7, 107,
  140
pessimism 41–2, 140; *see also*
  dystopianism
Pet Shop Boys 127
phatic images 65
Philips 29
Pichaske, David 28
Pierrot in Turquoise 26
PinUps 66, 138
Pink Floyd 41, 139
Pitt, Kenneth 20, 25–6, 32, 35, 90

Pixies 104
Playboy magazine 131–2
'Please Mr Gravedigger' 22
political left 48; and sixties
  culture 7–9, 28
political music 96–7, 107, 144; *see
  also* black music
political nihilism 49
political/personal fusion 7, 107,
  140
political right: and sixties
  culture 7–9, 28; *see also* New
  Right
politics 4; Bowie's
  comments 36–7, 131, 132
Polyphonic Spree 195
Pop Art 47–56, 58, 84, 85, 195
Popswop Annual 41
popular culture: reinvention in
  fifties and sixties 7, 8, 9–15, 26;
  and Second World War 130–1;
  see also high/low culture
popular music 4, 6; in fifties
  and sixties 5, 7–9, 15–19;
  relationship to rock music
  29–31; *see also individual genres
  and performers*
post-human environment 122–5
postmodernism 87, 144, 179,
  195; Bowie as postmodern
  performer 5, 38–81, 82, 119,
  121, 127, 128, 132, 144, 195;
  fandom as postmodern
  community 172–83
Powell, Enoch 37, 133
Power Station studios 76, 91
presentism 124–5
Presley, Elvis 9, 16, 54, 162, 164
Press, Joy 10
'Pretty Thing' 106–7
'Pretty Things' 106

Prince 87

progressive rock 40–6, 52; *see also* art-rock

protest: political and social 19, 107; *see also* political music; rebellion

provocation 150

Pulp 126

punk 74, 78, 89, 97, 107, 119, 130, 147, 148

Q music magazine 105–6, 108–9

Queen 91, 96

queerness *see* bisexuality; gayness

R and B 14, 15

race and ethnicity 34–5, 39, 84, 94, 143–4; fans 154, 155, 163, 181–2, 183, 191; *see also* black music; fascism; Thin White Duke, The

radical feminism 142

radicalism 5, 7, 8, 9, 17, 27–8, 37, 49, 82, 87, 144, 192; *see also* gay politics

radio 13, 14

Radiohead 139

Ray, Johnnie 14

RCA 13, 73, 90, 91, 125

Ready, Steady, Go! (television programme) 14

Reality 144–5

Reality tour (2004) 175

Rebel Without A Cause (film) 11

rebellion: fans and 188–90; popular culture of fifties and sixties 8, 9–10, 12, 18, 27, 28, 118

reconciliation 79–81

Reed, Lou 49, 50, 55, 99, 135

Reeves, Martha 35

reflexivity 82, 86, 97, 115, 117, 157, 159, 163

religion: fans' attitude to Bowie 63, 153, 164–6, 168, 183–5; themes in Bowie's music 62–3, 116

REM 145, 175

'Repetition' 142

representation 65; *see also* images(s)

resistance, camp as 53

Reynolds, Simon 10

Richard, Cliff 15–16

Richards, Dave 143

Ricoeur, Paul 157

Rise and Fall of Ziggy Stardust and the Spiders from Mars, The see *Ziggy Stardust*

Rock Against Racism 133

rock music 10–11, 14, 29–32, 53; Bowie's deconstruction 56–66; Tin Machine 103–10; *see also* art-rock; Brit pop; folk-rock; glam rock; metal music; progressive rock; punk; rock 'n' roll; stadium rock

rock 'n' roll 10, 15–16, 17, 64, 69, 104, 112, 113; *see also* rock music

'Rock 'n' Roll Suicide' 57, 62

Rodgers, Nile 91, 115, 143, 144

Rolling Stone magazine 45

Rolling Stones 9, 15, 16, 18, 19, 28, 31, 64, 69, 96, 162

Romantics 112

Ronson, Mick 43, 45, 55, 62, 63–4, 69, 97, 116, 135, 172

Roxy Music 41, 172

Royal Academy of Arts 124
'Rubber Band' 23
Russell, Jamie 67

Saatchi, Charles 124
Said, Edward 93
Sales, Hunt 104
Sales, Tony 104
Savage, Jon 18
*Scary Monsters (and Super
    Creeps)* 76–7, 79, 80, 88, 141,
    148
science fiction 56, 62
Scott, Ken 62
'Scream Like A Baby' 79
Second World War in popular
    culture 130–1
security, search for 100, 105, 115
Segal, Lynne 10, 178
Seidler, Victor 170
self, selves: bohemianism
    and 114; and change 87–8;
    creation and reinvention 3,
    4, 30, 39–47, 78–81, 87–8, 128;
    fans' production of 156–72,
    180, 183–5, 191; fragmentation
    of 64–6; politics of 35–7
self-expression 28–9
Sensation exhibition (1997) 124
'Sense of Doubt' 140
September 11th 2001 144, 145,
    193
Serious Moonlight global
    tour 91–3
sex camp 53
sexism 108, 109
sexual ambiguity and
    ambivalence 41, 44, 63, 64,
    68–70, 96, 126, 127; fans 148,
    171–2

sexual identity 13, 67–8
sexual politics 8, 60, 66, 80, 111,
    126
sexuality 2, 12–13, 14, 28–9, 89,
    113; postmodern Bowie 44, 49,
    58–64, 82, 85; *see also* gender;
    masculinity; sexual ambiguity
    and ambivalence
'She's Got Medals' 20–1
Simon, Paul 94
Simpson, Kate 36
Sinatra, Frank 14
Siouxsie and the Banshees 45,
    112
skiffle 14
Slade 63
'Slow Burn' 179
Smith, Patti 4, 67
Smiths, the 22
Snowman, The, introduction by
    Bowie 98
social and technological
    change 3–4, 19, 39, 119, 229;
    fans and 161–6
social studies 156
Society for the Prevention
    of Cruelty to Long-Haired
    Men 17
sociology, and glam rock 49
Solanas, Valerie 99
Sonic Youth 104
soul music 71
Sound+ Vision 98
Sound + Vision tour (1990) 115
Space Oddity 29–36
'Space Oddity' 15, 34–6, 63, 77,
    177
spectacle 49, 88, 91
Spiders, the 66, 129
Springsteen, Bruce 96, 145, 184

Stacey, Jackie 167
stadium rock 80, 92, 97
Stage 142
Stallabras, Julien 123
stars and stardom 7–8, 9, 18,
    44, 48, 192; Bowie as 2–4, 8,
    24, 137, 142; commodification
    and 13, 14, 15, 82, 86, 89–90,
    91, 94; fans and 153, 162,
    164, 166–7, 168, 182, 190, 191;
    postmodern Bowie and 54–5,
    56–66, 72, 73, 74, 77
Station to Station 72, 133
Status Quo 96
Steele, Tommy 15–16, 20
Steiner, George 155
Stewart, Rod 41, 63
Stooges, the 41
'Strangers When We Meet' 128
Stroller, Mike 101
structuralism 156
style 16–17, 49, 89
Stylistics, the 72
subcultures 13, 18, 21–2, 51,
    87, 88, 104, 118; *see also*
    bohemianism; mod movement
suburbia 111–12; utopianism of
    Deram album 22–4
Suede 126
Sun 193
Supergrass 125
'Supermen, The' 46
Sweet, the 63
'Sweet Thing' 69–70
Switzerland 99, 104, 129, 141

taboo-breaking 124
Taylor, Ian 49
technological change *see* social
    and technological change
teen pop 40–1, 52

'Teenage Wildlife' 77
teenagers 11–13
television 14, 17, 41, 53, 116–17,
    119; *see also Top of the Pops*
Templar, Simon 63
Temple, Julien 13, 103
Tennant, Neil 127
terrorism 145, 193
Thatcher, Margaret, and
    Thatcherism 83, 133
theatre 148; *The Elephant Man* 98,
    99
theatricality 2, 21, 26, 56, 57, 63,
    64, 79, 80, 119, 132
'There is a Happy Land' 22
Theweleit, Klaus 134
Thin White Duke, The 2, 52, 72,
    133–4, 137, 140, 142, 181
Thompson, J. B. 156
Thompson, Tony 91
Three Degrees 72
Thus Spake Zarathustra
    (Nietzsche) 46
Tin Machine 103–10, 115, 126,
    134, 143, 150
Tin Machine 98, 105–7
Tin Machine II 107–8
Tonight 101–2, 106
Top of the Pops 63–4, 97, 147, 172,
    184, 186
transformation *see* change
Transformer (Lou Reed) 135
tribalization, fans and 173–4, 183
2001: A Space Odyssey (film) 35

UFOs 26, 71
uncertainty 12, 128, 193; *see also*
    ambiguity and ambivalence
'Under Pressure' 99, 100, 116
underground 8; *see also* avant-
    garde *and individual groups*

United States *see* American
    influence
'Up The Hill Backwards' 78
utopianism 22–4, 32, 35, 58, 59,
    60, 68, 69, 71, 126

Vandellas, the 35
Velvet Underground 41, 47, 135
Velvet Underground and Nico,
    The 55
Vermorel, F. and J. 59
Vernon, Mike 24
Vietnam war 19
Virilio, Paul 65, 124
virtual communities 173
Visconti, Tony 32–3, 34, 36, 43,
    45, 72, 73, 77, 88
visual art 5, 118, 119, 121;
    Bowie's painting 121, 148; *see*
    also Brit Art; Pop Art
visual image *see* image(s)
Volosinov, V. N. 156

Wakeman, Rick 36, 55
Walkerdine, Valerie 149
Wall, David 49
Walser, Robert 109–10
Warhol, Andy 5, 47, 49, 50, 51,
    52, 53, 54, 55, 57, 61, 82, 99,
    102

'We Are Hungry Men' 21
websites 154, 173, 174, 195; *see*
    also internet
Werner, Craig 34
'What's Really Happening?' 80
'When I Live My Dream' 22
Who, the 15
Wild Boys, The (William
    Burroughs) 67, 68
Wilde, Oscar 112
Williams, Raymond 85, 156
Williamson, James 101
Wilson, Brian 101
Wilson, Colin 9
Wilson, Elizabeth 114
Wolfe, Tom 144
Wollen, Peter 51
women fans 154, 155–6, 157,
    169–72, 178
Woodmansey, Mick 45, 62
'Working Class Hero' 107

Young, Neil 41, 42
Young Americans 71–2
youth cultures 7, 49

Ziggy Stardust 2, 33, 52, 53,
    56–66, 71, 72, 78, 180
Ziggy Stardust 56–66, 78, 86, 93,
    98

Printed in Great Britain
by Amazon

22131608R00126